Women of the
Resistance

Women of the Resistance

Eight Who Defied the Third Reich

MARC E. VARGO

McFarland & Company, Inc., Publishers
Jefferson, North Carolina, and London

LIBRARY OF CONGRESS CATALOGUING-IN-PUBLICATION DATA

Vargo, Marc E.
　　Women of the resistance : eight who defied the Third Reich / Marc E. Vargo.
　　　　p.　　cm.
　　Includes bibliographical references and index.

　　ISBN 978-0-7864-6579-8
　　softcover : acid free paper ∞

　　1. World War, 1939–1945 — Underground movements. 2. World War, 1939–1945 — Biography. 3. World War, 1939–1945 — Participation, Female. 4. World War, 1939–1945 — Women. 5. Women guerrillas — Biography. 6. Women spies — Biography. 7. Women political activists — Biography. 8. Women and war — History — 20th century. I. Title.
　　D802.A2V29   2012
　　940.53092'52 — dc23　　　　　　　　　　　　　　　2012031406

BRITISH LIBRARY CATALOGUING DATA ARE AVAILABLE

© 2012 Marc E. Vargo. All rights reserved

No part of this book may be reproduced or transmitted in any form or by any means, electronic or mechanical, including photocopying or recording, or by any information storage and retrieval system, without permission in writing from the publisher.

Front cover photographs: Sophia Magdalena Scholl (1921–1943) was a German student, active within the White Rose non-violent resistance group in Nazi Germany (Wikipedia Commons); white rose © 2012 Shutterstock

Manufactured in the United States of America

McFarland & Company, Inc., Publishers
　Box 611, Jefferson, North Carolina 28640
　　www.mcfarlandpub.com

For my mother,
Doris Vargo

Table of Contents

Introduction	1
1. Vera Atkins and the Special Operations Executive	7
2. Sophie Scholl and the White Rose Movement	27
3. Monica Wichfeld and the Danish Resistance	52
4. Noor Inayat Khan and the Wireless Network of Paris	81
5. Yukiko Sugihara and the Escape of the Polish Jews	106
6. Virginia Hall and the Vichy Underground	124
7. Hannah Senesh and the Palestinian Commandos	157
8. Christine Granville and the Polish/French Resistance	184
Notes	213
Bibliography	219
Index	223

Introduction

The moonlight illuminates him: a man clad in black and wearing a beret, a rifle slung over his shoulder, stealing through the snow-covered forest to plant explosives on a railroad line. This is the classic image of the World War II resistance figure that literature and the cinema have long presented to us.

As to the female agent, when she has been portrayed, it, too, has been in a clichéd fashion. Particularly in the Hollywood narrative, she has been a *femme fatale,* that alluring and mysterious woman who seduces, then exploits, an unsuspecting Nazi officer in a smoke-filled cabaret while a chanteuse pours out her heart beneath a silver spotlight. Alternatively, she has been the hard-edged assassin who eliminates the enemy, effortlessly and adeptly, with a single bullet to the heart. But while such compelling, even glamorous, representations are entertaining, the fact is that most of the women in the underground were neither enchanting sex sirens nor cold-blooded killers, just as a considerable share of the men were not guerrilla fighters. In reality, the diversity of those who served in the resistance, like the sheer range and ingenuity of their deeds, eclipsed such one-dimensional renderings.

Of the two sexes, female agents were perhaps the more fascinating because their gender roles prior to the war had limited them to the drawing room, the kitchen, and the nursery. In the face of the supreme threat posed by the Third Reich, however, they stepped outside of tradition and into treacherous territory, performing deeds they never before could have imagined. By all accounts, their participation demonstrated the intelligence, fortitude, and resiliency of women whose skills and potential abilities had heretofore gone unrecognized and unrealized.

In terms of their circumstances, women who joined formal resistance organizations as full-time agents tended to be relatively young, single, and childless.[1] Such women were more likely to be able to travel behind enemy lines on a moment's notice and to remain largely inaccessible to family and friends for months at a stretch. Wives and mothers, by comparison, did not enjoy such latitude owing to their marital and parental responsibilities. Then, too, they often were hesitant to take part in activities that might invite retaliation against their loved ones. In writing about the French Resistance, the authors of the book *Behind the Lines: Gender and the Two World Wars* elaborate on this sense of protectiveness:

> [M]any women were reluctant to take risks which could place families or dependents in jeopardy. This was especially true for those who found themselves single heads of households in the absence of men taken prisoner of war or away from home for other reasons. The arrest of the remaining parent could leave small children utterly without care or resources.[2]

On those occasions when a wife or mother did play a part in clandestine operations, it often began as a family affair, with spouses and other relatives being involved as well. It was a matter of trust. Whereas a friend or comrade-in-arms might prove to be undependable if interrogated and tortured by the enemy, family members could nearly always be counted on to make a herculean effort to conceal a relative's involvement in the resistance, especially if that relative was a wife or mother.

As to their clandestine deeds, women of the underground, unlike their cinematic facsimiles, usually did not play hands-on roles in violent missions.[3] With the exception of certain communist cells, guerrilla warfare was typically considered a man's domain, with women serving in a support capacity. For instance, in the maquis — bands of fighters that operated mainly in the mountainous regions of France — women often assumed the role of "forest wives," sustaining in a traditional manner the groups' male fighters. They cooked for the men, gratified their sexual needs, and created comfortable surroundings as much as the rugged settings would permit. In other organizations, women functioned as wireless operators, devised false documents, produced and distributed underground newspapers, and sheltered Jews and escaped prisoners-of-war. As well, they provided treatment for injured operatives and cared for the families of male resistance fighters who were away on missions or incarcerated. In most cases, though, they served as couriers or liaison agents, conveying messages between underground cells or between an organization's headquarters and its units in the field. Not only were women adept at this risky business, but they also were less likely than their male counterparts to be suspected, and thus arrested, by the enemy.

On this topic, capture, it is worth noting that female agents, when they were apprehended, were often treated differently than their comrades of the opposite gender. Although the male-dominated Gestapo did not hesitate to interrogate, torture, and execute either a man or a woman, the latter was more apt to suffer personalized forms of maltreatment, most notably sexual abuse.[4]

"[T]he violence inflicted upon women's bodies by male interrogators was often gender-based," writes historian Juliette Pattinson in her book centering on British agents. "Personal testimonies indicate that female political prisoners experienced punishment with distinct sexist and sexual overtones."[5] She continues,

> Women arrested for their Resistance activities were strong, independent women who destablised conventional notions of what it means to be a woman: weak, dependent, inferior and submissive. Nazi views of ideal femininity, underpinned by the glorification of domesticity ... were challenged by these women.[6]

To be sure, the female resistance agent was poles apart from the subservient "Aryan" woman who embraced with nationalistic zeal her role as a breeding machine for the Master Race, this being her principal function as set forth by National Socialism. And the Gestapo's male officers, dutifully embracing this tenet and perhaps feeling personally threatened by progressive, independent women, reacted savagely. "Being sexually aggressive was a way to reclaim their masculinity and to refeminise their prisoners," says Pattinson.[7] It was the predictable response of a troglodyte mentality and it was doomed to fail. The fact is, the women who served in the underground — strong, smart, and skilled — remained undiminished by the men of the Gestapo who sought to dominate and demean them.

Regarding another facet of the female resistance figure, her socioeconomic status, a considerable share of the women belonged to the middle class, with another portion being comprised of the less financially secure. As to those who were among to the upper class, they were not represented in great numbers, although women of prosperity and privilege did join the underground on occasion. And among them was a handful of legendary faces.

Josephine Baker, for instance, the dazzling African American headliner of Paris cabaret revues, was a fêted performer when she decided to engage in clandestine work. In collaboration with a captain from French military intelligence, she used invisible ink to transcribe more than fifty secret messages onto sheet music. She then traveled from her home in occupied France to Lisbon, Portugal, where she forwarded the documents by ship to the Allies in London. And this was not a one-shot operation. The feisty performer continued traveling to Portugal and sending intelligence reports to Britain, with her inspired methods of concealment including, among other tricks, pinning documents to her brassiere. In effect, she was challenging the Gestapo to search her, convinced that its haughty officers would be too intimidated by her fame, if not by her voluptuousness, to actually touch her. "I call that courage," her comrade later said.[8] As it turned out, the French government agreed, decorating the luminary after the war.

Two years later in the picturesque city of Arnhem, Holland, an aristocrat and her teenage daughter, a ballet enthusiast, likewise took considerable risks to oppose the fascists. The Baroness Ella van Heemstra and thirteen-year-old Audrey — she would become known to the world as Audrey Hepburn — were ensconced in a splendid white mansion on the family's ancestral estate when the Nazis confiscated their money, investments, and jewelry. Affronted, mother and daughter set about helping to destabilize the occupying forces. "[T]he Baroness Ella van Heemstra began to work actively with the Dutch resistance, even to the point of hiding Underground workers in their home," writes Donald Spoto.[9] Meanwhile, Audrey performed in improvised ballet recitals in local homes to raise money for the resistance, the windows of the houses being blacked out and applause forbidden so as not to draw the attention of the Nazis who patrolled the streets. She also carried secret messages to and from resistance agents in her ballet slippers, and on one occasion served as a liaison between a downed Allied pilot hiding in the forest and his rescuers in the city.

"I knew the cold clutch of human terror all through my early teens," the actress later recalled. "I saw it, felt it, heard it."[10] More important, she prevailed over her fears and acted on her principles.

In the pages that follow, we meet eight women who likewise surmounted their trepidation to become involved in the resistance operations of several nations. Collectively, the women — European, Asian, and North American — possessed many of the characteristics we have discussed. Most were single and did not have small children. Then, too, their lives prior to their underground years were marked by traditional female endeavors, although some of the women were already evincing a desire to break away from such gender-restrictive conditions. In terms of their deeds with the resistance, the eight served as couriers and wireless operators, devised escape routes for prisoners-of-war and downed Allied airmen, supervised the training of operatives, and oversaw covert operations. They also sheltered Jewish families as well as forged travel documents, ration coupons, and identification papers. One of them, in an exceptionally bold stroke, even helped to forge a non-violent protest movement within Nazi Germany itself. And in those unfortunate cases where the enemy captured them, the women's ensuing treatment, or maltreatment, was consistent with that endured by the much larger number of women who served in resistance organizations and were also apprehended.

It should be noted, however, that in one important respect — socioeconomic status — the figures profiled in this book differed from the typical resistance agent. Like Josephine Baker and Audrey Hepburn, they were, by birth or by marriage, financially secure and socially prominent in the years before the war. As such, they represent women who, as a class, have seldom been considered together in works about the resistance.

Among these courageous women are Christine Granville, a Polish countess, and Virginia Hall, an American citizen and the descendent of an East Coast shipping tycoon. Others include Sophie Scholl, the daughter of the mayor of Forchtenberg, Germany, and Hannah Senesh (Szenes), a Hungarian-born Zionist and the daughter of the renowned playwright and critic Béla Szenes. Also revisited are Monica Wichfeld, whose childhood was spent on a sprawling estate in Ireland, and Yukiko Sugihara, who hailed from a progressive family in Japan. Both Wichfeld and Sugihara proceeded to marry foreign service officials, a Danish attaché and a Japanese diplomat, respectively, which further enhanced the women's social standing. And lastly, we examine the life and wartime experiences of Noor Inayat Khan, a descendent of Indian nobility and Sufi mystics as well as a respected poet and author in her own right.

Ultimately, these women, without exception, took astonishing risks and made extraordinary sacrifices in spite of the fact that they were not personally threatened by the enemy. That is to say, none were backed into the proverbial corner, all of them being situated in non-occupied nations or territories at the outset of the war—Ethiopia, Palestine, England, and so forth. All the same, they chose to serve in Nazi-occupied nations in the course of the conflict. Groomed to become socialites, they instead became spies and subversives, a radically different and potentially deadly trajectory for which their prewar debutante days had not prepared them. It was, however, a trajectory to which they readily adapted. All told, the indomitable women we are about to meet joined the resistance because of their profound commitment to eradicating totalitarianism and ensuring a world of liberty, humanity, and honor. They were, by any measure, women of passion and principle.

1

Vera Atkins and the Special Operations Executive

At the height of World War II, a Scottish journalist by the name of George Millar decided to join the Special Operations Executive, or SOE, a formidable covert organization based in London. As a journalist, he had spent time in occupied France covering the exploits of the maquis, the guerrilla warfare outfit, and now he wished to undergo paramilitary training himself and be dropped into the same territory as an operative. But he was in a fix: he was infatuated with a young woman and found his desire to spend time with her competing with his commitment to the SOE's rigorous training program. So it was that the lovesick journalist, upon giving the matter considerable thought, decided to seek a compromise by devoting himself fully to the SOE's training course while asking the organization's highest ranking female member, the thirty-six-year-old Vera Atkins, for permission to leave the compound so that he might enjoy a few moments with the object of his affection. A force of nature, the no-nonsense Atkins was a woman be both feared and adored.

"I have fallen in love," Millar told Atkins in a face-to-face meeting at SOE headquarters. He thought it best to be straightforward about the matter.

"Are you serious?" she replied. "Oh, the bloody English! We never have bother of this outrageous sort with the French," she said. The French "just copulate, and that is that."

But the besotted Millar persisted, imploring that she allow him "a few hours, or days, around London."

"Well, leave it to me, you poor sap. I'll pinch you every bit of spare time I can wangle," Aktins said. "What's she like?"

"Small, fair, but more Spanish than English in some ways," he replied.

"A security risk," Atkins said.

"Don't worry," Millar said, now delighting in the banter. "[S]he doesn't know a thing."[1]

A woman of her word, Atkins did indeed make good on her promise for the young correspondent to visit his new lover, and shortly thereafter Millar was parachuted, as he had requested, into a treacherous area of occupied France. As for his memory of Atkins, he always recalled her with great fondness, as did so many who knew her, she being the steely spymistress of the SOE whose stern demeanor concealed a very human heart. Yet she had not always been so tough-minded, or, for that matter, had she always been known as Vera Atkins. In fact, she wasn't even British-born — she hailed from Romania — although she kept such particulars under wraps throughout the war, even from many of her colleagues. By all accounts, she was a twenty-four carat woman of mystery.

In this chapter, we will meet the indomitable Vera Atkins. Imbued with intelligence, fortitude, and a profound social conscience, she was both an admired and misunderstood figure during Britain's war years. In recounting her life, we will become better acquainted with this remarkable woman who was well ahead of her time, which, as it turns out, was very much to the benefit of the world at large.

The Rosenbergs of Romania

Vera Atkins was born into lavish circumstances in Galati, Romania, a seaport on the Danube River. Her mother and father, Hilda and Max Rosenberg, were recent arrivals in the Central European country, Hilda having been born and reared in South Africa, a British colony at the time, and Max hailing from Germany.

As to the couple's affluence, Hilda's ancestors had amassed a fortune in South African diamond mines in the nineteenth century, while Max, in the early years of the twentieth, had established a Romanian shipping company. Using its vast distribution network, he shipped timber far and wide, the result being that the company's profits soared and seemingly assured the couple's future prosperity. With shining optimism, Hilda and Max, who already had a son, decided during this auspicious period to bring into the world another child.

In her comprehensive biography of Vera Rosenberg Atkins, *A Life in Secrets,* journalist Sarah Helm recounts that the pair celebrated the birth of their daughter Vera on June 16, 1908.[2] In a touching expression of fatherly love, Max decided to name a ship in the child's honor, such was the adoration into which she was born.[3] By all accounts, it seemed her life would be a privileged one; certainly it began with a childhood that was positively enchanting.

It was in an affluent Gatali neighborhood that Vera lived with her family in an "elegant single-storey villa, shaded by linden trees," writes Helm.⁴ Here, the cheerful, blonde-haired girl enjoyed the run of the villa, brimming with vitality as she basked in the affection that her family showered on her. A carefree existence, it was a sunny period for her and her loved ones, although this should not be taken to imply that life was perfect for the Rosenbergs or that it was entirely free of concern. Among other issues, there existed the potential for anti–Semitism to encroach upon their contentment, although this had not occurred to an appreciable degree presumably because their wealth and influence in Romanian society shielded them from it. Unfortunately, their financial circumstances, and after that their social acceptability, would decline in the years ahead and intolerance would enter their lives. But during these, the early years of Vera's childhood, the Rosenbergs were well-liked by those around them and treated with respect.

Three years later, Hilda and Max brought into the world another child, a boy. It also was at this juncture that they decided to purchase a new estate, and it was a truly grand one. An impressive six thousand acre property, Crasna, as it was known, contained a magnificent chateau dating back to the seventeenth century, with an entrance hall boasting an enormous stone staircase and intricately carved walls. Impressive, too, were the grounds, which included a stable for the family's horses (Vera would become an avid equestrienne (as well as a lake, a tennis court, and thousands of acres of lush vegetation.⁵ A sumptuous residence, it was a home that young Vera appears to have adored and one in which she would enjoy some of the warmest moments of her childhood. Only with the arrival of World War I would her satisfaction be interrupted, a turn of events that occurred while she and her family were en route to a summer holiday on the Dutch coast.

The Rosenbergs, sans Max, stepped off the Orient Express in Berlin in the late summer of 1914 only to discover that war had broken out.⁶ Taking stock of their unsettling circumstances, Hilda decided they should board with some of Max's relatives in K(ln until the conflict was resolved. Like a large swatch of the population, she appears to have believed the war would be a brief one, a fleeting setback on the family's expedition to the seacoast. As historian Paul Fussell has noted, it would be several weeks before the public would come to the disturbing realization that the conflict would not, in fact, be "over by Christmas."⁷ As it stretched into a debilitating four-year ordeal, Hilda seems to have become exasperated, and understandably so. She was in the unenviable position of being marooned with her children in a war-torn country. Young Vera, on the other hand, does not appear to have been as upset by this unexpected diversion. Her lengthy stay in the foreign nation even carried distinct benefits, providing her, for instance, with a familiarity with the German language and a knowledge of German society. It was an education that would serve her well in the years ahead.

When the war drew to a close, Hilda and the children returned to Romania, where Vera resumed her education at the estate. Her subsequent studies, most notably those in her teenage years, would take her to private schools in Switzerland and France, as well as to England in her early twenties to attend a business college. Providentially, these experiences, like her extended stay in Germany, would help prepare her for the clandestine work she eventually would perform against the Third Reich.

In terms of another important aspect of Vera's young adult years — her love life — it appears to have been a colorful one. Among her relationships were an ill-starred romance with a young British pilot aboard a cruise ship bound for Egypt, an affair with a White Russian prince, and, according to an acquaintance, "a blissful summer in the company of another young woman."[8] Political affairs, on the other hand, do not appear to have held much interest for her; that is, until she chanced upon Count Friedrich Werner von der Schulenburg, a German envoy to Romania, with whom she enjoyed a lengthy affair. Unlike many of his fellow countrymen, Schulenburg was not enamored with Adolf Hitler or National Socialism, and in this regard he and Vera were in complete agreement. In terms of the relationship itself, besides providing Vera with the pleasure of an adult romance with an erudite gentleman, it also offered her a window into the inner workings of the German government. No doubt it was an edifying experience in light of the fact that National Socialism was on the ascent.

It was during this same period that the Great Depression descended on Romania, with one of its casualties being Max Rosenberg and the fortune he had amassed. Following the financial meltdown and Max's death in 1932, the remaining Rosenbergs not only were less affluent but also more subject to discrimination. This is because the flames of anti–Semitism were intensifying, flames that would reach alarming heights in the years to come. Presumably, it was for this reason that the three Rosenberg children, in the course of the 1930s, decided to change their surname to Atkins, Hilda's maiden name.

As it happened, more unwelcome change would enter Vera's life when, two years later, her relationship with Count Schulenburg came to a halt as the German government transferred him to Moscow to serve as ambassador. She therefore began spending time with other well-placed gentlemen in Bucharest, among them a handful of British intelligence agents who were functioning covertly in the capital city. "[S]he was evidently at ease with such shadowy figures," writes Helm, based on her research into this period of Atkins' life.[9]

Another author, William Stevenson, has also written about these years,

1. Vera Atkins and the Special Operations Executive 11

the 1930s, and he alleges that Vera went so far as to help these operatives in secret missions that stretched far beyond the borders of Romania. He claims, for instance, that an influential figure in Britain's Industrial Intelligence Center who made Vera's acquaintance in Romania became so "impressed by her mind, her mastery of several languages, her dedication, and her fierce anti–Nazi stance" that he dispatched her on "fact-finding missions to several European countries, secretly reporting her findings to a few trusted souls in Britain."[10] Such theatrical assertions are intriguing.

As to what we know with a high degree of certainty, based again on Helm's meticulous research, is that one of Vera's companions in the Romanian capital was Leslie Humphreys, a British intelligence agent whose cover was that of a businessman. It was to him that she passed information from a job she landed as an interpreter at an oil company in Romania.[11] Because Germany was striving to acquire Romanian oil in its buildup to war, her position with the petroleum company, one that required her to translate a range of documents, allowed her to keep an eye on the Germans' progress in this regard. Naturally, such inside information was valuable to the British. Meanwhile, conditions for the Jewish citizenry of Romania continued to deteriorate, eventually culminating in an untenable situation for the Rosenbergs.

With the forecast for the nation's Jews being grim, Vera and her mother decided in 1937 to flee the country and after a treacherous journey arrived in England in the autumn of that year. Whereas Hilda was a citizen of a British colony, South Africa, Vera was a citizen of Romania, a nation that was aligned with Germany. For this reason, she was permitted to enter England but was denied British citizenship. For years to come, she would struggle to obtain it.

Like countless Jewish immigrants from Central Europe, the young Romanian appears to have kept a low profile during the early months of the war. Even so, any well-connected person who wished to find her could do so. And this proved to be in Vera's favor when, in February 1941, she received a note from Leslie Humphreys, her former contact in Bucharest. The impression she made on the covert agent during their time together appears to have been an indelible one, and now that she was in England he hoped to bring her into the intelligence fold more officially. Vera was not only smart and trustworthy but also fluent in French, German, and English, as well as her native Romanian. Clearly, she possessed an amalgam of qualities that could be of considerable value to British Intelligence.

For his part, Humphreys, since the outbreak of war, had been serving with Britain's MI6 (Military Intelligence — Foreign) — also known as the Secret Intelligence Service (SIS) — orchestrating sabotage operations behind enemy lines. Recently, however, he had joined a handful of insiders who were creating a more radical organization, one that would incorporate elements of MI6 and other clandestine groups into a far more audacious enterprise. Known as the

Special Operations Executive, the SOE was "a potent and venturesome outfit," says William Casey, former director of the Central Intelligence Agency, one that would gain a reputation as "the most swashbuckling of the British organizations."[12] It was this new agency into which Humphreys wished to bring Vera.

In what would signal an abrupt change in the trajectory of her life, Humphreys invited the thirty-two-year-old Romanian to interview at the organization's headquarters in London, and she promptly complied. Not only would the job improve her chances of obtaining British citizenship, but, more importantly, it would place her in a position to oppose the Third Reich in a meaningful way. Predictably, given Vera's intelligence and social dexterity, the interview went well and she was hired on the spot, initially as a secretary for the clandestine agency.

The Special Operations Executive

The Special Operations Executive was a distinctive wartime organization that was widely regarded as "Churchill's baby."[13] Unlike a sizable share of his government, the prime minister, from the outset of the war, grasped the unprecedented threat that Hitler's war machine posed to the West and the need for Britain to do everything in its power to halt it. Traditional methods, in his opinion, simply would not suffice.

"From the moment he took office," writes historian Anthony Cave Brown, "the most basic of all Churchill's concepts about how Germany would be defeated was that there should be created throughout German-occupied Europe 'an army of the shadows.'"[14] As to the role Britain might play in shaping such a force, Churchill's idea was a clever one: the British government would create a special covert organization that would serve as a catalyst for the domestic resistance movements that were springing up in German-occupied nations. Its intent would be to aid and abet these grassroots opposition groups, employing "the resource of the weak against the strong," in the words of historian M. R. D. Foot.[15]

Hugh Dalton, dubbed Dr. Dynamo by his colleagues, was named the director of the SOE. In a memoir he penned after the war, he explained that the organization was designed to move beyond the tactics of sabotage, heretofore the focus of clandestine British operations, and embrace more unconventional methods:

> [S]abotage was a simple idea. It meant smashing things up.
> "Subversion" was a more complex conception. It meant the weakening, by whatever "covert" means, of the enemy's will and power to make war, and the strengthening of the will and power of his opponents, including in particular, guerrilla and resistance movements.[16]

Despite widespread anxiety about the war, many in the British intelligence community objected to the SOE's approach. They viewed its methods as underhanded and unseemly, arguing that its tactics were on a par with those of the Nazis. For that matter, even the Nazis themselves would eventually howl about the organization's agents, likening them to terrorists in spite of the fact that the British operatives' deeds were never aimed at civilians, and, in fact, were specifically designed to avoid injury to noncombatants.[17] Despite the controversy, Churchill stayed true to his instincts and put his full weight behind what he proudly called his "ministry of ungentlemanly warfare."[18]

The SOE was officially, if secretly, launched in July 1940 and fast became a daring and adventurous outfit. It also expanded rapidly, establishing branches in Asia, Europe, Africa, and North America in addition to its main offices at 64 Baker Street in London. By the final years of the war, the organization would employ over thirteen thousand people around the globe, five thousand of whom would be agents in the field.[19] The preponderance of the staff would be involved in concocting clandestine operations, recruiting and training agents, procuring and distributing supplies, and providing security for agents. The workforce would also research lifestyles in occupied nations, track political developments in relevant countries, and decode messages. It was an enormous undertaking and one that the SOE would accomplish in near-total secrecy.

As a secretary for the organization, Vera Atkins' unique traits were soon on display and helped spark her rapid ascent. It was only a matter of time before the bright and brisk Romanian came to the attention of Maurice Buckmaster, the head of the SOE's French Section, or F Section. It was this division's function to oversee underground operations in occupied France. A tall, wiry Eton graduate, the buttoned-down Buckmaster was a well-meaning gentleman whose previous job had been with the Ford Motor Company division in France. "[A] man who was more often praised for affability than for keenness of mind," writes Rita Kramer, the amiable Buckmaster had a genuine respect for women and was quick to ask the self-assured and opinionated Atkins to serve by his side.[20] Certainly she was qualified to work in the French Section, and not just because of her decisive demeanor. Buckmaster, by this point, appears to have known that she possessed the life experiences as well.

As we have seen, Vera had lived in Germany throughout World War I, an ordeal that familiarized her with that nation's society and language. She also had enjoyed close personal relationships with politically-informed German men, most notably Count Schulenburg, the envoy who provided her with an insider's view of Hitler's rise to power. Additionally, she had a South African mother who had bred into her British attitudes and values. And Vera had formed relationships with British intelligence agents in Bucharest, as well as completing a secretarial program in London where she acquired organizational skills while further absorbing the British way of life. Along the way, she had lived and studied in Lausanne and Paris, where she enhanced her expertise in the French language and enriched her knowledge of French culture. In short, her background was a propitious mélange of formal education and personal experience in Romania, Germany, Switzerland, France, and England, which, coupled with her intelligence and determination, promised to make her a singular asset to the SOE's French Section.

Before long, Buckmaster elevated Vera, if informally, to the role of deputy director of the F Section. In time, he formally appointed her "Intelligence Officer — F Section." Although it was Buckmaster's job to oversee the training and dispatch of operatives into occupied France, Vera appears to have become so adept at these tasks that in time she was virtually running the F Section while Buckmaster more or less served as its figurehead. "Coolly handsome, very tough, shrewd, quick," recalled one of her former operatives, Vera "was regarded by many people as the critical force in [the] French Section."[21] Behind closed doors at the SOE, the consensus seems to have been that she was smarter and more cunning than Buckmaster. She also was considered tougher, with her firmness solidifying as the demands on the F Section multiplied and intensified in the course of the war.

Described as "brilliant"[22] and "indefatigable,"[23] Vera appears to have been a quick study and a classic workhorse, grasping virtually every aspect of the F Section during her eighteen-hour workdays. She even went so far as to memorize the minutiae of her agents' personal lives and cover stories, which was no easy task considering there were 470 operatives. And she learned to take in stride the nonstop chaos of the F Section itself. "In Baker Street's years of almost chronic crisis," writes journalist Max Hastings, "Vera was the woman never seen to lose her head."[24]

By all accounts, the pressure on the French Section was tremendous and often pushed the staff to its limits. This was due mainly to the section's daunting mandate: its principal mission was to prepare the various factions of the French Resistance to take action when the Allies invaded occupied France on D-Day. Along the way, the F Section was to supply armaments and agents to help the French underground engage in day-to-day covert operations against the enemy. And this is what came to define Vera's life during the war years. So it was that the former socialite became a robust, single-minded leader of a widespread network of spies carrying out covert maneuvers behind enemy lines.

Based on what we know about the SOE during this period, Vera was exemplary at her task, as was the F Section itself. A few months after she joined it, the division had its first major victory, one that served notice to MI6 and other rival domestic agencies that the upstart organization was having an impact on the war. It happened when a handful of F Section agents parachuted into France, where, with a small number of expertly-placed explosives, they managed to demolish a crucial power station. The consequence: railways in the Bordeaux region were brought to a standstill and work at one of the Germans' principal U-boat facilities had to suspend operations.

As the war stretched on, Vera, whose influence in the SOE was mounting, was among those who pressed for advances in the organization itself, with one her more significant campaigns centering on the inclusion of female operatives into the French Section. As it stood, the British government had historically relegated women to support roles in wartime, such as performing manual labor in munitions factories or providing nursing care in infirmaries. But the War Cabinet, at Vera and the SOE's urging, secretly agreed in 1942 to authorize the use of females behind enemy lines on the premise that the Germans might be less suspicious of women than of men. Then, too, it was thought that women could acquire specialized skills unique to their gender. "[F]or clandestine purposes," says Foot, "there were several tasks that women would perform a good deal better than men."[25] Vera, being among those who selected, trained, and dispatched these women into France, performed her role with the utmost care.

Regarding the means of recruiting women to serve as operatives, they appear to have been largely the same as those used for men. In a couple of respects there were differences, however, most notably in the areas of physical attractiveness and social class. In the SOE, some believed that the Gestapo might be less likely to arrest women who were blessed with stunning features and who appeared to be members of the smart set, the leisure class; that male officers of the Nazi secret police would not wish to risk being reprimanded by their superiors for behaving toward seemingly well-connected women in a way that might be considered disrespectful, intrusive, or otherwise offensive. On this premise, the French Section, on occasion, intentionally enlisted women who were comely and well-heeled, many of whom it drew from the First Aid Nursing Yeomanry (FANY). A nursing unit, FANY was viewed as a "somewhat socially exclusive" support service that appealed to women of the privileged class who wished to serve their country.[26] It was Vera who helped prepare these stylish women, along with the section's other female newcomers, for undercover work in occupied France.

To this end, Vera spent countless hours briefing each one on everything the woman might need to know to live undetected behind enemy lines. She taught the agents about current practices in occupied France, such as curfews and ration regulations, and she provided them with French clothing and accessories. According to writer Shrabani Basu, Vera also furnished them with fake letters, tickets, and other items to keep with them while working undercover.[27] If an agent were arrested, these authentic-looking objects could help convince the enemy that the operative was a French citizen. Invariably, Vera was businesslike with these women, deliberately trying to avoid becoming too attached to them. Even so, she was still human and indeed did become fond of them, particularly since their lives, to a very real extent, were in her hands. In virtually every case, she saw her agents off at the airfield herself.

Throughout the war years, Vera appears to have more or less lived in her Baker Street office, toiling throughout the day and evening hours. For reasons of national security, she could not disclose to her mother the nature of her work despite the fact that the two still lived under the same roof in Chelsea. Of course, this left Hilda to wonder about her daughter's lifestyle. Once, when a dog-tired Vera returned home at daybreak, her mother just shook her head. "Well, I hope at the end of all this he makes an honest woman of you, dear," Hilda said.[28]

All of which brings us to Vera's love life. For the most part, it is unclear if she had one during the war, her practical attitude toward sex notwithstanding. No reports exist of romantic encounters during this time. Dedicated to her job, her focus was first and foremost on her agents. And although a rumor did circulate which suggested that she may have been intimately involved with her boss, Maurice Buckmaster, the affair, if it existed, was never confirmed. Given Vera's self-assured, brusque manner and her prominent role in the SOE, it is possible that the men with whom she was in daily contact simply felt too intimidated to ask out her out.

George Millar, for one, the Scottish journalist whose recollections opened this chapter, adored Vera but admitted that he felt threatened by her. "She terrified me," he said.[29] An episode also has been recounted in which a Frenchman whom Vera had trained in espionage decided to invite her on a date. "He nerved himself to make a pass," it was said, "but in the end could not go through with it — he was too frightened of her."[30]

As the war progressed and the demands on F Section mounted, so, too, did the hardworking Vera's responsibilities. And these duties involved both desk work and legwork.

She maintained a signal log, for instance, a record of communications being sent into, and received from, occupied France, and which only a few SOE officials were allowed to view because the information could be extremely damaging if it were to fall into the wrong hands.[31] It could easily cost agents their lives. For this reason, the log's custodian had to be above reproach, a person trusted within the walls of the Baker Street organization, and this is why Vera was the F Section official who was selected to preserve the documents.

At designated locations in London and elsewhere, Vera also met with each F Section agent upon the individual's return from an assignment in France. During these secret reunions, which were more akin to friendly interrogations, she debriefed the operative so as to learn about the ever-changing conditions that existed behind enemy lines. The more she knew about the situations into which she would be dropping her agents in the weeks ahead, the more she could tailor her preparations and better help them avoid detection. Up-to-date information was critical in covert operations.

The accounts of those agents who came back to Britain also appear to have helped Vera recruit new operatives behind enemy lines and expand the F Section's reach inside of France. Among other things, returning agents were in a position to supply her with the names of French citizens who had agreed to help undermine the Germans either by joining the resistance or offering their services in other ways. Surely such grassroots support was key to the F Section's success, since its activities in France relied on the participation of the local populations. Villagers were "crucial in providing safe houses for agents [and] letter boxes for couriers," says Shrabani Basu, just as local farmers were vital in providing fields into which agents could be parachuted and barns into which their armaments could be stored.[32] It was a risky business by any measure, as well as a splendid partnership between the British and French people. It demonstrated that ordinary men and women could evince extraordinary behavior when called upon to do so. This had long been Vera's contention.

As the war stretched onward, her belief that women, in particular, would make suitable agents in the field, that they possessed the right stuff, was confirmed persuasively. According to historian Marcus Binney, the "resourcefulness and success" of Vera's earliest female operatives proved that she had been correct on this score.[33] Ultimately, she and the SOE would send thirty-nine women into occupied France, each of whom would carry out deeds of striking temerity. Surely Vera was herself successful in virtually everything she did for the SOE, and she did an enormous amount with the exception of serving behind enemy lines. This is because the agency's regulations forbade her from doing so, just as it prohibited Buckmaster and other high-level figures from traveling abroad. Such people simply knew too much about the organization's operations. Were the Germans to capture a Vera Atkins or a Maurice Buckmaster, their disclosures under torture could fell the entire Special Operations Executive.

A debacle that did damage, but not destroy, the organization occurred in the summer of 1943 when Maurice Buckmaster welcomed a new recruit, Henri Déricourt, into the operation. Many now believe that Déricourt knowingly furnished information to the Germans that resulted in several SOE agents being arrested, tortured, and in some cases, executed. To be sure, it was a dark period for the Special Operations Executive.

And yet, while the SOE was alarmed and perplexed over the abrupt disappearance of these operatives, the organization, by its nature, was accustomed to living with ambiguity and so it continued moving forward and making remarkable headway. This was due not only to its determination but also to its pragmatic style of operation. The staff's unwavering agreement on the organization's aims appears to have focused its priorities and enhanced its esprit de corps. To its credit, the SOE lacked the internecine warfare that consumed the energies of many other groups during the war. In describing the down-to-earth nature of the agency, one of its officers said it seemed less like a gathering of geniuses than "just shrewd, sensible people working very hard."[34] By all accounts, they were a collection of individualists, even mavericks, from diverse backgrounds. And Vera invariably came up for praise, being appreciated by, among others, those keyed-up operatives she primed for life behind enemy lines. "[W]onderfully soothing," is how one of them portrayed her.[35]

In 1944, Vera and her staff would toil most feverishly, this being the most crucial, and the most hectic, year of the operation. This is because the invasion of France was fast approaching and D-Day, as we have noted, was F Section's ultimate mission. Its overarching mandate had always been to help prepare the French Resistance for the Allied invasion.

Throughout the war, the SOE, through its F Section, had airdropped supplies into France on an ongoing basis. During the month of May 1944, however, it dispatched its greatest share: a full twenty-five percent of the total amount it dropped during the entire war. In terms of manpower, the French Section now possessed its largest number of agents, nearly all of whom were on the ground in France and laboring side by side with a far greater number of French Resistance fighters to prepare the country for the Allied offensive.

So it was that the Allies, on June 6, surged onto the beaches of Normandy. Although Vera, firmly planted at SOE headquarters in London, could do little more than monitor events from afar, her agents on the ground ramped up their efforts, pulling out all stops to aid the Allied troops that poured into the country by land and by sea. Surely their accomplishments were stunning. One of Vera's female agents, a courier by the name of Pearl Witherington, took the reins in one region and led a unit of fifteen hundred maquis against the Germans. Elsewhere in France, F Section agents siphoned oil from the wheels of trains carrying the equipment of Germany's Second SS Panzer Division and replaced it with an abrasive solution that brought the trains to a screeching halt. Still other agents, in concert with scores of French Resistance members, ambushed this same Panzer division yet again as its soldiers tried to trek northward to Normandy, thereby delaying the division's arrival by over two weeks. By this time, the Allies had secured the Normandy coast and established a footing in France. It was a pivotal development that marked the beginning of the end of the battle for France, with the SOE, most notably its French Section, having achieved enormous success. It also was an accomplishment in which Vera shared enthusiastically, albeit one that signaled the end of her days as a leading figure in the organization.

As it happened, when the F Section was created the decision was made that French officials would assume control of it when Allied forces gained a stronghold in France; that is, when opposition no longer needed to be covert but could be performed overtly. And this meant D-Day. At this juncture, Vera Atkins, Maurice Buckmaster, and their associates in the F Section were to give over their London offices to their French counterparts and move into a suite the organization had set aside for them in a nearby building. But now that the time was at hand, Vera evidently had second thoughts. Although she had gotten along famously with her French equivalents throughout the war — she had worked with them hand in hand under the most trying of circumstances — she became recalcitrant. "Vera Atkins flatly refused to leave Baker Street," says Hastings.[36] No doubt her obstinacy stemmed from the fact that the war was not yet over and she still had well over a hundred agents in the field. So she remained an immovable object in the months leading up to the conclusion of the war. Certainly no one at the SOE had the nerve to eject her.

As the historical record reveals, Germany, in the early hours of May 7, 1945, surrendered to the Allies, thereby bringing to a close the war in Europe. By the end of the summer, most members of the Special Operations Executive had left the organization, with the F Section, in particular, being essentially vacated. Buckmaster had returned to his prewar position as an executive at the Ford Motor division in France, and the preponderance of his F Section staff members had returned to their former jobs or secured new ones. Vera, however, remained in her office at the Special Operations Executive. Having a strong sense of personal responsibility, it seems she could not bring herself to leave her post until she knew what had become of 118 of her agents who had not come back from the war. These were people she had helped select and train, the same men and women to whom she had bid farewell at the airstrip night after night. And she was determined to find them or at least find out what had happened to them.

Descent into the Death Camps

Vera began by writing letters to a British Army command center in Germany, according to Sarah Helm's research into Atkins' postwar activities.[37] As it stood, though, the officials had little information about Vera's missing agents for the same reason that news about so many people was hard to obtain in that place and time: parts of Germany had been reduced to rubble and the nation's communication system was in tatters. All the same, she kept writing letters and in other ways searching for any shreds of information she could dig up about her operatives.

Several months after D-Day, Vera's persistence paid off when she discovered that the father of Violette Szabo, one of her missing couriers, had approached the Red Cross and the British military in an effort to learn about the fate of his daughter. When answers were not forthcoming, he got in touch with a Member of Parliament, a development that placed the government in a bind since the matter promised to become awkward if it reached the House of Commons. It would be tricky because it was still largely unknown that the nation had sent women behind enemy lines.

Vera chose this time to approach her superiors in London and request that she be allowed to travel to Germany to check on her lost operatives. Politically uncomfortable questions would no doubt continue to arise until it was obtained. Accordingly, British officials, not without certain misgivings, permitted her to embark on a series of investigations in Germany over the next year. Eventually, as her inquiries progressed and produced tangible results, the British government would promote her to Squadron Leader in order to provide her with more muscle in her investigations. Along these same lines, it would assign her to Britain's War Crimes Investigation Unit so as to further increase her resources and clout.

As to the specifics of Vera's mission, she set off in December 1945, traveling to the German town of Bad Oeynhausen. Formerly a fashionable health resort on the Weser River, it was at Bad Oeynhausen that the British Army had set up a postwar command center. From here, she journeyed to outlying areas to question the perpetrators and victims of crimes believed to have been committed in concentration camps and other facilities. As well, she distributed questionnaires and spoke at length to an array of eyewitnesses. In doing so, she remained both objective and professional despite the disturbing accounts that rolled in. "Vera was always composed," it was said of her demeanor during these inquiries.[38]

As it happened, Atkins began obtaining results almost immediately, findings that were at once illuminating and disconcerting. Early on, for instance, she received word suggesting that a handful of her female agents may have been sent to Ravensbruck concentration camp in northern Germany. An infamous facility designed specially for women, Ravensbruck was known for thrashing them, starving them, and all too often killing them, says Robert Jay Lifton.[39] It was also a camp in which no British women were thought to have been interned. So it was that Vera, pursuing her lead, was able to verify conclusively that three of her female operatives had indeed been transported to the ghastly camp and shot to death. Among the victims was Violette Szabo, the young woman whose father had sought out a Member of Parliament in a heartwrenching effort to find out what had become of his daughter.

Vera further secured information suggesting that the Nazis, in 1944, had sent another group of her female agents to Natzweiler-Struthof, a concentration camp where captives were used in medical experiments, worked to death, and otherwise maltreated or killed. A notorious facility hidden away in the mountains near Alsace, France, Natzweiler-Struthof was among those installations the Nazis designated for use under Hitler's top-secret directive known as *Nacht und Nebel,* or "Night and Fog."[40]

Intended mainly for political dissidents and resistance figures, this edict called for those who opposed the regime to be abducted and hauled off to special concentration camps without being charged with a crime or placed on trial. At no point were the authorities to give information to the abductees' families or comrades-in-arms about what had happened to them, nor even admit they had been seized. In this way, those who contested the Nazi ideology could be removed from view without due process or public outcry, with their disappearances serving to intimidate their loved ones and accomplices into docility in the face of the regime. Once the *Nacht und Nebel* abductees were placed in the camps, these being secret compounds situated in remote areas, the prisoners were commanded to remain silent at all times. On their shirts, a bulls-eye was stitched over their hearts and signified that the guards could kill them at any moment and for any reason. "In the precise and detailed registers of the camps," writes historian Martin Gilbert, "the initials *NN* against the name of a prisoner signified that he had been taken out of his barrack and shot."[41]

Based on the physical descriptions she obtained from witnesses, Vera compiled a list of F Section women whom she thought might have been the victims of the *Nacht und Nebel* directive and unlawfully sent to the Natzweiler-Struthof facility. She next tracked down and questioned eyewitnesses in Belgium, France, Germany, and Luxembourg. Based on the numerous accounts she collected, she was able to establish that four female agents of the F Section had indeed been put to death at Natzweiler-Struthof. At the ensuing trial that was held in the spring of 1946, Vera was the first to take the stand and provide testimony against the murderers and their accomplices.[42]

In the summer of 1946, she moved on to Dachau, where she commenced an inquiry into events at that concentration camp. And so it went, with the indomitable spy mistress moving from site to site in her single-minded pursuit of her operatives.

As a result of those gray months she spent trudging through the ruins of postwar Europe, Vera was able to establish what had become of 117 of her 118 missing agents. All of the former were dead. "The 118th had been, unknown to her," reports the *New York Times,* "a compulsive gambler who vanished not far from Monte Carlo while carrying three millions francs of secret service money."[43]

Besides tracking down news of her operatives, Vera also collected and prepared evidence for use in the mounting number of war crimes trials that loomed on the horizon, a grim task to be sure.[44] She was dedicated to bringing to justice those who had committed such heinous crimes against humanity. Of these cases, perhaps the most notable was her interrogation of Rudolf Hoess, the former commandant of the Auschwitz extermination camp.

With an interpreter in tow, Vera told Hoess she had reason to believe he had supervised the slaughter of a staggering number of people, perhaps as many as a million. "Oh, no, 2,345,000," he corrected her, seeming to take pride in his kill rate.[45] Of course, he was incriminating himself with such a vainglorious admission. As the historical record shows, Hoess soon joined the ranks of the dead, with the Polish Supreme National Tribunal, two weeks after his trial, ordering him to be hanged next to a crematorium at Auschwitz. It marked the demise of one of the most notorious mass murderers in history, the man who introduced the use of cyanide gas, Zyklon B, to hasten the extermination of the European Jewry. And it was Vera's interrogation that helped send him to the gallows.

Unlike Rudolf Hoess, the indefatigable Atkins would go on to enjoy a long and prosperous life. One burden she would have to bear, however, concerned a smudge on her reputation owing to the British operative Henri Déricourt. He was the ostensible double agent who worked for SOE and evidently MI6, and who appears to have handed over several of Vera's agents to the Nazis. Surprisingly, when he was taken before the court, he was acquitted. As to the reason, it was speculated that British Intelligence, upon taking him on during the war, knew he would betray some of its agents in order to win the Nazis' trust and it allowed him to proceed. In other words, British Intelligence may have accepted his evidently premeditated betrayals of its agents as the human cost of using him as an effective agent against the German war machine. Vera, however, does not appear to have known about this scheme, if indeed it actually existed. She seems to have been referring to Déricourt when, in 1949, Jean Overton Fuller interviewed her on three occasions. During one of their talks, Fuller mentioned a woman in France who had been guilty of betraying an SOE agent but whom the courts had set free. Vera, being familiar with the case, expressed her dismay that the woman had been exonerated. Then Aktins said something else. "She dropped a reference to another acquittal, an acquittal which had particularly sickened her," writes Fuller. "She did not name a name, but I remembered the words and the tone and later realised that her reference had been to Déricourt."[46] Fuller adds that "Miss Atkins had spoken of Déricourt as 'rotten.'"[47]

In the end, it appears that Vera was not a player in what some believe to have been the odious machinations of MI6, SOE, and Henri Déricourt, but instead was out of the loop in this episode in modern espionage history. Even so, she remained under a cloud of suspicion owing to her involvement with the Special Operations Executive and the belief, in some quarters, that British Intelligence had knowingly allowed some of its agents to be sacrificed. Thus, despite her diligent, courageous, and altruistic work both during and after the war, she fell victim to conjecture that was exceedingly unfair to her. Unfortunately, it would persist in some measure for a long time to come and would be joined by other unfounded rumors.

Unexpected Strengths

After World War II, Vera appears to have found herself peppered with questions from Members of Parliament, historians, and filmmakers about the Special Operations Executive. Seeking her out, too, were those who had served alongside her in the French Section. The latter were penning their memoirs and were in need of her recollections, opinions, and insights. But although Vera assisted them, she did not encourage them. For that matter, she did not seem to understand why they would choose to revisit their clandestine activities.

"[M]ust you write a damned book?" Vera asked resistance agent George Millar, adding that she found it to be a rather "cheap idea."[48] Her concern, she explained, was that the public might misconstrue the book to be a scheme to cash in on his wartime deeds and she knew this was not his reason for writing it. All the same, she did proceed to help him and others, although she had no plans to publish a chronicle of her own. In much the same way, she tirelessly petitioned the British government to bestow awards on her agents who had served with distinction, but at no point did she seek such recognition for herself — not that the powers-that-be would have granted it at that time.

In this regard, the French bestowed on Vera a much-deserved Croix de Guerre in 1948, but the British gave her no such honor in the years immediately following the war. Decades later, in 1995, the French government again paid tribute to her, making her a Commandeur de la Légion d'Honneur. But it was not until 1997 that the British government finally recognized Vera's accomplishments — it was now a half century after the war — and bestowed upon her the Commander of the Order of the British Empire (CBE).

The fact is, there were those in Britain who regarded Atkins as a somewhat controversial figure as well as an uncomfortably unconventional one. As a hardy, self-sufficient woman who chose not to marry, for instance, her sexual orientation came into question after the war.[49] It seems there were those who wondered if the never-married, middle-aged woman might be drawn to her own gender, which, of course, was a socially unacceptable trait in that era. In fact, Vera may or may not have preferred other women, but if she did it was never confirmed. Certainly there is no indication of her having formed such a bond during her sixty-three years in Britain.

More darkly, some people during the 1950s speculated that she might be a Soviet spy, a suspicion reflecting the overheated political climate of the times.⁵⁰ This being the era of the Red Scare in the United States, political paranoia was likewise running amok in Britain. In Vera's case, she occasionally made politically liberal remarks that those around her mistook as leftist. Then, too, her history may have put her in the line of fire: she was a Romanian Jew by the name of Rosenberg who had escaped to Britain, changed her name, and become part of a top-secret spy network. For those with vivid imaginations and a taste for conspiracy, it was easy to concoct sinister theories about her. Unfortunately, such speculation was more than just talk; it also carried real-life consequences. Sarah Helm explains that it was during this period that the domestic security branch of Military Intelligence, MI5, opened a dossier on Vera to determine if she might be a Communist mole.⁵¹ And due to the suspicion that she might bear leftist leanings, Atkins was denied one job and looked upon with a degree of doubt in another position that she did hold. It seems that those who did not know her envisioned Vera committing an array of dubious deeds. It is therefore little wonder that she chose to offer scant information about herself to anyone who dared to probe. Yet such discretion itself may have fueled the conjecture, causing her to be perceived as a woman with a cache of secrets.

As the 1950s gave way to the 1960s, such speculation subsided and was supplanted by a renewed interest in her knowledge of the Special Operations Executive. It was information she readily provided. And she did more. Emblematic of her generous nature, Vera redoubled her efforts in the 1970s to keep alive the memory of the exceptional men and women of the SOE's French Section. To this end, she solicited funds for memorial projects for her fallen agents, with one of the ventures being situated on the grounds of the former Natzweiler-Struthof concentration camp. Another centered on establishing an annual commemorative service in the French town of Valençay in the Loire Valley, a region where numerous covert missions took place.

When she was not traveling in England and France as a part of her campaigns on behalf of her operatives, the adventurous Atkins journeyed to other parts of the world while also taking pleasure in her social life. "[S]he entertained and probably partied more in her seventies and eighties than she had since her Romania days," writes Helm.⁵² Despite her sociability, however, Vera seems to have remained a bit guarded and to have possessed a certain solemnity, a fleeting shadow that appeared on occasion. Some thought it reflected her remorse at having sent so many men and women to their deaths in occupied France, while others attributed it to the months she spent slogging through German concentration camps, interviewing the perpetrators and victims of the atrocities and attending the ensuing war crimes trials.⁵³

It is plausible, of course, that Vera's caginess and gravity may also have had their roots, at least in part, in her years in Romania, a time when she suddenly found it dangerous to let others know that she was a Jew by the name of Rosenberg. Being born into a wealthy family, basking in a childhood of enormous privilege, and enjoying a young adulthood spent courting Russian princes and German emissaries no doubt provided her with a solid sense of security and perhaps a feeling of invincibility. When her nation formed its profane alliance with the Third Reich, however, she found herself confronted with a reversal of fortune that caused her to become stigmatized and ostracized. It was a shock that may well have ruptured her worldview, with the consequences including a painful awareness of the illusory nature of security in one's life and an enduring tendency to avoid close examination by others.

That said, it appears that the same trauma also may have had a beneficial effect, setting into motion a constructive personal transformation. The fact is, Vera's initial response to the Nazi threat in Bucharest was to conceal her Jewishness and flee from her homeland. But later, when given the chance to go on the offense in London, she seized the opportunity, joining the SOE and steeling herself to fight vigorously against Hitler's malevolent command. Her experience of powerlessness in Romania, then, may have acted as a catalyst, prompting her to accrue a remarkable degree of authority in Britain.

As we have seen, Vera arrived in London in 1937 a dispossessed immigrant who was refused British citizenship, yet within five years she had become a leading figure in one of the most effective intelligence operations in Western Europe. And she made this leap in spite of numerous obstacles, not the least being the fact that she was a female in an era of male ascendancy. To be sure, the gender discrimination she faced appears to have been significant.

Vera was not granted the title Intelligence Officer in the SOE until 1943, for instance, even though she had essentially been running the French Section for nearly two years by that point. Along these same lines, she was not promoted to Squadron Leader in the WAAF until after the war, when it behooved the British government to boost her authority in the field so she could obtain the information it needed for the prosecution of Nazi war criminals. And when she was finally granted British citizenship, it came only after a second and prolonged tussle. Had Vera been a man, it could be argued that she would have been more quickly appointed an intelligence officer and promoted to squadron leader, and perhaps granted British citizenship at an earlier date. As it was, she had to wait longer and accomplish more to receive the same recognition as the men around her. As to those advances she did attain, it helped that she had complete confidence in herself, a certitude that caught the attention of her male colleagues and intimidated some of the more timid ones. Vera was well aware that she "could master anyone in trousers," in the words of one of her male agents.[54]

In such ways Atkins left behind the social trappings of her Romanian past and climbed to heights in London beyond what she could have imagined only a few years earlier. And through her charisma, energy, and passion, she inspired other women to push themselves to their own limits. These included, most significantly, her thirty-nine female agents, two-thirds of whom returned home after a war in which they had pulled off astounding feats behind enemy lines. In so doing, they had helped subvert the Nazi regime and hasten its downfall.

On June 24, 2000, Vera died of complications associated with a broken hip. She was ninety-two years old. Her obituary in the *New York Times* was suitably respectful, and it contained an oft-heard anecdote: Vera was the inspiration for the character of Miss Moneypenny, the secretary in Ian Fleming's series of James Bond novels.[55] Yet while it is true that Vera, like the fictional Moneypenny, was an urbane figure in the upper echelon of a British spy agency, this similarity applied only at the beginning. The real Vera promptly set aside her notepad and advanced to such a degree that she came to be regarded as the person who ran the French Section of the SOE itself.

In the end, it was Atkins' perfect balance of heart and mind that made her so adept in her role at the Special Operations Executive. A woman with a strong and distinctive personality, she possessed brilliance, resilience, and compassion, with the latter including, first and foremost, her abiding concern for her agents.

In her final years, Vera reflected on the qualities that made these men and women, seemingly ordinary citizens from all walks of life, agree to take part in missions of extreme peril from which they might never return. She decided it came down to their fundamental principles. "These people had no doubts about the importance of defeating Nazism," she said. "They undertook risks feeling it was a duty; they made a voluntary sacrifice."[56] She also remarked on the fortitude, unforeseen reserves of it, that came to the fore when these same individuals found themselves in life-threatening circumstances. "Ordinary people," she said, "sometimes reveal quite unexpected strengths."[57] Certainly this was a maxim that applied to Vera herself, a Romanian socialite who became Britain's premier spymistress and whose spirited work for the SOE helped to ensure an Allied victory in Europe. By all accounts, she, too, displayed unexpected strengths, and in so doing attracted a host of international admirers in the course of her long, distinguished, and dynamic life. Vera Atkins truly was a woman of valor.

2

Sophie Scholl and the White Rose Movement

On a summer day in 1942, scores of professional men and women in Munich, Germany, discovered in their mail a startling item: a hard-hitting political tract by an anonymous source, a treatise that objected stridently to the principles and practices of the Third Reich. In an era when red banners emblazoned with swastikas hung solemnly from edifices throughout the city, it was unthinkable that anyone, or any group of people, would dare to disseminate such a bald statement rebuking Adolf Hitler and his totalitarian regime. Yet it happened on this day.

"Nothing is so unworthy of a civilized nation as allowing itself to be 'governed' without opposition by an irresponsible clique that has yielded to base instinct," read the opening words of the one thousand-word text.[1] Thus began an eloquent case against the German leadership, with considerable culpability being placed upon the shoulders of the citizenry for tolerating the errant and excessive deeds of its government. The treatise then proceeded to provide an account of the harm the Führer and his minions had inflicted upon the nation, and it did not limit its damage assessment to the political sphere. It penetrated the realm of the individual as well, even to the plane of the soul. "[B]y means of gradual, treacherous, systematic abuse," the tract declared, "the system has put every man into a spiritual prison."[2] It was, by any measure, a damning indictment of both the fascist regime and the complacent populace that had enabled it, yet the treatise did not confine itself to condemnation; it also issued a call to action as a way to begin altering the situation. Borrowing from the passive-resistance approach that a segment of the black population in the United States was using in its own fight against oppression, the tract proposed a similar method: "Offer passive resistance —

resistance—wherever you may be, forestall the spread of this atheistic war machine before it is too late, before the last cities ... have been reduced to rubble, and before the nation's last young man has given his blood on some battlefield for the *hubris* of a sub-human."[3] Concluding with an excerpt from an allegorical play by Goethe, *The Awakening of Epimenides*, the text implored its readers to make copies of the tract and disperse them throughout the city.

During the ensuing months, more leaflets with further arguments against fascism and Germany's misguided course were distributed by the same source — it identified itself as the White Rose — with the tracts being dispatched not only to citizens' mailboxes but also to university campuses and even to beer halls. In time, they appeared on the streets of cities across Germany as well. Of course, such episodic bursts of defiance in the face of the deadliest regime in modern history were very dangerous; those comprising the White Rose were taking a monumental risk given that the Nazis tolerated no form of dissent. "[A]ny form of opposition carried the risk of death," writes Frank McDonough.[4] Yet by putting forth a series of rational, polished, and persuasive arguments against National Socialism, the White Rose was setting an example. It was illustrating that it was still possible in Nazi Germany, the belly of the beast, for men and women to take a stand against the totalitarian regime. The intention was to reawaken in the German people the collective social conscience which the White Rose hoped was lying dormant in them. It was, in effect, an opening salvo, a first step designed to prompt the German citizenry to restore its self-respect and moral standards through non-violent, yet meaningful, acts of noncompliance.

As to the source of this bold new movement, it was not comprised of hardened men and women with backgrounds in political activism. Rather, it was a twenty-one-year-old biology major at Munich University, Sophie Scholl, along with her brother Hans, a twenty-three-year-old medical student at the same school. Joining them was a handful of friends. An idealistic collection of devoted Christians, many of them medical students, they were revolted by National Socialism and refused to retreat into silence as the regime gave free rein to its malevolence. So they set out to challenge it.

For Sophie, in particular, her commitment to the resistance movement was an act of passion, one that revealed an independence of spirit that began in her home with her nonconformist Lutheran parents during the interwar period, the years between 1918 and 1939. An interlude during which a destitute and demoralized Germany struggled to rise from the ruins of World War I, it also was a time when Sophie and her loved ones found themselves witnessing their nation's reinvention as a toxic, immoral force and feeling compelled to arrive at a proper ethical response to its unsightly transformation.

Independent Spirit

Sophie Scholl was born on May 9, 1921, in Forchtenberg, Germany, the daughter of intelligent, warmhearted, and progressive parents.[5] Her father, Robert Scholl, had been a conscientious objector in the First World War, one of the few pacifists in Germany at the time. Refusing not only to fight in the war but to even carry a weapon, he fulfilled his obligation to the state by serving with the Red Cross at a military hospital near Stuttgart. It was at this infirmary, moreover, that he made the acquaintance of Magdalene Müller, a nurse and lay minister in the Lutheran Church, who, like him, was gentle and introspective. Well-matched, the couple soon married and started a family.

The Scholls gave birth to five children in as many years: Inge, Hans, and Elisabeth, who were slightly older than Sophie, and Werner, a year younger. A happy, boisterous family, the Scholls lived in a spacious, well-appointed home in Forchtenberg throughout the 1920s, where Robert served as the bürgermeister, or mayor. In this capacity, the forward-thinking official, deeply committed to the needs of the constituency, brought about several advances for the community. He ensured the construction of a railroad line that linked the town to the outside world and he oversaw the erection of an agricultural storage facility to help the local farmers. This being wine country, a region that boasted a surfeit of vineyards, the facility was a definite asset. He also improved the town's infrastructure, as well as arranged for a gymnasium to be built as a way of fostering the health and fitness of the townsfolk. And yet, such innovations notwithstanding, a share of the local population did not find Scholl's forward-looking approach desirable but instead remained provincial in its views. "Liberal concepts, thoughts of progress and change, were bad things for the conservative peasant," explains Inge Scholl, "a thorn in the old-timers' sides."[6] Due in part to this inflexibility, this discomfort with modernization, Robert Scholl was defeated in his 1930 reelection bid.

Leaving behind the small town, the family, in due course, settled in the city of Ulm in southern Germany. Situated on the Danube River, Ulm had two claims to fame: it was the birthplace of Albert Einstein and the site of the tallest cathedral spire in the world. In this walled Bavarian city, Robert went into business as a financial advisor and tax consultant, an endeavor that proved so lucrative that eventually he was able to move his family into a sprawling apartment in Cathedral Square with a spectacular view of the edifice itself.

As to the Scholl's home life in the 1920s and 1930s, it was one of conviviality, bustle, and remarkable freedom of thought and action. Robert and Magdalene encouraged their children to think for themselves and to voice their opinions, with the couple welcoming novel and controversial ideas. It was, moreover, an open-mindedness and respect for diversity that extended to the Scholls' friends. Often gathering in the home were writers, artists, and intellectuals who engaged in rollicking discussions centering on art, literature, philosophy, and politics. The atmosphere being that of a Paris salon in the twenties, it was precisely the type of free-thinking milieu the Nazis found threatening and eventually forbade — not that its prohibition fazed Robert Scholl. By all accounts, he was very much an individualist, a man who refused to be intimidated by the coercive tactics of Hitler and his underlings, or "beasts and wolves" as he referred to them.[7] "The Germans have a word for individuals with Robert Scholl's kind of personality —*Einzelgänger*, a man who goes his own way, alone," say Annette Dumbach and Jud Newborn. "He brought up his children in the same manner."[8] Certainly Robert's abiding respect for personal freedom infused the household during the Führer's rise to power, and it no doubt had an impact on young Sophie, who was regarded at home and at school as a self-directed child. She also was considered reflective, insightful, and measured.[9]

"Sophie was thoughtful, even reserved at times," write Dumbach and Newborn.[10] Not one to behave impulsively, she pondered complicated issues before arriving at a judgment, and it may have been for this reason that her father was said to consider her the most prudent female in the household.[11] Yet he respected her for other reasons as well. "He especially admired her humility and her incredible calmness under pressure," says McDonough.[12]

Sophie, with her dark eyes, short hairstyle, and tomboyish manner, excelled in school, where she was a bright student with an armload of friends. She also adored art and enjoyed sketching the human figure, as well as being drawn to athletics and other outdoor activities. Like many German youths of the era, she took pleasure in swimming, hiking, and especially camping, with its camaraderie and sing-alongs, and it was for this reason that she joined an outdoorsy group for girls which was sponsored by the Nazi Party. Known as the *Jungmädel* or Young Girls League, it was attracting a considerable share of girls between the ages of ten and fourteen during this period in the early 1930s, and they included many of Sophie's friends and classmates. But while she enjoyed the group's outings, Sophie showed little concern for its ideological underpinnings, which were, at any rate, deemphasized in this juvenile age group. We do know that she disagreed with the league's anti–Semitism, rejecting it outright and continuing to enjoy friendships with Jewish students at her school. She also carried on inviting them into her home just as she had done before Hitler came to power. To Sophie, the Young Girls League appears to have been a social and recreational group, nothing more. For her older brother Hans, on the other hand, Nazi youth groups were an entirely different matter, and his intense involvement in one of them would eventually have consequences both for him and Sophie.

In 1933, Hans became a member of the male version of the Young Girls'

League. Known as the *Hitlerjugend* or Hitler Youth, he quickly became captivated by the simplistic, sanitized version of Nazi ideology that the organization promulgated, and in due course rose to the position of Youth Leader. As was typical of young men in such roles, he touted with grand passion the purported values of National Socialism, and he did so at school and at home. Yet his membership, like his tendency to pontificate on the subject, was not always well-received by those around him. Robert Scholl, for one, was troubled when Hans and Sophie — indeed, when all of his children in due course — joined Nazi youth groups, which is not surprising in light of the older man's wisdom and pacifism. Even so, he did not prohibit them from participating, believing it best that they pursue their own experiences and draw their own conclusions. Just as he respected their freedom of choice, though, he was also comfortable with his own right to express himself and thus repeatedly voiced his revulsion for Adolf Hitler and the Nazi Party. And the result was often a heated argument.

"[W]e are people who have our own free opinions, our own political ideas, our own beliefs," Inge Scholl recalls her father telling the family. "A government that so much as touches these things is not entitled to our confidence."[13] But the younger Scholls were not ready to hear his warning. They thought their father was behind the times, a man from a bygone era, with this being a misinterpretation the Nazi leadership purposely fostered. The fact is, the Party controlled, from the shadows at times, virtually every aspect of the youth organizations, and this included manipulating the naïve participants into viewing any signs of their parents' disapproval of National Socialism as symptomatic of advancing years, of senescence. As to the proper response, they were encouraged to disregard their parents' opinions and look to Adolf Hitler as their father.

While the Nazi Party sought to control the hearts and minds of the nation's young people, even to the point of alienating them from their families if necessary, it persisted in instilling in German girls the doctrine of reproduction and childrearing as their fundamental duty to the Fatherland. Furthermore, it continued advancing this position even as the government became increasingly militaristic, an unambiguous prelude to war. Simply put, the Nazi leadership did not plan to make use of women in the impending conflict, at least not militarily, and this was conveyed to Sophie when she progressed to another National Socialist organization in 1935. Designed for girls between the ages of fourteen and eighteen, it was known as the *Bund Deutscher Mädel* or League of German Girls, and it taught that a woman's role remained a maternal one even during wartime. "Girls were reminded," says Michael Kater, "that they were not made of the stuff that could fight in the trenches or that they could not share in the 'tough, masculine romanticism' and camaraderie which allowed boys to sing the old fighting songs of storm troopers."[14] But not only did the League of German Girls contend that females, first and foremost, were to churn out future generations of Aryan children, the organization went so far as to bring in physicians to examine them periodically to make sure they were hale and hearty and thus on the path to becoming healthy mothers. It was an ideology that reflected "German conservative thinking," says Kater, "but with the biological functions vastly exaggerated."[15]

As Sophie gained more exposure to, and experience with, the League of German Girls, her enthusiasm began to wane. She did not embrace its underlying ideology, and, as we have noted, she had always eschewed its policy of prohibiting Jewish girls from participating. Nor was she alone in her disenchantment.

It was in 1935 that Hans likewise became disillusioned with his youth group and with National Socialism itself, a change in spirit his family noticed after he served as an honorary flag bearer at a historic Party Rally in Nuremberg in September of that year. While at the assembly, he came face to face with the more sinister side of Nazism, a darker and truer version that was far removed from the sunny simplicity of the Hitler Youth. In Nuremberg, he encountered adult Party members who were fanatical in their nationalism and vehement in their hatred of Jews, Roma (Gypsies), gay men and women, and other sets of people. Returning home, he was observed to be "exhausted, distraught and demoralised."[16] Thereafter, he and his father no longer argued about National Socialism, and Hans subsequently resigned from the Hitler Youth.

As Hans was shaking off his remaining connections to the Nazi political machine, Robert and his wife Magdalene continued nurturing their friendships with modern or "degenerate" artists, writers, intellectuals, and other nonconformists, steadfastly refusing to distance themselves from these fellow Germans whom the Reich was demonizing. As for Sophie, her fondness for sketching was still intact and therefore the presence of artists visiting her home delighted her. She took a special interest in their views and creations, and in time she acquired a love of avant-garde art, brushing aside the Nazis' official condemnation of it.

Well into 1937, Sophie's interest in her Nazi youth group continued to fade, as did that of a number of other young people, their disenchantment mounting in proportion to the increase in explicitly authoritarian measures within the groups themselves. Then, too, racial intolerance was being stressed more than ever before.

Hans, during this same year, completed a compulsory six-month stint with the National Labor Force and began his mandatory military service. Because the latter was situated at Bad Cannstatt, which was near his home in Ulm, he was able to stay in touch with old friends and occasionally enjoy with them a respite in a youth group that was free of Nazi influence. An organization the Party had banned, the *Deutsche Jungenschaft* or German Boys Federation still had a few branches in that smattering of German cities which had managed to cling to the vestiges of culture. For those who belonged to it, the Federation offered an opportunity to experience life freshly, away from the strangling dictates of Nazism. "On weekends they went on hikes," writes Inge Scholl.[17] They also went on camping trips, took photographs, collected folk songs, and composed music.[18] Literature was an important part of their activities as well, the young men evincing a genuine love of books. In essence, it was a throwback to the German youth movement that existed prior to the rise of National Socialism, one that celebrated nature and harmony and fraternity. Now, however, the Gestapo set out to quash this middle-class, freestanding boys' group, the upshot being that the entire Scholl family soon found itself changed irrevocably.

It happened in the fall of 1937 when the Gestapo began arresting anyone suspected of being associated with youth organizations that the Nazis had proscribed, a turn of events that placed Hans in their sights. Since he was serving in the military at this time, the Gestapo seized him at his barracks and locked him away. But this was not the end of it. Gestapo agents also showed up at the Scholl household in Ulm and took into custody Sophie, Inge, and Werner, rushing the children to the city of Stuttgart for questioning. Although Sophie was released the same day she was arrested, officials detained and interrogated Inge and Werner for several more days before discharging them. Worst of all, however, was Hans' ordeal, one that was initiated by a sexual allegation against him.

In November of that ill-fated year, the Gestapo charged Hans, who was nineteen, with having previously formed a sexual relationship with another teenage boy, a fellow member of the Hitler Youth. During an interrogation session in an unrelated investigation, the other boy had reported it to his inquisitor. By this point in time, Reichsführer-SS Heinrich Himmler had publicly condemned same-sex relationships as "a symptom of racial degeneracy destructive to our race."[19] Even more menacing, he had put forward the regime's solution: "we have returned to the guiding Nordic principle that degenerates should be exterminated."[20] Subsequent to this, the Federal Security Department for Combating Abortion and Homosexuality was established at Gestapo headquarters in Berlin, with vigorous efforts being set into motion to identify and prosecute those believed to be drawn to their own gender. The Nazis had officially launched their unholy war on gay men, and Hans Scholl was caught in their net.

Imprisoned and interrogated for seven months, a term that included solitary confinement, Hans ultimately acknowledged that he had, in fact, enjoyed a homoerotic relationship with another young man during the period when he was a Hitler Youth leader. Hans had been sixteen years old at the time.[21]

Although he and the other boy had been near in age and the pair had willingly engaged in the affair, the Gestapo was unyielding. It was especially perturbed that Hans had been a Hitler Youth leader at the time and thus a role model for German youths, an exemplar of the fascists' notion of morality, meaning Aryan and pure of heart, or heterosexual. The situation appeared to be dire.

Determined to liberate his son, Robert Scholl worked tirelessly to persuade Hans' superior in the military to intervene, and in fact succeeded in securing the officer's cooperation. Furthermore, it proved helpful to the defense, with the court appearing to be comfortable with the notion of handing over Hans to a military official. Then, too, it was advantageous that Hans' former boyfriend, the one who had divulged their relationship to the Gestapo, supported him during the legal proceedings in June 1938, stating that their attachment had been consensual and that he harbored no ill feelings toward Hans.

In the end, young Scholl was acquitted. The judge concluded that the same-sex relationship had been an isolated affair, one that would not recur, and that Hans could still be an asset to the Fatherland. The judge did not voice the widespread expectation that war was on the horizon and that all able-bodied young men, like Hans, would be needed for battle. Still, whatever the court's motive for acquitting him, Hans was free at last, although for him and the entire Scholl family the trauma had decisively turned them against the regime. For Sophie and Hans, in particular, their anger over his arrest and protracted incarceration would lead them to sympathize with the other victims of Hitler's madness as well as to realize that there existed a need for the voice of opposition to be heard from within Nazi Germany itself.

The White Rose

During the ensuing years, Sophie graduated from high school, completed a program in kindergarten instruction at the Fröbel Institute, and fulfilled a requirement that all young Germans work for the National Labor Service for a period of one year. Whereas the latter had formerly been a six-month stint, the regime, owing to the war, had now doubled the amount of service time. For Sophie, it consisted of farm work, and it was a job in which she had no interest. Equally off-putting was the fact that the Nazi administration, which she loathed, was mandating it while stalling her university education.

In terms of the assignment itself, it proved to be a discouraging experience during which she lived away from home for the first time and found herself unpopular with the other young women with whom she toiled. They considered her bookish and aloof, and she regarded them as dim-witted and vulgar.[22] As a result, she spent much time alone. This yielded certain benefits, however, most of all the opportunity for contemplation, and this was important to Sophie at the moment. With Germany embroiled in war, she found herself forming questions of religion, faith, and meaning. In the pastoral setting, she had the conditions to reflect upon such matters.

Paralleling her growth in this regard was that of Hans, who was far away at this time and in very different circumstances. All the same, he, too, was being drawn toward the spiritual. Although a Lutheran, he had begun seeking insight through the writings of influential Catholics such as Carl Muth and Theodor Haecker, both of whom he and Sophie would eventually come to know personally. He also was attracted to the works of Sören Kierkegaard, Leon Bloy, Georges Bernanos, and others.[23] On both moral and political levels, however, he was especially impressed by the words of a German Catholic bishop, Clemens Graf von Galen, excerpts of whose sermon condemning Hitler's program to euthanize disabled citizens were being covertly released in the summer of 1941 in the form of leaflets. Using a hectography machine to duplicate the texts, three university students disseminated the controversial homily — one student was an acquaintance of the Scholl family — with the young mens' courageous actions serving as an inspiration to Sophie and Hans. Indeed, the Galen affair would culminate in the Scholls' own leaflet operation once the two siblings were together in Munich as university students.

For Hans, it was in January 1939 that he entered college. Enrolling in the medical education program at Munich University, he planned to become a physician. Alongside his formal studies, however, the government required that he serve periodically as a medic in field hospitals as a member of the Student Medical Corps, which was associated with the German army. It was while he was fulfilling this obligation, moreover, that he befriended several medical students like himself, young men and women who likewise took a dim view of the Third Reich and supported, in spirit at any rate, the resistance movements of those war-torn countries to which they were dispatched. Pleased to find himself in close contact with sympathetic colleagues — they lived together in barracks and worked side by side in field hospitals — Hans formed solid ties with a number of them and made these kindred spirits a part of his life back at the university.

As for Sophie, she embarked on her studies in biology at Munich University in May 1942. Because Hans was attending the same school, the two were able to spend a considerable amount of time together, the upshot being that she became well-acquainted with his circle of friends. It was, of course, a circle comprised mainly of anti–Nazis with whom he had served in the Student Medical Corps.

It was during this same month, Sophie's first month at college, that she was said to have begun casting about for a duplicating machine, with this strongly suggesting that she was helping Hans put together the resistance operation.[24] Certainly equipment of this type would be necessary to reproduce the immense quantity of tracts the White Rose was planning to dispense. Here we are referring to the leaflet campaign that was described at the outset of this chapter, the one whose texts reproached Nazism and advocated passive resistance. A bold operation that could be construed as treasonous, it urged non-cooperation with the German government during a time of war. As could be expected, those who were behind it were dead-set against surrendering to mindless nationalism; they were guided by a higher ethic. As for Sophie's determination to secure a mimeograph machine, it implies that, like Hans, she was in on the ground floor of the movement.

In terms of its formal aspects, Hans came up with the name *Rose Weisse* or White Rose. Later, when the Gestapo interrogated him about it, he claimed that he did not have a clear memory of how he had come to choose it. Recently, however, historian Jud Newborn has made a persuasive case that Hans was attempting to protect a comrade through his calculatedly fuzzy answer. "[H]e was probably trying to divert the Gestapo's attention away from his dear friend Josef Söhngen — the 'bachelor' bookseller who secretly nurtured the White Rose resistance by providing a meeting place and an endless supply of banned books from his cache to boost their morale," writes Newborn.[25] Were Hans to have told the truth, the Gestapo no doubt would have arrested Söhngen and quite possibly transported him to a concentration camp because he appeared to be a gay man who was abetting a resistance movement.

As to the forbidden book, it was titled *Die Weisse Rose* and was written by a German anarchist whose nom de plume was B. Traven and who also wrote *The Treasure of the Sierra Madre*. Traven's ambitious novel, *Die Weisse Rose*, centered on an Indian village that sought to insulate and thereby protect itself from a cruel and exploitative American oil company that had usurped its land.

In regard to the composition of the White Rose resistance movement, it was made up of Sophie, Hans, a handful of medical students, and several others. Most were in their early twenties, and included the following:

- Alexander (Alex) Schmorell, medical student. Born in Russia and baptized in the Russian Orthodox Church, Schmorell was the son of a prominent physician. Schmorell's childhood and adolescence were spent in a wealthy milieu, one that prized culture and urbanity. Handsome, extroverted, and well-liked, he and Hans were very close.
- Christl Probst, medical student. Born in Germany to affluent parents, Probst was quiet, bookish, and reflective. Catholic with a Jewish stepmother whom the Nazis had persecuted, he was married with young children. Because he was a husband and a father, the White Rose sought to avoid placing him in hazardous circumstances.
- Wilhelm (Willi) Graf, medical student. Born in Germany and long opposed to National Socialism, the regime had once imprisoned Graf

for belonging to a Catholic youth group, the *Grauer Orden* or Gray Order. The son of a wine merchant, he was reserved in manner and philosophical in approach, and he was deeply devoted to Catholicism.

Additional members came to include young women, among them Traute LaFrenz, Katharina Schüddekopf, and Marie-Luise Jahn, with secondary support being provided by such figures as Kurt Huber, a philosophy professor at Munich University, and Falk Harnack and Jürgen Wittenstein. Together with the enmity these people felt toward the regime, the preponderance of White Rose members shared two other characteristics, features that were socioeconomic and religious in nature.

Most of the participants were the products of affluent, refined families that were prominent and well-connected in their communities. Accordingly, these members were well-insulated given the time and place. Certainly their backs were not against the wall; they were not forced by personal circumstances to rise up against the regime. And this is important to bear in mind in that it signifies that they made a choice. Theirs was an act of conscience, not an act of self-defense. "If they had not wanted to oppose Nazism," says McDonough, "they could easily have slipped into a 'Brideshead Revisited' student lifestyle of self-gratification."[26] Instead, they dared to stimulate social and political change.

The other common characteristic, a religious orientation, is particularly telling. Sophie and Hans were Lutherans who had found meaning in the writings of Catholics, while nearly all of the remaining members were lifelong adherents of the Catholic faith. For the White Rose, Christianity was not a mere vestige of its participants' upbringings; the members' religious convictions were thoughtful and sincere, with their understanding of Christ's teachings and of their responsibilities as Christians serving as a guiding light. Their beliefs permeated the movement's values, then, and constituted a fundamental message. "[D]evotion to God was a unifying and dominant factor," writes McDonough. "They all emphasized Christianity as the basis for moral regeneration in a post–Hitler Germany."[27]

Understandably, Sophie appears to have become even more spiritually-inclined as the Holocaust progressed. We know that she became aware of the liquidation of the Jews and was aghast with horror. We know, too, that she was searching for a Christian response to the ruthlessness that surrounded her. And we know from her diary entries that she was struggling to be closer to her experience of God, more enveloped in its reality, even as she contended with secular diversions. "I destroy what distracts me from you and force myself to turn to you," she writes, "I'm happy with you alone."[28]

It is worth noting that Sophie's spiritual and moral qualities also infused the White Rose itself. It was she, more than any other member, who gave the movement its compassion and its humanity even as its male members generated the arguments against National Socialism and strategized the dispersal of their tracts. "Sophie Scholl, she was the heart," says former member Franz Müller, "Hans and Alex were the thinking behind the White Rose."[29]

A high school student in 1942, Müller had found himself stirred by the actions of the movement and volunteered to help disseminate its tracts in the city of Ulm, home of the Scholl family. Like other participants, he was drawn to the activists' overarching objective, which journalist Toby Axelrod has described in the following terms:

> The first goal of their campaign was to spread the word that there were Germans who were opposed to Hitler. They knew they could not overthrow the government, and they did not encourage a revolution. But they could spread information and encourage other Germans to question the dictatorship.[30]

And spread the word they did. In June 1942, the White Rose distributed its inaugural tract at Munich University and in the city's suburbs. And to Sophie, it appears to have come as a surprise. While on campus, she came across a leaflet denouncing Adolf Hitler and National Socialism while criticizing the German population for tolerating its country's moral disintegration. It called for the citizenry to undertake passive resistance as a way to hinder the Nazi war machine, which the treatise portrayed as godless and depraved. The tract expressed the same opinions as those of her brother, Sophie realized, and the writing style also matched that of Hans.

Hurrying to his rooms, she found that he was away at the moment, but she discovered evidence linking him to the tract and confronted him as soon as he returned. And her suspicions were correct: Hans and Alex were the source of the text, and Hans had refrained from telling her because he did not want to implicate her. It was far too dangerous, in his judgment, for his younger sister to be involved in the hands-on preparation and dissemination of the tracts. But Sophie, writing off his concerns, insisted on contributing to the mission at this most crucial of moments, and Hans had little choice but to agree to her demand. Soon, she would be joined by others.

On this summer day when the first tract was distributed, many of those who found copies of it turned them over to the Gestapo.[31] Undaunted, the White Rose persisted in circulating them, releasing three new texts in the course of the ensuing four weeks, all of them smart and hard-biting in their cases against National Socialism. Determined to enlighten the public, the White Rose informed readers that Germany had murdered three hundred thousand Jewish civilians in occupied Poland, along with other groups the Nazi leadership judged to be inferior. For many German citizens in 1942, it was the first time they had heard about such atrocities. The tracts further deliberated on the nature of evil and the individual's duty to intervene, and in this context urged their readers to disrupt the Nazi apparatus through peaceful noncompliance.

During this period, Sophie remained very much at the fore of the White Rose movement. Among other tasks, she helped formulate its tactics, oversaw its finances, and hand-cranked the duplicating machine alongside Traute LaFrenz. Her resistance activities came to a temporary halt in the middle of July, however, as they did for the other White Rose participants, due to the government's demands on them.

At this juncture, Hans and his medical school colleagues, among them Schmorell and Graf, were ordered to travel to the occupied Soviet Union to serve as medics. Sophie, meanwhile, was directed to perform mind-numbing work in a factory that manufactured munitions. Here she worked alongside other German women as well as those from the occupied Soviet Union, the latter being forced to comply. And while Sophie felt affection toward the Soviet women — she both respected and pitied them — she could neither understand nor empathize with the German women in the industrial plant. "The sight of so many people in front of so many machines is depressing and reminiscent of slavery," she wrote to a friend, "except that these slaves have appointed their own slave driver."[32] The whole set-up appears to have struck her as absurd.

Disconcerting, too, was the regime's continued suppression of speech that was in any way unfavorable toward National Socialism, a heavy-handed restraint that directly affected Sophie and her loved ones. It was during this period, for instance, that Robert Scholl ran afoul of the regime when he made a comment in his office, one that his secretary, whose allegiance to the Führer was unwavering, felt obliged to report to the Gestapo. "This Hitler is God's scourge on mankind," Robert remarked, with the mere utterance of these words constituting a crime in the totalitarian state.[33] So it was that a trial was held in early August, the outcome being that the elder Scholl was found guilty of treachery, his professional credentials were revoked, and he was sentenced to a four-month prison term.[34] Because of such outrageous experiences, Sophie's antagonism toward the regime, which already was strong, further intensified.

It would not be until November 1942 that the White Rose would be able to regroup, when the medics returned from the eastern front and Sophie completed her factory duties. True to form, the members were keen to resume their resistance work. "Their double life was launched once again," write Dumbach and Newborn.[35] As before, they set out to promote passive resistance, but they also decided to expand their operation by procuring more funds and sharing information with other underground groups. Regarding the latter, Hans Scholl and Alex Schmorell established contact with a Berlin-based operation, one that was itself in touch with a cadre of people who were plotting to assassinate the Führer. Of course, this was not the only outfit conspiring to murder him, and, as we know, none of them succeeded. As to why the White Rose wished to establish such communication, it was not the case that it, too, was itching to kill Hitler — the White Rose was non-violent — but rather it wished to stay abreast of others' plans in this regard. That said, merely because the White Rose eschewed violence does not mean its members did not fantasize about it. Even Sophie told a friend that if she chanced upon Hitler on the street and had a gun, she would kill him. "If men can't manage it," she said, "then a woman should."[36] Again, though, the White Rose movement, bound to Christianity as it was, had no intention of actually moving in such a direction.

The beginning of 1943 brought a new tract, one written by Hans but that included the contributions of Sophie and other members of the movement. To make the operation appear larger and more influential, the White Rose decided to list the name on the treatise as that of the Resistance Movement in Germany.[37] The participants then reproduced ten thousand copies of the text and distributed them far and wide, with Sophie and her comrades mailing or hand-delivering copies to destinations in Köln, Frankfort, Vienna, Innsbruck, and Salzburg. Sophie also traveled to Ulm, where she helped Hans Müeller disperse them in that city, and she journeyed to Stuttgart and did the same with hundreds more tracts.

It was at this taut stage that the Gestapo resolved to obliterate the movement. Forming a task force to track down and prosecute the participants, it placed in charge of the team a man by the name of Robert Mohr, who, in short order, concluded that the leaflet operation was based in Munich. Not only had the first tract been distributed primarily at Munich University, but the ensuing investigation was able to determine that the resisters' supplies had also been obtained in that city. Accordingly, Mohr instructed local stationery shops to report to the task force anyone attempting to buy large quantities of paper or duplicator ink. Widening his net, he also posted Gestapo agents at train depots on the assumption that the resisters would travel by rail to distant cities to disseminate their tracts. And he placed notices in Munich newspapers offering rewards for information regarding the identities and whereabouts of White Rose members.

But the movement was not naïve. When purchasing paper and ink, Sophie and her comrades procured only small amounts from a variety of shops so as not to arouse suspicion. To further avoid detection, they distributed their tracts under cover of darkness, usually in areas where the texts would be discovered by foot traffic the next day, such as in doorways of buildings or in public plazas. They took advantage of the comparative anonymity of post offices, too, mailing their tracts to a range of people, from members of intelligentsia and to arbitrary addressees. And they made an effort to divert attention away from their home base by posting tracts from one city to another, thereby taking Munich out of the picture entirely. All in all, theirs was an effective operation, especially considering that its participants, until the advent of the White Rose, were inexperienced in covert political activities. Furthermore, they gained greater expertise as their operation progressed.

The prospect of a German victory in the war, on the other hand, was starting to dim at this time. Tensions within Germany were running high, particularly in the early days of February 1943, due mainly to the Battle of Stalingrad and the shockwaves it sent through German society.

Five months earlier, in August 1942, Germany's formidable Sixth Army had invaded the Soviet city of Stalingrad only to find itself surrounded by the Soviet military by November of that year. "Over the next eight weeks, the Red Army tightened the noose," writes historian William Hitchcock, "and pummeled them to pieces."[38] Prolonging the Sixth Army's agony, moreover, was a directive from Berlin demanding that it carry on no matter what the human cost, a command that came from the top. "Hitler refused to allow them to surrender," says Hitchcock.[39] Ultimately, the Red Army prevailed, retaking Stalingrad at the end of January 1943. In all, two hundred thousand German and other Axis soldiers were killed in the battle, while another ninety-one thousand were marched out of the city, most of them failing to survive and return to their homeland.[40] As the historical record reveals, it was a shocking loss for Germany, a profound humiliation for Hitler, and a turning point in the war itself. Furthermore, it served as a wakeup call for the German people, a substantial portion of whom concluded that the Führer, through his lust for power, was steering their beloved Fatherland to the slaughterhouse. "The people were angry at Hitler," write Dumbach and Newborn. "[T]hey felt manipulated and ill used."[41] For the White Rose movement, however, it was a turn of events that produced a rare experience of hope in that it indicated that the public might at last be receptive to its message.

Building on this opportunity, some of the male participants of the White Rose movement, Hans Scholl among them, began painting anti–Nazi messages on public facades in Munich at night. Some of the graffiti was hostile to Hitler while other messages called for a return to freedom. The powerful image of a red line crossing out a swastika was also painted onto walls. Clearly, the White Rose was expanding its methods beyond disseminating its tracts which advocated passive resistance, although it continued to regard the latter as its principal means of opposition.

In early February 1943, Kurt Huber, livid at Hitler's obsession for world supremacy and the ensuing recklessness that had led to the Stalingrad defeat, insisted on penning the next tract, the sixth in the series. Unlike the movement's young adult members, Huber was nearly fifty years old and had witnessed the Germany of his youth disintegrate owing to the twisted fixations of the Führer. In view of that, the piece he wrote was a scorcher, even more vitriolic than those the White Rose had previously released, and its line of reasoning was both logical and supported by the evidence. Specifically, the tract portrayed Hitler as an amateur in the art of war, a dilettante who had no firm grasp as to how to execute a battle, let alone a war of historic dimensions. It accused Hitler of having on his hands the blood of hundreds of thousands of young German soldiers, and it predicted that he would continue using the nation's young people as cannon fodder until he was forced to cease. It was a revolutionary cry, an appeal to the citizenry to help save the remnants of their nation from a dictator with gravely impaired judgment, an unsound man who would drive Germany into the dirt rather than relinquish power or forfeit his misguided designs for the once-great nation.

While Huber was drafting this tract, Sophie, in early February, paid a visit to her family in Ulm. From her diary and letters, it is evident that she had been under profound stress and was suffering from physical and mental symptoms. To a friend she wrote, "I'm just not myself at the moment, and it's an entirely novel sensation. My thoughts flit to and fro without my being able to control them properly. I'm suffering from some pretty bad headaches."[42]

Regarding her mood, it seems to have been rather unstable as well, based on Sophie's descriptions of it in her letters and diary. "As soon as I'm alone," reads one diary entry, "melancholy suppresses any desire in me to do anything at all."[43] Yet also during this period she describes feelings of lightness and elation. Surely one can appreciate such variations in mood given her resistance activities and the danger inherent in them, even as she attended classes at the university and sought to present herself in public as an ordinary first-year student. Yet there may have been another contributor to her symptoms as well.

"The students took stimulants to stay awake," writes Toby Axelrod, who proceeds to raise the possibility that stimulants may have been partly responsible for the Scholls' ill-fated actions a few weeks later.[44] Certainly it is no secret that members of the resistance in various European countries did at times require stimulants to stay awake, alert, and energized so that they could carry out their tasks, deeds that were often precarious and required sustained concentration. They were taking the drugs, then, for altogether practical purposes. But it is well-known, too, that stimulants ranging from caffeine to amphetamines, both of which were available in Europe during World War II, may produce precisely those side effects Sophie described, particularly if they are used excessively—"flitting" thoughts, diminished attention span, headaches, and mood swings. Of course, if stimulants were indeed a factor in Sophie's internal discomfort, she does not appear to have realized it based on her journal entries and letters. And if stimulants impaired her judgment or rendered her more impulsive during a mission on February 18, again we will probably never know for certain. What we do know that is she and Hans planned the operation in advance, and that it was similar to their previous ones except it was to be conducted in broad daylight and they were the only two people who knew about it. It was not, in itself, a spur-of-the-moment operation, even if it did end with a precipitate act on Sophie's part.

It all started a few days earlier when she and a small number of others set about making mimeographed copies of Huber's sixth tract. They gathered in the Scholls' rooms in Munich, where they spun out hundreds of leaflets that supposedly would be dispersed by mail or by hand. Hans even bought upward of a thousand stamps at a local post office ostensibly to be used for the mailings.

As these preparations were being made, he met with Christl Probst and asked that he write a seventh tract. Probst was hesitant, however. He sensed that the Gestapo was closing in on them and thought it wise to lie low for the moment, a sentiment shared by other White Rose members. His loyalty to the movement being unshakable, however, he ultimately agreed to perform the task as a favor to Hans, Probst's assumption being that authoring a leaflet would keep him out of visible association with the movement and thus not expose his wife and children to danger. Like the earlier tracts, it would be typewritten and anonymous when it was distributed, thereby shielding his identity. Accordingly, Probst drafted a text in longhand and slipped it to Hans, who pocketed it.

On February 16, Sophie paid a visit to a modern artist who wished to sculpt her. His name was Wilhelm Geyer, and he was a devoted friend who was aware of her White Rose involvement. The two met at the studio of Manfred Eickemeyer, an architect and resistance supporter who occasionally permitted the movement to print its tracts in the basement. While Sophie and Geyer were commiserating about the dreadful state of affairs in Germany and elsewhere on the continent, she made a rather startling admission. She said that she thought the Gestapo was about to silence her, and she hoped it would happen in a public place where there would be witnesses.

Sometime later, the Gestapo seized Geyer and questioned him about his contact with Sophie, and the transcript of the ensuing interrogation session reveals that Geyer recalled a statement Sophie had made to him during their final conversation at the studio. "So many people are dying for this regime, it is high time that someone died opposing it," she said.[45]

On the same date that Sophie met with Geyer, Hans, late that night, showed up at the door of Josef Söhngen, a treasured companion as well as the bookseller who had been furnishing him with banned books. The pair spoke at length while downing a bottle of wine, according to McDonough.[46] In the course of their conversation, Hans divulged that he and Sophie were planning to leave mass copies of the sixth tract at Munich University during class time, meaning that the setting would be swarming with students. An ambitious plan, Söhngen recognized at once that it also was hazardous in the extreme. For this reason, he tried to dissuade Hans from going through with it, but to no avail. Söhngen later recalled that Hans, as the two saying their goodbyes that night, seemed in his manner to intimate that it would be their final farewell.[47]

The Munich Mission

On Thursday morning, February 18, Sophie and Hans arose and breakfasted, then packed a valise with something in the order of eighteen hundred of copies of Huber's sixth tract and made their way to Munich University where classes were in session.[48] When they arrived, they scrutinized the area. "The *Lichthof*, the large inner courtyard of the university with a glass-vaulted ceiling, was empty of people," write Dumbach and Newborn, the students and faculty being in the lecture halls at the time.[49] Even so, Sophie and Hans soon found themselves face to face with two of their White Rose comrades, Willi Graf and Traute Lafrenz, who were on their way to a neurology lecture in another building. Like the other members of the movement, the latter were unaware of the dicey mission upon which the Scholls were embarking, although Lafrenz subsequently recalled feeling a bit troubled when she noticed they had with them a valise.

Once they had entered the Lichthof, meaning "light yard" in German, Sophie and Hans split up, each of them hurrying about the building's sunlit interior court and placing stacks of leaflets near the statues that adorned it. Next, the Scholls dashed to the second floor, where they deposited more tracts near the exit doors of the lecture halls, and they also left copies at the tops of the staircase. Finally, the pair reached the third floor and repeated the process, after which they began rushing out of the building; that is, until Sophie remembered that there was still a bundle of leaflets in the valise. On impulse, she ran back to the third-floor balustrade — it was a marble banister that overlooked the central court below — and with a sweep of her hand she sent the batch soaring through the air, fluttering down to the main floor. As fate would have it, a custodian by the name of Jakob Schmid happened be on a lower floor at this moment and caught sight of the flurry of leaflets. He shouted and raced up to the third floor.

Amid this blur of motion, Sophie had the presence of mind to dispose of an item she had with her, namely, the key to Manfred Eickemeyer's studio, the architect who had allowed the White Rose to duplicate its tracts on the premises. Hans did not possess the same quickness of thought, however, and thus failed to discard a piece of incriminating evidence he was carrying: the hand-written draft of the seventh tract that Christl Probst had given him to review. And it was now that the custodian laid eyes on the two siblings.

Although Sophie and Hans insisted they knew nothing about the spectacular flurry of tracts that had inundated the interior of the building, they soon found themselves under arrest and at the local Gestapo headquarters in the former Wittelsbach Palace. Here, Robert Mohr, the task force leader who had been appointed to ferret out the members of the White Rose movement, took charge. He and his staff set about questioning the pair separately, even though Mohr believed that both of the Scholls were probably innocent. They appeared calm and unruffled, not cornered and guilty. "[T]he young man and woman made an extremely relaxed impression," say Dumbach and Newborn.[50] But even as Mohr was assuming they were two clean-cut students who happened to be in the wrong place at wrong time, new and disturbing information began coming to light.

First, the history of the Scholl family revealed run-ins with the Nazis. Only a few months earlier, as he have noted, the Gestapo arrested Robert Scholl, charged him with treachery, and forced him to stand trial. And before that, the agency arrested Hans and charged him with participating in a forbidden organization and engaging in sex with another boy while serving as a Hitler Youth leader. The Scholls' background, then, revealed that they did not toe the line when it came to the regime's imperatives.

Second, a search of Sophie and Hans' rooms in Munich turned up an inordinately large number of postage stamps, precisely the type that the White Rose had used on its previous mailings. Worsening matters, a postal worker, as the Gestapo had requested, had recently tipped off the agency about a young man who had purchased a sizable quantity of stamps. These facts appeared to link Hans to the resistance movement.

And third, Hans tried, while at Gestapo headquarters, to tear up the draft of the seventh tract that Probst had given him. Evidently, Hans had forgotten to remove it from his pocket before starting the mission. But he was not fast enough. The Gestapo seized and reassembled it, with the text's existence contributing to Hans' culpability. Unfortunately, it also led the Gestapo to Christl Probst. Officials, it turns out, were able to trace the text to Probst through the handwriting, the agency having obtained a writing sample in a letter he had sent to Hans and that was discovered in the Scholls' rooms. Accordingly, the agency promptly hunted down Probst and arrested him, too.

As the investigation continued to rush forward, the Gestapo peppered Sophie and Hans with questions, albeit it with no real success. Interrogated for a grueling seventeen hours, the pair, to their credit, refused to divulge the names of other White Rose members or even admit that such members existed. They also tried to protect one another. Hans insisted that Sophie had not participated in the movement; that, in fact, she did not even know about it. His efforts fell short, however, since the Gestapo had found in the Scholls' rooms the ledger in which Sophie, in her own hand, had recorded the expenses of the White Rose operations. In much the same way, Sophie attempted to bear all of the blame so as to remove Hans from the situation, but again the Gestapo could not be deceived. In the end, Sophie, Hans, and Christl Probst confessed, since the evidence against them was damning. The regime then charged the three with high treason and ordered them to stand trial.

Ominously, the proceedings were set to take place in a so-called People's Court rather than in a traditional German criminal court, the regime having contrived the former in 1934 exclusively to contend with those who disputed the Reich.[51] According to journalist William Shirer, the People's Court had the dubious distinction of being "the most dreaded tribunal in the land."[52] Although the government could have granted Hans a military trial since he was still connected to the Student Medical Corps, which was itself associated the German army, the regime denied it in favor of this more despotic arrangement. Of course, this was a very bad sign, and it appears that Sophie, Hans, and Christl Probst knew it. It also seems that they suspected they would soon face an executioner. In this regard, the twenty-one-year-old Sophie asked a prison official before the trial how death would be delivered to her, so convinced she was of its inevitability.

Certainly the fact that the regime needed a show trial at precisely this moment did not bode well for the proceedings' outcome. As it stood, it had only been twenty days since German troops laid down their arms at the Battle of Stalingrad, which, as mentioned earlier, was a profound reversal of fortune that caused a considerable swath of the German population to become disillusioned, if not furious, with Adolf Hitler. Accordingly, this same segment of the citizenry began contemplating what it had previously thought to be an impossibility, namely, the prospect of defeat in yet another world war, and it also set about examining its blind allegiance to the Führer. The upshot: the abrupt, pervasive shift in public sentiment unnerved the regime, since mounting doubt on a national scale might well contain within it the seeds of mass rebellion. Nazi leaders therefore decided to prevent such a development by demonstrating yet again how the authorities would deal with attempts at collective opposition to the Reich. They would eliminate it with "extreme prejudice," in the jargon of the military, and the White Rose would serve as a timely example.

So it was that powerful figures in Berlin, Heinrich Himmler and Martin Borman among them, demanded an immediate trial for the three Munich students, the swift legal proceedings and executions that were to ensue being intended as a stern warning to the public, especially to college students across the nation. Because the plan was to instill fear in the populace, however, and not to invite sympathy for the students, the regime decided that the three should not be killed in public. Rather, their lives would be snuffed out behind the walls of Stadelheim Prison.

Regarding the trial, it was set for the following day, Friday, February 19, with a sadistic showman of a judge presiding. Roland Freisler was his name, he was President of the People's Court, and his belligerence was renowned. "[P]erhaps the most sinister and bloodthirsty Nazi in the Third Reich after Heydrich," according to Shirer, the judge shrieked at defendants and in other ways insulted and demeaned them in the course of their legal proceedings.[53] Given his poisonous invective, his torrents of insults and over-the-top punishments, it should come as no surprise that Freisler was an admirer of the Stalinists' extreme judicial methods — or, for that matter, that Adolf Hitler was an admirer of Freisler's methods. In fact, the Führer found Freisler's acrid theatrics so appealing that he watched films of them for his own amusement. Unfortunately, the judge's spectacles on the bench, while constituting first-rate Nazi entertainment, nearly always led to the brutal executions of those who appeared before the court ostensibly in the name of justice.

As it came to pass, the trial of Sophie, Hans, and Christl Probst was typical of a People's Court proceeding, particularly one presided over by Roland Freisler. The tribunal was structured in such a way that a jury was not involved, only four associates who were present to assist and support the judge, meaning that Freisler would arrive at the verdicts himself. As we have noted, however, the verdicts, like the sentences, had already been determined in Berlin even before the trial was scheduled. As for legal representation, the regime assigned Sophie, Hans, and Christl Probst a defense attorney, a Nazi Party member whose contributions were negligible since his objective was not to win their acquittal. And witnesses were another matter. Witnesses for the defense had no place in Freisler's courtroom, none being called to testify on behalf of the Scholls or Probst. Then, again, this was not all that unusual in trials over which this particular judge presided, since many potential witnesses were reluctant to publicly support a defendant for fear of repercussions from the regime. As to witnesses for the prosecution, Freisler does not seem to have believed he needed these either, since he did not call to the stand Jakob Schmid, the custodian who had spotted Sophie and Hans at the university and reported them to the authorities. In any event, the defendants had already confessed.

As to the nature of the proceedings, the trial was coarse and quick, since multifaceted and nuanced arguments were not to Freisler's liking despite the fact that he possessed a sharp legal mind. The tenor of the proceedings was also characteristic of those over which Freisler officiated; that is to say, one of wrath and doom.

Sophie was the first defendant to appear before the judge and she was said to be on crutches. "Sophie Scholl was handled so roughly during her interrogation by the Gestapo that she appeared in court with a broken leg," writes Shirer in his classic work on the Nazi era, *The Rise and Fall of the Third Reich*.[54] Subsequent accounts by other writers, however, have not reported an injured leg. But whatever abuse Sophie may have endured at the hands of the Gestapo, she was not intimidated by it and instead sought to defend the White Rose movement during the tribunal. At one point, she went so far as to tell Freisler, calmly yet bluntly, that Germany had already lost the war and that he lacked the backbone to admit it.[55] To say that it was bold of her to dress down the Nazi judge is an understatement; it was an extraordinary move on her part, her refusal to be cowed by the unprincipled official who held her life in his hands. Furthermore, she continued sounding off even after her appearance before the judge had concluded and she was escorted back to her seat; this, despite the protocol of the court. As Freisler continued to attack the White Rose movement and mock its seeming futility, Sophie erupted yet again. "Somebody had to make a start!" she cried out from across the courtroom.[56]

Hans, for his part, appears to have decided not to allow himself to be stage-managed by the People's Court. Refusing to be maneuvered into a public quarrel with the partisan judge, he did not defend his actions with the resistance. At the end of the trial, however, as Freisler was proclaiming with relish the punishment of Christl Probst, the third defendant to stand before him, Hans shouted out a statement on this comrade's behalf. The judge did not respond to it, however, except to state that Hans was in no position to defend his friend since he had refused to defend himself.

Sadly, Christl Probst was crushed by his arrest and trial. Not only did he have a wife who was ailing and in the hospital, but the couple also had three young children, one of them an infant. It was because of his responsibilities as a husband and father, then, that he made a plea for leniency. His young family was depending on him. Probst also told the court that he had been suffering from bouts of depression, and that his emotional instability may have accounted for some of his deeds with the White Rose. But Freisler was unmoved, and he refused to grant the young man's request for leniency.

In the course of this travesty of justice, Robert and Magdalene Scholl, accompanied by their son Werner, rushed into the courtroom. They had been kept in the dark about the entire matter and only now had learned that their children had been arrested and put on trial. Robert Scholl shouted to Freisler, who at once ordered the guards to eject the newly-arrived family members from the courtroom.

Wrapping up his performance, Freisler delivered a guilty verdict for the three defendants and announced their sentences: they were to be beheaded by guillotine. He justified the extreme punishments with the dubious claim that anything other than their deaths would diminish public support for the war.[57]

After the trial, Sophie, Hans, and Christl Probst were given an opportunity not usually afforded to those about to be killed, one that involved the behind-the-scenes maneuverings of sympathetic guards. The three were offered a few moments together to share a final cigarette. As well, they were allowed to briefly join their parents one last time.

As Sophie was saying goodbye to her mother, she reminded Magdalene yet again of the purpose of the White Rose movement. It had been an attempt to spur the German people to begin standing up for what was right, Sophie said, an initiative that would "cause waves."[58] As for Hans, who was now tearful, he asked his father to send farewell wishes to a list of friends he had prepared.

Back in their cells, the three students wrote letters to their loved ones, although the Gestapo failed to deliver them. They also spoke to clergymen, Sophie and Hans meeting with a Protestant minister and Probst with a Catholic priest.

A few hours later on the same day as the trial, the moment arrived for their executions. Standing beside a guillotine was the executioner dressed in a traditional black coat and wearing a top hat. Two guards stood on either side of the macabre device, their task being to hold the condemned in place as the blade was released.

Sophie was to be decapitated first, and she went to her death with grace. For her, the end was mercifully fast: a mere forty-eight seconds elapsed from the moment she left the holding cell until the time she was declared dead.[59] Hans Scholl and Christl Probst were executed a few minutes later. According to the official record of the event, Hans made a declaration as he was being led to the guillotine, one he evidently intended for all of the other prisoners to hear. "Long live freedom!" he shouted.[60]

During the weeks and months that followed, the Gestapo ruthlessly pursued and seized over eighty people suspected of having been associated with the White Rose movement in Munich and other cities where it had attracted adherents. Twenty-six people were tried in four separate proceedings. Among those the Nazis executed were the medical students Alexander Schmorell and Willi Graf, as well as Professor Kurt Huber. The regime placed under house arrest Robert and Magdalene Scholl, and they jailed Josef Söhngen, the bookshop owner, and Josef Müller, the teenage participant from Ulm. They also imprisoned Falk Harnack and Katharina Schüddekopf. As for those who were acquitted, they included Sophie's friend, the modern artist Wilhelm Geyer, and the architect Manfred Eickemeyer, in both cases owing to lack of evidence. Heartingly, Traute Lafrenz eventually was released from prison, after which she moved to Berkeley, California, and completed her medical degree. Jürgen

Wittenstein, Hans' friend who introduced him to Alex Schmorell, likewise moved to California, where he practiced medicine.

Looking back at the White Rose movement, it is stunning that a handful of young adults in the heart of Nazi Germany would dare to stand in protest of the totalitarian state in which they lived, contesting their government's ruthless efforts to slaughter minorities and assimilate other nations. Yet they believed it was their obligation to do so, that it was their Christian duty to raise their collective voice in response to the injustice and inhumanity that surrounded them. Yet in the minds of many, there seems to remain an uncertainty as to whether Sophie and her comrades truly expected their non-violent resistance movement to lead to widespread opposition that would help bring the regime to its knees. Historian Hans Rothfels, for one, does not think so. "[T]he Munich students can hardly have believed that a spontaneous rising on their part could alone alter the course of events," he writes. "They were, on the other hand, firmly convinced of something else, of the necessity of bearing witness to their faith and of clearing themselves as well as the name of Germany."[61] That said, Sophie and her comrades did appear to believe that their active, visible opposition to National Socialism was a means of balancing, at least on a small scale, the passivity of the German people in permitting the regime its atrocities. Theirs was a small way of redeeming the citizenry, of revealing that not all Germans were Nazis or Nazi sympathizers, as well as being a means of expressing publicly their Christian values. But Sophie, in particular, also seemed to believe that the White Rose movement, while in itself unable to produce immediate, sweeping change, was a beginning, a starting point. It was the germ of a protest movement, in her view, a fact that is clear in her statements during the trial and in her last words to her mother. And she was correct; the movement did spread.

As the war progressed, the tracts of the White Rose continued to find their way across Germany and other European nations, turning up at universities and even concentration camps. The Allies also got their hands on them and airdropped copies over Nazi Germany, the objective being to inspire a massive student revolt against the Third Reich. Thus, while the White Rose movement, in and of itself, did not lead to the fall of Hitler, nor did it expect to do so, its message expanded with the passage of time and with the continued deterioration of conditions in the Fatherland. "It is said that the appearance of the leaflets pierced the silence," writes Sue Halpern in the *New York Times*, "moving some Germans to hope and others to active opposition."[62]

Equally impressive was the behavior of Sophie and her White Rose comrades. In the face of the jaw-dropping viciousness doled out by Hitler and his minions, those in the peaceful resistance movement took no destructive action in response. They injured no one, nor did they threaten to do so. Instead, they did something more dangerous to the totalitarian regime: they educated the public through carefully considered arguments set forth in written treatises. And even when they found themselves confronted with their own executions, with murder at the hands of political thugs, they remained composed. "Their actions established that human dignity can be maintained in the midst of a sea of inhumanity," says Hans Mommsen, speaking of the German resistance movement.[63]

The personal conduct of Sophie Scholl and her comrades, as well as their wartime efforts to bring the light of knowledge into the darkness of their day, is a lesson we should treasure. During a period of ignorance and intolerance in Nazi Germany, they emerged as a shining example of intelligence and humanity, their integrity transcending the era in which they lived and serving as an inspiration to us today.

3

Monica Wichfeld and the Danish Resistance

A Danish national treasure, Monica Wichfeld won renown for her subversive deeds with her nation's resistance movement. Brimming with self-confidence and conviction, she was a woman who approached life on her own terms, a woman who acted on the basis of her own notions of right and wrong no matter what the consequences. It is therefore not surprising that she repeatedly came into conflict with the society of her day. Certainly she faced a mountain of criticism for one such transgression that took place during the 1920s, an indiscretion that was amorous in nature.

It seems the free-spirited Monica, who was married to wealthy Danish landowner Jørgen de Wichfeld, found herself the target of gossip because of a love affair she was carrying on with a neighbor, a dashing young aristocrat with an impressive pedigree. His name was Kurt Reventlow and he was a stunner. Ignoring the scandal that dogged her, Monica continued romancing the passionate nobleman for the next nine years, even as she gave birth to two more children by her husband. In her view, the affair was her own business and she refused to let her neighbors' tongue-wagging diminish it.

In the 1930s, Wichfeld again demonstrated her indomitable spirit when her family fortune began to dwindle. Rather than bemoaning the ravaging effects of the Great Depression on her standard of living, she promptly set up shop in Paris and began concocting a fragrance she named after herself, *Monica 55*. It was an essence she obtained through master perfumer Coco Chanel, and within a matter of months Wichfeld had succeeded in transforming it into a popular commodity. Throughout the remainder of the decade, the fragrance yielded a handsome profit for her family.

Then, in the 1940s, Monica's individualism reached its most defiant expression when the Germans marched into Denmark. Outraged by the takeover, she joined the Danish Resistance and spent the next two years destabilizing the occupying forces. She was eager to take on the Germans despite the fact that they constituted one of the deadliest regimes in human history.

In this chapter, we look back at this extraordinary woman, one whose actions reveal the manner in which a privileged figure in Denmark, rather than taking refuge in her vast estate, stepped forward and challenged the evil that surrounded her. In so doing, her bold actions served all classes of Danish society, not just her own, with her deeds helping to preserve the hope for a return to a free and self-governing nation.

Halcyon Days

Born Monica Massy-Beresford in a London hospital in July of 1894, Monica was reared in luxury at Saint Hubert's, her family's ancestral estate in the Irish countryside. A sprawling property, it was located near the town of Belturbet on the southern border of what is today Northern Ireland. The estate boasted a secluded Victorian manor with a tower and stables, and it was situated by a lake, Lough Erne, which to the delight of the Massy-Beresfords was the site of the Irish Regatta. The family had only to step outside their door to enjoy the annual yachting competition. And it was here, in this fresh, verdant setting, that Monica spent her childhood and adolescence in what truly was a charmed existence.

As for her personality, she was a bright, inquisitive child who was fiercely loyal to her family members, especially her brothers. But she also could be impatient, as well as headstrong, blunt, and defiant. "Monica was a rebel — a difficult child," wrote her adult daughter Varinka many years later.[1] All too often, Monica intimidated the staff at Saint Hubert's, with the estate's nannies yielding to her demands because they knew it would be pointless to resist. This should not be taken to imply that Monica was a bratty child, however. She was not. It is merely to point out that she evinced an iron will at an early age and felt comfortable exercising it.

Predictably perhaps, her willfulness was on display when, as a high-spirited eleven-year-old, she was sent to a nearby school and found herself bored by the instructor's methods. Certainly her solution was not helpful: she proceeded to lead the class in taunting the hapless teacher, the upshot being that Monica was unceremoniously removed from the school. After an ensuing stay at a boarding school likewise failed — she was expelled after a month — her mother hired a private tutor, a no-nonsense Scottish disciplinarian by the name of Miss Graham who knew how to handle unruly girls. Through this woman, Monica became well-versed in history and music, acquired the art of conversation, and learned the importance of self-control. With Miss Graham, she also traveled to Paris, where she gained exposure to French culture and assumed a touch of sophistication. The trip signaled the beginning of Monica's emancipation from her provincial Irish background and a step into international society, even as Europe teetered on the brink of World War I.

In 1914, when war did break out, the twenty-year-old Monica moved to London and took a job at a canteen that catered to servicemen. In the meantime, two of her three brothers were dispatched to the Western Front, where her favorite, Jack, was struck in the forehead with shrapnel and killed. A personal tragedy that had a lasting impact on Monica, it caused her to relinquish her religious beliefs and to become an avowed foe of Germany and its people.

Still, the trauma over Jack notwithstanding, wartime also held pleasant surprises for her. It was during this period, for instance, that she met her future husband at a gathering at the Café de Paris in London. His name was Jørgen de Wichfeld and he was the honorary attaché to the Danish Embassy in London. Handsome, impeccably attired, and sporting a monocle, the diplomat was both intelligent and refined. Educated in Switzerland and Denmark, he also was well-traveled, and, to his credit, owned a splendid estate known as Engestofte situated on the Danish island of Lolland in the Baltic Sea. As it turned out, the worldly envoy made an indelible impression on Monica, with the couple marrying two years later at Saint Margaret's Church (Westminster) near the Houses of Parliament in London. Certainly their guest list was impressive. Besides numerous counts and countesses, Baron Bror Blixen-Finecke was invited, along with his wife Karen Blixen, who would later find fame under the pseudonym Isak Dinesen, the author of *Out of Africa*. The Archbishop of Armagh, Primate of Ireland, officiated at the ceremony, which was a stunning affair by any standard.

In neighboring Germany, by comparison, the situation was not nearly so sunny during this, the early interwar era, with the populace struggling to rebuild the country in the wake of its humiliating defeat in World War I. Because the Treaty of Versailles held Germany accountable for the total cost of the conflict, the nation was saddled with a staggering war debt it could not possibly repay, a turn of events that contributed to widespread frustration and ultimately to the emergence of intense German nationalism. At this early date, however, the country's fateful march toward militancy was still in its nascent phase and thus went unnoticed by Monica, Jørgen, and other residents of Denmark. Oblivious to the approaching storm, the Wichfelds concerned themselves instead with settling into Engestofte, their pastoral domain.

By Monica's own admission, her first glimpse of Engestofte was unforgettable as the manor house rose into view at the end of a long driveway lined with lime trees and elms. Although she was accustomed to mansions with formal gardens, this one took her breath away. It consisted of a forty-room neo-classical mansion, along with separate cottages for elderly house staff, a school, a pair of churches, and a Chinese pavilion built over a mineral spring. In addition, it contained three thousand acres of fertile farmland, a park, a two-mile-long lake, a pier, and a procession of terraces leading from the manor house to the lakeshore. Of all of these, it was the lake she came to cherish the most.

Monica also was drawn to a neighboring property, one that held a magnificent edifice known as Hardenberg Castle. It was here that Hans Christian Andersen wrote *The Ugly Duckling* in 1844. The estate now was owned by the Reventlow brothers, two debonair Danes of German descent, the younger of whom, Kurt, had served in the German army during World War I. Despite Kurt's prominent lineage, Monica was initially unwilling to make his acquaintance because he had cooperated with the Germans, although she more than made up for her frostiness by eventually getting to know the charismatic aristocrat quite well. Intimately, in fact.

A few years her junior, Kurt was a handsome, virile, and dynamic man who drove a fashionable yellow Hudson, dressed in country tweeds, and loved jazz. Soon the two were spending their days together at Hardenberg Castle and at hotels in Copenhagen. As for Jørgen, he learned about the affair when Monica, in due course, told him about it, and his reaction was remarkably democratic: he decided the relationship was his wife's concern and thereafter looked the other way. Their neighbors, on the other hand, were not nearly as tolerant, gossiping incessantly about what they regarded as the wanton Irishwoman and her pusillanimous husband. True to form, Monica displayed the same independent spirit she had evinced as a child, brushing aside their chatter and romancing Kurt for the next nine years.

During this same period, she and Jørgen added to their family. They already had a son, Ivan, and now he was joined by a sister and brother, Varinka and Viggo. As for Kurt, the Wichfelds regarded him as a sixth member of the family and even named him one of Varinka's godfathers, an honor he shared with Grand-Duke Dimitri of Russia and Prince Aage of Denmark.

But then the tide began to turn. It seems the Wichfelds' lifestyle during the early years of the 1920s, one that fizzed with glamour and privilege, started to ebb as Monica and Jørgen's fortunes suffered due to Denmark's new tax structure. Exorbitant taxes were being levied on their properties and they could not afford to pay them. Worsening matters, new legislation required that they surrender hundreds of acres of their land for redistribution to the Danish people, with such hefty obligations rapidly swallowing up the couple's resources.

"The unexpected collapse of the Wichfeld family finances came as a bolt from the blue," writes Christine Sutherland in *Monica,* her biography of Wichfeld. "One day Monica was the wife of a rich landowner, mistress of a beautiful house, attended by a large staff of servants; the next day creditors were beating at her door."[2]

Ultimately, Jørgen and Monica leased their beloved Engestoft to a prosperous Danish family and moved to Italy, where Monica's mother owned a sun-drenched villa on the Riviera. Christened Campo dei Fiori, it overlooked the cliffs of Portofino. On its spacious grounds was a profusion of camellias, roses, azalea, and wisteria, as well as jasmine shrubs and tangerine, orange, and plum trees. As for the three-story villa, it included eleven bedrooms, meaning it could comfortably accommodate the Wichfeld family. An idyllic home, Campo dei Fiori was a godsend for Monica, Jørgen, and their children during their years of financial distress.

Despite her financial limitations, Monica still found the means to return to England for the occasional visit, where she mingled comfortably with luminaries such as Noel Coward and Talullah Bankhead and played tennis with Clementine Churchill, the wife of Winston Churchill.[3] As well, she visited friends and family in France, Scotland, and Ireland, although these excursions eventually became fewer.

As the Wichfelds' financial status continued to erode in the early 1930s — the Great Depression had now descended on Europe and deepened their economic woes — it became necessary for them to make further changes. So it was that Monica resolved to try her hand at business, a bold course of action for a woman in that era. Determined to improve her family's lot, she left her children in the capable hands of Jørgen and her mother, leased a flat in Paris, and obtained an essence from Coco Chanel that she transformed into a fashionable perfume. With the help of a chemist, Monica also created a fingernail protectant known as *No-Crax*, and with the collaboration of artisans in Venice designed a line of elegant costume jewelry. All of these ventures were successful, moreover, with their profits helping to sustain the Wichfelds throughout the 1930s.

It was during this period that Monica also brought to an end her long romance with Kurt Reventlow, a decision she had reached before moving to Italy. All the same, the pair continued to enjoy a deep affection for one another, with Monica wishing him well when, in 1935, he began wooing Barbara Hutton, one of the world's richest women and the heiress to the Woolworth fortune. From impetuous young lovers Monica and Kurt had matured into platonic friends, with the two occasionally meeting for drinks at the Hôtel Ritz in Paris or skiing together in the Swiss Alps. It was therefore regrettable that their bond was about to be tested by political events, occurrences that would reveal a profound disparity in their values.

It seems that Kurt, in response to rising tensions on the continent, decided to move to the United States. Rather than grant Monica's request and join a pro–Danish organization in Washington, DC, however, an organization designed to protect Danish interests during this ominous period, Kurt joined the leisure set in Sun Valley, Idaho, and later, California. Along the way, he also married a wealthy socialite, Margaret Astor-Drayton, with whom he enjoyed a lavish life on the West Coast throughout the war years. According to those who knew her, Monica, repelled by what she viewed as his unscrupulous, self-serving behavior, removed his photograph from her dresser and never spoke to him again.

As for her own course of action, Wichfeld found it necessary in 1938 to liquidate her business ventures in France due to the same political developments that had frightened away Kurt Reventlow. These included the proliferation of National Socialism in Germany and the metastasization of Fascism in Italy.

As noted earlier, the Treaty of Versailles created an insurmountable hardship for Germany after World War I, a burden that gave rise to a resentment in the German people and contributed to their determination to reclaim their country's former dignity and might. Theirs was a bitterness that Hitler exploited as he ascended to power. In Italy, meanwhile, Benito Mussolini sought to improve conditions in his nation by establishing a central ruling authority to control all aspects of the country's life while aggressively stifling dissent. Together, these totalitarian movements, along with the alliance that existed between their two leaders, proved deeply troubling to many Europeans, Monica among them.

War Breaks Out

Still living in Paris and with war now imminent, Monica decided to return to Italy to wait out the ordeal with her loved ones. To this end, she set about saying farewell to friends, one of whom, the distinguished financier Baron Maxwell Beaverbrook, made an unusual request of her.

According to Monica's brother Tim, the baron asked her to remain in touch with him upon returning to Campo dei Fiori, explaining that any information she could provide about conditions in Italy would prove helpful. And sure enough, Monica began gathering material about events in the authoritarian nation as soon as she arrived on the Riviera. What she found, among other things, was that numerous aspects of life in Italy were highly strained, as was the case in several other European nations. Given the political events of the era, this was to be expected.

Such pervasive unease intensified the following spring as war edged closer, with Monica becoming concerned about the fates of her friends in Denmark and the outlook for the Engestofte estate. Surely there was cause for worry given that Denmark and Germany shared a common border. Even so, she had reason to hope that the Scandinavian nation might not be drawn into the conflict, especially when, in 1939, it signed a non-aggression pact with Germany. Yet by all accounts, this did not ease her concerns about the costs to Britain if war broke out, a worry that proved justified when the British government declared, four months later, its intention to engage Germany in battle. For Monica, stuck in Italy, this marked the beginning of a long stretch of social isolation and feelings of futility.

Wichfeld would later tell others that her days in Italy, in spite of the luminous Mediterranean setting, were among the most unpleasant she had ever endured. As it stood, she had little choice but to linger at her mother's seaside villa while her friends and relatives on other parts of the continent suffered. Travel outside of Italy was simply too fraught with danger to consider leaving. Nevertheless, she did what she could to aid her homeland, most notably by continuing to dispatch to Great Britain, by way of the United States, information about conditions in Italy. Furthermore, her communiqués were quite useful, with some of them providing contextual material for BBC news broadcasts. Clearly, Monica had no intention of remaining inactive at this critical political juncture.

Idleness, in fact, had never been one of her traits, and her messages to London were only the beginning. In 1940, she was noted to become even more determined to aid the cause of freedom when Germany invaded Denmark, a turn of events that was supposed to have been prevented by Hitler's non-aggression pact with the Danish government. In truth, the accord had always been a sham.

It appears that Hitler, from the start, planned to overtake the Scandinavian nation because it formed part of a buffer zone between Germany and Britain. By occupying it, the Nazis hoped to prevent the Allies from passing through it and invading Germany. Denmark also was a stepping stone to Norway, another country Hitler planned to consume in his campaign to control the buffer zone. Then, too, Denmark possessed a railway system the Germans could use to receive supplies from neutral Sweden, and it boasted rich farmland they could seize to feed their own people. Denmark was therefore valuable to Hitler's war strategy and he did not wish to alienate its leadership or its citizenry. For this reason, the Führer sought to portray his takeover as a benevolent act, his hope being to win the cooperation of the Danish people.

"[W]e will do our utmost to make the operation appear as a peaceful occupation, the object of which is the military protection of the neutrality of the Scandinavian States," Hitler wrote in a top secret memo to his aides shortly before the incursion. "If, in spite of this, resistance should be met, all military means will be used to crush it."[4]

As it turned out, little resistance was encountered when the invasion was launched in April 1940 the operation being completed within a matter of hours. Afterward, Hitler assured the Danish government, as well as Denmark's king, Christian X, that they could remain in place while their country was occupied. Yet there was a tacit understanding that this arrangement would apply only so long as the Danes did not challenge the German presence in any way — not that Hitler had reason to worry. Denmark, a nation having a population of just over four million people, had no realistic alternative but to comply with the conditions set forth by Germany, a nation of seventy million with a formidable military.

So it was that the Danish people, in the ensuing weeks, struggled to adjust to the German troops that patrolled their streets, although they neither accepted the intruders nor deferred to them. For that matter, Christian X made it a point to ride his stallion through the heart of Copenhagen each morning and greet the citizenry, his aim being to reassure them of their nation's independence and his continued presence as their sovereign.

With regard to Monica, who was still living on the Italian Riviera, she appears to have been incensed by the takeover. Little did she know that, due to Il Duce's growing animosity toward foreign nationals like herself, she would soon have the opportunity to return to Denmark and lend it a hand.

This change in her circumstances began on a summer morning in 1941, when the chief of police of Rapallo, the town in which Campo dei Fiori was located, showed up at the villa and ordered her and her loved ones to leave Italy. Mussolini, it seems, had decided to expel British citizens. As could be expected, Monica was taken aback by the abrupt demand and evidently was opposed to it, which is not surprising since a hasty departure in the midst of a war was not only impractical but also dangerous. But after weighing their options for several weeks, as well as watching conditions in Italy decline along with their children's health, Monica and Jørgen decided the family should indeed take its leave. To this end, the Wichfelds, in September 1941, packed their belongings and boarded a train for the first leg of a long, nerve-wracking journey that would take them through the heart of the Weimar Republic.

On this precarious trip, the family first traveled to the Brenner Pass on the Austrian border, a daunting experience during which machine gun–wielding Nazis barged into their compartment and drilled them about their nationalities. The Wichfelds next passed through the Alps into Germany, where the following morning, they arrived in the ravaged German capital and had to disembark for several hours. Walking through the streets of Berlin, they could see that large swaths of the city had been bombed during Soviet and British sorties. They noticed, too, that the lobbies of its hotels teemed with Nazi commandants and their entourages. What most impressed the Wichfelds, though, were the clusters of papier maché trees that stood in odd locations, as well as the expansive camouflage nets that were suspended above one of Berlin's main thoroughfares, a street that led to Wilhelmstrasse, the site of Hitler's command center. Obviously, the ersatz trees and camouflage lattices were intended to confuse British bombers, a ruse that was not lost on Monica. Always eager to aid her homeland, she instructed her son Viggo to memorize the details of their surroundings, particularly the grid of the area underneath the canopy, so they could later pass on this information to British Intelligence in London, which they did. The family then boarded another train for the last leg of their journey back to Denmark, arriving late that night at a ferry station on the Baltic Sea in the midst of an air raid. The Wichfelds were fortunate to have made it back to Denmark given the conditions in Western Europe at the time.

Upon returning to Engestofte, Monica spent the first few weeks restoring the interior of the manor house — their former tenants had neglected it — after which she traveled about the island of Lolland reuniting with her neighbors. The visits were not mere social calls, however. With considerable discretion, she was sounding out these people, trying to determine who might be interested in helping her arrange opposition to the occupying regime. And what Monica discovered dismayed her, namely, that their well-to-do neighbors had no desire to oppose it. Worse still, some of them, proud members of the landed gentry, admired Hitler and planned to collaborate with the Danish National Socialist Party. They believed his professed goal of a more wholesome, more tightly-controlled society was a worthy one. Disgusted, Monica sent a heartfelt letter to her mother, who was now safely ensconced in London, saying she no longer felt at home in the Scandinavian nation, her adopted home. And yet, such feelings of alienation aside, Monica could take heart in the fact that most Danes shared her disdain for the regime.

Indeed, unlike the clique of privileged landowners who endorsed National Socialism, the majority of Danish citizens looked down on the Nazi ideology and were put off by the German presence in their land. As to the reason why organized resistance had not yet emerged, it was because Christian X and the government remained in power, at least outwardly, and daily life had thus far been largely unaffected by the German occupation. Also contributing to the inertia was the constant visibility of the Gestapo. "People were paralyzed, and the Nazi power was overwhelming," says historian Helge Seidelin Jacobsen.[5] For such reasons, the Danes initially expressed their discontentment through small, individual acts, such as singing a patriotic song in front of a German soldier or mocking a serviceman in a public place. On those few occasions when collective defiance occurred, it was usually rather innocuous and aimed at the Danish government for its deference to the Germans. It was not directed at the Nazis themselves, since any attempt at organized opposition to the regime would have prompted a rapid and ruthless retaliation. In this way, life ground on in the beleaguered country with comparatively little protest.

As the winter of 1941 progressed, the Danish people continued to endure stoically the German presence. Although the weather was harsh that season, a season during which the Nazis enforced nightly blackouts, food and electricity were still available in most parts of the country. The populace was not yet experiencing the marked deprivation it would face in the years ahead.

As for Monica, despite being isolated at Engestofte during these frigid months — even the channel between Denmark and Sweden iced over — she persisted in her quest to track down and join the resistance. Although she had given up on her politically misguided neighbors, she was sure that large-scale defiance must be forming elsewhere within the nation's borders, according to her family members.

In the spring of 1942, her search was bolstered when she came across a newspaper report that was said to intrigue and inspire her. Two parachutes, the article revealed, had mysteriously shown up in the nearby town of Haslev, which Monica correctly took to mean that some form of insurgency was indeed in the works.[6] Inspired by this twist, she redoubled her efforts to unearth the anti–Nazi underground and play a role in its operations.

"Monica was talking wildly about destroying telephone and telegraph wires," writes Flemming Muus about this pivotal moment in Wichfeld's life.[7] Jørgen urged restraint, however, advising her to wait until she was safely connected to a trustworthy, proficient organization before attempting such subversive deeds. And Monica concurred. It seems she was well aware that she could be most useful as a member of a well-established network — this is precisely why she had been trying to join the underground — and she was astute enough to realize the network should be a highly skilled one, since her life would depend on it. She was therefore excited when, a few months later, she discovered not one but three points of entry into the Danish Resistance, the first of them involving a new tenant at Engestofte itself.

It occurred one spring day when she and Jørgen rented a cottage on their property to three communists: the journalist Hilmar Wulff and his wife, along with their friend, the dissident poet Halfdan Rasmussen. Of this trio, Hilmar Wulff was the most politically active, playing an important role in the Danish Communist Party. Among other tasks, he took it upon himself to assemble a distribution network for two underground newspapers, a job he continued performing while living on the grounds of Engestofte. In fact, he not only carried on disseminating *Frit Denmark* ("Free Denmark"), a resistance newspaper, and *Land og Folk* ("Country and Folk"), the official publication of the Danish Communist Party, but he even duplicated the latter in the Wichfelds' cottage. Of course, he was risking his life by doing so since the occupying forces had outlawed all such publications, but he seemed convinced the gamble was worth it. Fortunately, he would soon be able to dispense with some of his secrecy because Monica would become aware of, and supportive of, his operation, a turn of events that began when she called on him one day at the cottage.

The reason for her visit was simple: she wanted to become better acquainted with her new tenant. It was nothing more than a social call. At this point in time, Monica was unaware of Wulff's resistance work; he had been careful to keep her and Jørgen in the dark about it. All the same, as she wrapped up her visit and prepared to leave, she turned to him and asked off-handedly if he was a reader of *Frit Denmark*. To her surprise, he replied that he was, whereupon she insisted he come to the main house so they could speak further.

Wulff later recalled that Monica, during their ensuing discussion, probed him about his political connections and in this way learned of his work distributing illicit newspapers. Encouraged by her discovery, she asked what she could do to help and he did not hesitate to tell her. Wulff explained that the underground press was in dire need of funds.

In short order, Monica set about calling on bank managers, clergy members, and friends, urging them to donate money to an unnamed yet worthwhile cause she was representing. As contributions rolled in, she and Wulff sent them to the Communists' treasury in Copenhagen. As well, she helped him distribute the banned newspapers and she wrote to acquaintances urging them to oppose the German presence in their communities. Despite the fact that she was performing such beneficial deeds, however, she does not appear to have felt that her work was sufficient and continued looking for ways to further contribute to the resistance. She was successful, moreover, with her search soon leading her to another entryway into the subterranean world of subterfuge and sabotage.

This next opening came in the form of an insurance agent. Tall, blond, and brawny, his name was Erik Kiersgaard and he was the cousin of one of Engestofte's tenant farmers. As it happened, Kiersgaard appeared at the manor house one day to assess the property, and Monica, as was her way, began inquiring into his politics. She had met him before and seems to have suspected that he might be a member of the underground, just as he had wondered if she might likewise be involved. In the course of their tête-à-tête, both disclosed that they were indeed in the movement, with Kiersgaard explaining that he was in the midst of forming a sabotage unit on a neighboring island. He added that he was in desperate need of a place to hide weapons and explosives, and he asked if Monica would be amenable to storing them at Engestofte. She readily agreed.

As to her third and most effective entry, it came through a friend of Viggo and Varinka. His name was Count Carl-Adam Moltke — "Bobby" to friends — and he was the son of Denmark's former Minister of Foreign Affairs. Intricately involved in the burgeoning underground movement, Bobby was in contact with its top echelon in Copenhagen, precisely the leaders with whom Monica wished to confer. Viggo therefore arranged for Bobby and Monica to meet at the country home of Bobby's mother, a countess and an acquaintance of the Wichfeld family, the purpose of the visit outwardly being a social one. It was after this get-together, as Monica was preparing to return home by train, that she made her move. She asked Bobby to accompany her to the depot, pumping him en route about his political connections and conveying her own determination to undermine the regime. Bobby later recounted how Monica grabbed his arm, spun him around, and asked him emphatically to arrange for her to gain greater access to, and more substantial involvement in, the resistance movement.[8] The startled young man agreed on the spot.

True to his word, Bobby, a few weeks later, set up a backstairs meeting between Monica and a prominent Dane in the underground movement, a gentleman who went by the alias Jørgen Møller. Trained by Winston Churchill's Special Operations Executive (SOE), a British organization created to buttress the resistance efforts of occupied nations, Møller was the chief of the paratrooper division of the Danish Resistance. His real name was Flemming Muus and he would eventually marry into the Wichfeld family. At this early date, though, he and Monica were strangers as they met at a discreet inn in Copenhagen, the Damehotellet, to discuss their mutual interests. By his own account, Muus found himself taken with her. "I was at once aware that I was in the presence of a truly great personality," he said.[9]

In the course of their conversation, Muus asked her to grant him a favor: he requested that she hide at Engestofte one of the SOE's top saboteurs, a man whose code name was Jacob, and that she allow this agent to use the estate as a base of operations for the recruitment and training of apprentice saboteurs. Eager to assist, Monica consented; she had no qualms about opening her doors to the agent and his protégées. And true to form, upon returning to Engstofte she arranged for Jacob to lodge at Hilmar Wulff's cottage, this being the safest setup since the cottage was situated a few miles from the manor house and the agent would thus go unnoticed by the house staff. In this way, Jacob was securely installed at the cottage a few weeks later, with his presence remaining a secret even from the Wichfeld family.

Along these same lines, Monica did not tell Jørgen or her sons about her pivotal meeting with Flemming Muus, or, more generally, about her membership in the Danish Resistance. Apparently, she considered it irresponsible to draw her loved ones into her illicit activities since such knowledge could cost them their lives if the Gestapo were to capture and interrogate them. Yet this was not the only reason for her silence. It was also to ensure that Jørgen and her sons, all of whom had likewise joined the underground, did not intrude into her subversive activities. "She knew perfectly well," write the

Muuses, "that her own husband was busy distributing illegal papers, and that her two sons had their own duties, but she let each one keep his secrets to himself, just as she herself wished to be free from interference in her work."[10] The one exception was Varinka, who Monica not only told about her activities, but whose help she enlisted for certain missions. In time, Varinka, operating under the code name Kirsten, would become a valuable member of the resistance movement as well, first in its propaganda department and later as the secretary of Flemming Muus.[11] At this early point, however, she and Monica were still novices, although they would soon become proficient as the political situation in Denmark deteriorated and the underground movement rose up in response to the Nazis' increasing exploitation and abuse of the Danish people.

To be sure, life in the Scandinavian nation went from bad to worse during the period when Monica began serving with the underground. In 1942 and 1943, the Danish people suffered increasingly severe food and gasoline shortages, with the winter months being especially hard. During these cold stretches, heating fuel became so scarce that many families had no choice but to chop up their furniture and use it for kindling. Worsening matters, the regime's disrespect for, and mistreatment of, the citizenry intensified as the occupation dragged on, thereby contributing to the public's growing resentment of the German presence. For such reasons, the Danish Resistance became better organized and far more aggressive, with its subversive actions now being directed at the occupying regime rather than at the Danish government. It ranged from the destruction of German vehicles to armed assaults on soldiers, with the underground press expanding rapidly as well.

With the activities of the resistance mounting, Muus decided it was time to promote Monica to a position of greater responsibility. By his own account, he not only had been impressed with her composure and ingenuity during their initial meeting at the Damehotellet, but he had since become even more impressed by the manner in which she protected Jacob, the saboteur he had sent to her estate. Muus therefore increased the number and importance of her duties. She had proven herself to be both capable and committed to the cause.

In the summer of 1943, he paired her with Jacob, who was still living an Engestofte. Due to the intensification of the war, it now became necessary to expand Jacob's responsibilities to encompass not only the training of neophyte saboteurs but also the supervision of that arm of the Danish Resistance which was based on the island of Lolland. Monica was appointed to serve as Jacob's second-in-command.

With her tenant Hilmar Wulff at her side, she began by recruiting several local people while Jacob geared up to train them in subversive acts, most notably the uses of high explosives. For several weeks, Monica hid these deadly devices in her house as preparations for the training were being finalized.

When the time came to select a location for the classes, the charismatic Wichfeld, employing her remarkable gifts of persuasion, convinced a local minister to allow his vicarage to be used. Since the locals seldom took notice of the church or the rectory, especially on weekdays, she assumed the comings and goings of guerrilla fighters would not be detected. And sure enough, numerous saboteurs were instructed at the vicarage during the ensuing weeks without the local residents catching on.

It was during this same period that Monica helped conceal arms and ammunition that the Royal Air Force dropped on her property. Unlike the more discreet estates on the island, Engestofte's proximity to a vast lake and its prominent manor house made excellent landmarks for British pilots, since both the lake and the house could be seen in the moonlight. These advantages were quickly put to use.

In this treacherous operation, Wichfeld oversaw the reception of paratroopers and their deliveries. Under cover of darkness, she and Varinka would retrieve the agents and their cargo and transport both to secure locations on the estate. In the days that followed, the agents would bury their caches of weapons in Engestofte's park, which was situated across the lake from the manor house. While they were doing this, Monica and her daughter, pretending to be enjoying leisurely boat rides, would row a mile and a half across the lake to lend them a hand or update them on the underground's latest feats. Always sympathetic to fellow smokers, Monica also used these visits to give cigarettes to the agents.

As the RAF stepped up its airdrops and other missions, it became necessary for Wichfeld to reorganize her end of the operation, a task that entailed creating an office for herself and bringing in extra help. For starters, she moved out of the bedroom she shared with Jørgen and into a salon on the top floor of the mansion, after which she instructed her husband and sons to avoid that section of the house she had appropriated. As to why she chose the salon, Monica evidently favored it because it had a door leading to an outside staircase from which she could secretly receive visitors or, if necessary, use as an escape route. And the salon offered a further advantage, namely, direct access to two floors of attics that could be used to harbor insurgents. Satisfied with this arrangement, she thereafter spent innumerable hours in her new surroundings, holding meetings in her office while sheltering guerrilla fighters in the garrets.

As for the extra help she needed, Monica handpicked three trustworthy and reliable acquaintances from the island. The first was Pastor Mancussen, the small, unassuming Lutheran priest who had loaned her his vicarage. He was in the early stages of tuberculosis when he joined her team. She also selected Hans Christian Hovmand, a brash young veterinarian who agreed to use his van to convey explosives. And lastly, Monica chose Gerner Nielsen, the head of the island's sanatorium.

Together, she and her trio of comrades helped other resistance members bury weapons in Engestofte's park. Then, too, they assembled bombs to be used in demolishing the Nakskov Shipyard on the far end of the island, a coup that prevented the Nazis from using it. A shining example of Danish defiance, the obliteration of this vital facility was one of thousands of subversive deeds that took place during the summer of 1943, a season that witnessed an astonishing fifty to eighty acts of sabotage each night in the small but spirited nation.

It was now that Danish patriots vandalized German vehicles, slashing their tires and painting their windshields. "The letter *V*, the sign for British victory, appeared on fences and walls all over Copenhagen," says historian Ellen Levine.[12] And patriots staged nationwide strikes in an effort to paralyze the daily functioning of the occupied country. Even more provocative, insurgents blew up bridges and destroyed railroad tracks so as to obstruct the movement of German troops, while the Danish Navy, in an unprecedented act of defiance, sank its own ships rather than allow the Nazis to commandeer them. To be sure, Danish rebelliousness became truly formidable during this season, although, as before, such boldness met with equally fierce measures on the part of the Germans.

At the height of the Danes' rebellion in August 1943, Hitler ordered his minions to put a stop to the protestations in Denmark, which he dismissed as a "ridiculous little nation."[13] And his underlings took their task to heart, declaring martial law, seizing control of the press, and enforcing strict curfews. They also revoked the right to free association, with no more than five citizens permitted to assemble on a given occasion, and they sequestered Christian X and the royal family. As if this were not enough, they banned strikes and made punishable by death the participation in any protest whose actions interfered with the objectives of the regime. Regarding saboteurs, the Nazis summarily executed them, along with anyone suspected of sheltering them.

Despite being faced with such repressive measures, however, the Danish people refused to be cowed. More the opposite: the government abruptly resigned and parliament refused to meet for the remainder of the occupation. But while these acts were effective in conveying the Danish leadership's aversion to the Reich, they left a dangerous administrative void. For this reason, Denmark's principal resistance organizations promptly united to form an interim government of sorts, a militant administration known as the Freedom Council of Denmark, of which Flemming Muus was a founding member. The Council proclaimed its raison d'être in a public manifesto that contained this statement:

> The Freedom Council of Denmark consists of representatives of those Danish movements which jointly and in conformity with the will of the people will actively fight the German occupying force until Denmark is once more a free and independent country.[14]

The Reich's response was predictable. "The Germans reacted with force," says Ellen Levine. "Soldiers patrolled the streets, and the Schalburg Corps, a Danish Nazi SS force, was used to terrorize the populace."[15] By any measure, it was a bloody period, particularly for the nation's guerrilla fighters, many of whom resolved to get out of the country as swiftly as possible since the regime was stepping up its efforts to seize them. Monica, for her part, turned her attention to helping these patriots escape. Like other members of the underground, she had learned to be versatile in her actions.

Wichfeld's involvement in this aspect of the resistance began when Denmark's main newspapers, under Nazi control, published the photographs of several underground figures and offered rewards for their capture. Shortly thereafter, one of them showed up, uninvited and unannounced, at Hilmar Wulff's door in need of protection. In a curious twist, the man arrived at precisely the same moment that Monica dropped by the cottage, an awkward state of affairs which prompted Wulff, in a panic, to tell her the fugitive was his cousin. Wichfeld was evidently amused by the claim. Being on top of the news, she recognized the man at once from the press accounts. Next morning, she sent Varinka to the cottage with a valise filled with women's clothing, hair dye, and, of course, cigarettes, such that the resistance fighter was able to masquerade as a woman and make his way to neutral Sweden.

In the weeks that followed, Wulff continued using the cottage as a haven for fugitives, with Monica assisting them at every turn. Oftentimes this meant refashioning their appearances as she had done with the earlier gentleman. Certainly altering one's look could be a life-saving tactic in the underground, with British Intelligence having subjected one of the Danish underground's top leaders, Flemming Muus himself, to a facelift before dropping him in Denmark. His surgical transformation was effective, as was the case for many other members of the underground whose appearances were modified.

In addition to disguising agents on the run, Monica also gave them cash despite the fact that her own financial circumstances were still far from ideal. As well, she provided them with up-to-date information about resistance operations and furnished them with transportation when she was able to arrange it.

"[I]n every case Mrs. Wichfeld rallied round with advice and practical assistance," Wulff said after the war.[16] In the end, she even helped Wulff and his wife flee the country.

Furthermore, Monica did not limit her escape activities to the tiny cottage at Engestofte. As mentioned earlier, she also harbored fugitives in her own quarters, usually in the garrets but occasionally in her salon. The most notable was a master saboteur the Gestapo was bent on capturing because he had disrupted the transfer of German troops to Norway. With this notorious guerrilla, Monica shared her salon while helping orchestrate his escape on a fishing boat to Sweden.

Perhaps riskiest of all, however, were her efforts to help a Jewish family flee when the Nazis set out to liquidate this segment of the population. It was an intercession that would put her conscience to the test.

The "Jewish Problem"

Shortly after the Germans invaded Denmark, at a time when the Nazis were attempting to win the Danish leadership's compliance with the occupation, SS leader Heinrich Himmler met with the Danish Chief of Police, Thune Jacobsen, to discuss the Scandinavian nation's so-called Jewish Problem. Himmler swiftly discovered that there was nothing to discuss, however, with Jacobsen telling him, bluntly, "The Danish population does not consider this topic a problem."[17] Thereafter, it was understood that Denmark's tolerance of German troops would depend in part on the Germans' tolerance of Danish Jews, a state of affairs that irked Hitler to no end, the Führer purportedly finding their enduring freedom to be "loathsome."[18] All the same, the Reich deferred to Denmark's pro–Jewish position; that is, until August 1943, when open fighting broke out between the Danish people and the occupying forces, a rupture that provided Hitler with a pretext for setting into motion a deportation plan for the subjugated nation's Jewish citizenry.

Although the details of his strategy remained a secret in September 1943, it was evident to most everyone that the systematic persecution of the Jews was about to commence. It was during this month, then, that Niels Bohr, the renowned Jewish scientist who had published his theory of atomic fission three years earlier, fled to the United States and enlisted in the atomic bomb project at Los Alamos, New Mexico. It also was during this month that Monica Wichfeld found herself questioning, and ultimately rejecting, the stance of the Danish Resistance which discouraged its members from helping Jews.

On this subject, the underground believed the Nazis, who were ruthlessly trying to suppress the resistance movement, would become even more vicious if they discovered it was harboring Jews. For this reason, it advised against providing direct aid to the Jewish population, which, at least in the early days of the occupation, was believed to be a comparatively safe group under the country's agreement with the Germans. As for the small number of Jews who did require help during the early years of the occupation, the Danish Resistance guided them into the hands of citizens who were unaffiliated with it; certainly the nation was full of ordinary men and women who were willing to assist a fellow citizen in distress. In this way, the underground ensured that Danish Jews received the support they required, while, at the same time, decreasing the likelihood that the resistance itself would become the target of even deadlier reprisals by the regime.

As it turned out, it was this position of non-intervention that triggered a moral conflict in Monica one September morning when she saw a well-dressed lady, visibly distressed, rushing up the driveway toward the manor house. The woman, a Mrs. Kann, was the wife of a local real estate agent and had come to solicit her help in rescuing a Jewish family in Copenhagen that was being hounded by the Nazis. The family's name was Kauffman, and it consisted of a mother, two daughters, and a son, all of whom needed a place to hide. Earlier that morning, Gerner Nielsen, the administrator of the sanatorium and one of Monica's comrades, had agreed to shelter two of the children, so Wichfeld was being asked to protect Mrs. Kauffman and her little girl, Hanne.

Naturally, Monica was well aware of the underground's stance on assisting Jews and proceeded to explain its position to Kann. Disconsolate, Kann left Engestofte only to return a few hours later even more desperate because the family's plight had worsened. The Kauffmans' capture and deportation to a concentration camp appeared imminent.

With this new and disturbing information, Monica, as she had done so often in her life, decided to follow her conscience rather than the existing rules. And so it was, to Mrs. Kann's immense relief, that Monica agreed to open her doors to the imperiled Jewish family, a choice that not only violated the procedures of the resistance movement but also placed her own life in jeopardy.

As with numerous escapees before them, Wichfeld began by altering the Kauffmans' appearances. Since she could not convincingly disguise the mother and daughter as men, she decided to dress them in blue maid uniforms and pass them off as domestics. To enhance the illusion, she provided them with rooms in the servants' quarters, while instructing them to refrain from speaking to the house staff as much as possible. Most important, she insisted they have no contact with anyone outside of Engestofte, either by phone or by mail, since this could tip off the Nazis. They were to keep their presence a secret from everyone.

This last condition proved too much for Mrs. Kauffman, who, in a startling lapse of judgment, tried to breach it. Having left behind some of her favorite dresses in Copenhagen — she had departed in a hurry — she wrote to her maid with instructions to send them to Engestofte. Wisely, Wichfeld had been keeping tabs on the Kauffmans and was able to intercept and burn the letter.

While Monica was protecting the displaced Jewish mother and daughter, she also was working behind the scenes to devise their escape from Denmark, a tricky endeavor that was complicated by Mrs. Kauffman's insistence that she and her three children travel together. Monica managed to cobble together such an arrangement, however, with a convoy of sedans arriving at the estate a week later, one of which carried the son and daughter. Although the two youths appeared tired and frightened, Mrs. Kauffman looked even worse as she and her daughter Hanne emerged from the manor house to join them. It is heartening to note, though, that better days were ahead for the family. The

Kauffmans traveled to the harbor town of Hestnaes on the Baltic Sea, then on to Sweden, where they were granted asylum. In every respect, Monica's scheme had worked.

Unfortunately, her own fate would not be as favorable. It would be tragic, in fact, the result of a reprehensible incident in which a seasoned agent erred badly. Although it has never been determined if his slip up was caused by alcohol, stress, or a combination of the two, it is known that the consequences of his carelessness were disastrous for scores of Danish patriots, Monica among them.

The man at the center of the fiasco was Jacob, the underground agent who Flemming Muus had placed at Engestofte. In December 1943, Muus dispatched him to the city of Århus on Denmark's Jutland peninsula to help a fellow resistance member with a special assignment. While there, Jacob shared a flat with two other agents, one of whom, Henrik Ibsen, was a Norwegian paratrooper who had just arrived in Denmark. The other was Kai Lund, a wireless operator whose performance had been less than stellar and whom the SOE was recalling to London.

During their stay, the three men were at the Århus apartment one evening when Jacob, for reasons unknown, dispensed with the underground's stringent precautions and placed several long-distance phone calls to resistance figures in other parts of Denmark. His actions were reckless, of course, since the Nazis were notorious for tapping telephone lines, hence the underground's rigorous security measures regarding phone usage. All the same, Jacob made his calls while the Nazis eavesdropped, the consequence being that the regime gained valuable information about the underground as well as identifying three potential sources of additional material, namely, the three men themselves. A contingent of Gestapo agents, ten in all, stormed the flat within minutes and apprehended Jacob and his comrades, all of whom submitted without a fight; this, despite the fact that they were heavily armed in the event of such a raid.

Once in custody, Henrik Ibsen was fortunate in that the Nazis questioned him for a few days, then released him; being new to Denmark, he had no useful knowledge to divulge. Kai Lund and Jacob, on the other hand, were interrogated and tortured for several weeks until finally they talked. Lund, for his part, gave away vital codes the Germans could use to intercept and interpret underground transmissions, while Jacob disclosed even more damaging information: he furnished the Gestapo with the names of forty-four men and women in the resistance with whom he had worked during the past six months, as well as implicating over a hundred Danish families. Of those he identified, Monica Wichfeld's name was among the most prominent, the woman who had not only housed and protected him during his stint in Denmark but who also had served as his second-in-command. Shortly after Jacob's confession, a dreadful event occurred.

Capture and Confinement

The final chapter of Monica's life began on a bright, cold morning in January 1944, when two dozen German police officers stealthily surrounded Engestofte's manor house, machine guns in hand. A blanket of snow covered the estate's park, while inside the mansion the Wichfeld family, in the quiet of the winter morning, slept. But evidently all was not quiet for Monica, at least not within her own thoughts. Ever since Pastor Mancussen, highly unnerved, had showed up at Engestofte a week earlier and insisted they talk, she had reason to suspect that the Nazis might apprehend her. The minister had come to tell her about a rumor he had heard from a parishioner, the gist of which was that the Nazis had succeeded in breaking Jacob and the agent had told them everything. Naturally, Monica knew what this meant but she refused to panic. And she also refused to flee. "I have joined the struggle for Denmark," she told Mancussen. "I am willing to pay the price."[19]

At precisely eight o'clock on that fateful winter morning, a German criminal lawyer and two plainclothes officers barged into the house and ordered the servants to take them to the Wichfelds. In separate rooms, they found Monica, Jørgen, Viggo, and Ivan, and gathered them together. Varinka was in Copenhagen on this day. In Monica's salon, the room she had transformed into an office, the intruders discovered a stack of maps on which Danish cities that had been liberated were circled in red.

"You are obviously pro–Allies," barked one of the officers.[20]

"What do you expect me to be, pro–German?" Monica replied with a laugh.[21] She plainly did not wish to give the enemy the pleasure of seeing her squirm.

At gunpoint, the Germans took the Wichfelds outside, where they placed Monica in the lawyer's car and ordered Jørgen, Viggo, and Ivan into the back of a tarpaulin-covered troop carrier. They drove the family to the harbor town of Nakskov, whose shipyard, as noted earlier, Monica and her three accomplices had helped bomb the previous summer.

As to the circumstances of these comrades-in-arms, the Gestapo arrested Gerner Nielsen that same day and charged him with protecting two Jews, namely, the Kauffman children. As the Nazis ransacked his office, he stole into an adjoining room and telephoned Pastor Mancussen, alerting him to the raid. As a result, when the Gestapo arrived at the vicarage to arrest the minister, he already had escaped. The third member of Monica's team, Hans Christian Hovmand, the young veterinarian, was not so lucky. Like Nielsen, he, too, was captured.

In Nakskov, meanwhile, Jørgen, Viggo, and Ivan were questioned and released, whereas Monica was interrogated twice by two sets of Gestapo agents and transferred to Vester Faengsel (West Prison) in Copenhagen. In this bleak

Victorian edifice, she was confined to a six-by-ten-foot cell and subjected to daily interrogation sessions lasting up to eight hours at a stretch. But she revealed nothing, determined to take her knowledge of the resistance to the grave. All the while, her family lived in anguish.

Distraught over his mother's confinement, Viggo decided to return to Copenhagen to make sure she was all right. In the midst of a blizzard, he traveled by horse-drawn sleigh to the capital only to find that the Gestapo would neither allow him to see her nor give her the cigarettes he had brought for her. For that matter, he discovered that they were refusing to let her smoke, their aim being to amplify her discomfort. Outraged, Viggo lambasted two Nazi officers, the upshot being that he, too, was thrown into Vester Faengsel and charged with abetting the opposition. When Monica learned that he was being held in the same prison — the news came via Morse code tapped on her cell wall — she smuggled her cigarette lighter to him by means of a corruptible guard. When Viggo received it, he knew just what to do: unscrewing the small compartment in its base, he found a message of reassurance she had hastily scribbled on a piece of tissue.

As the weeks mounted, Monica's interrogation sessions persisted but to no avail. It was for this reason that the regime decided to ramp up its efforts by assigning to the case a highly efficient Gestapo agent, Heinrich Nagel. He was among their best interrogators, a man whose methods had produced several notable confessions.[22] As ordered by the Reich, Nagel set about conducting grueling marathon sessions with Monica, but like her previous questioners, he found himself unable to erode her defenses. In an effort to lure her into talking, he even placed a pack of Chesterfields on the table in front of her and offered them to her if she would divulge the names and locations of her accomplices. But still she refused, chucking the cigarettes across the room where they came to rest under a radiator.[23] In the end, the Nazis were both exasperated by, and impressed by, her mettle. Abandoning their efforts to pry information out of her, they finally left her to languish in her prison cell.

For a total of four months, Monica remained locked away in Vester Faengsel awaiting trial, although she was not forgotten by the underground during her incarceration. Indeed, at the beginning of the third month of confinement it hatched a plot for her escape, one that was set into motion by a former cabaret dancer, Claire Buchardt-Hansen, who now operated a café at Gestapo headquarters in Copenhagen and despised the regime.

In this daring scheme, Buchardt-Hansen established contact with a Nazi official who was involved in Monica's case. The man's name was Renner and the underground believed he could be bribed because he had elastic morals, was notoriously materialistic, and kept a mistress who insisted he lavish on her expensive jewelry. Resistance figures evidently thought he could use the money, and they were right. Through negotiations with Buchardt-Hansen, Renner agreed to an arrangement in which, for a sizable sum, he would escort Monica out of prison in his government car, ostensibly for a meeting elsewhere in Denmark. At a pre-arranged spot, he would stop the car and feign being ambushed by half a dozen underground agents.

The ersatz trap was set to occur on a bridge where an ambulance would be waiting to whisk Monica away. She would be taken to a safehouse, enjoy a brief visit with her daughter Varinka, and be spirited away by speedboat to Sweden. As for Renner, he would claim that guerrilla fighters had overpowered him, with his prisoner escaping during the melee. He was confident his superiors would fall for the story, and perhaps they would've had he not made a foolish mistake at the eleventh hour.

It appears that Renner, upon receipt of a cash advance for his complicity in the plot, decided to celebrate his good fortune by getting drunk. He became so inebriated, however, that he passed out in a restroom at Gestapo headquarters only to be discovered by the SS with Danish currency stuffed in his pockets. The next day, he admitted everything, the result being that the Reich sent him to a convict brigade on the eastern front. Unfortunately for Monica, the rescue attempt had been her only hope.

The Nazis did not drop the matter, however. They dressed up a Gestapo agent to resemble her, and, with several agents in tow, drove to the bridge hoping to nab the six resistance members they knew would be waiting there. But while the operatives were indeed present, Flemming Muus and Varinka Wichfeld among them, they had been careful to conceal themselves in case their plan went awry. And this proved to be an astute move. When the Germans arrived, the resistance agents realized the disguised figure was not Monica, so they remained in hiding until the Gestapo departed. Still unwilling to let go of the matter, the regime re-arrested Jørgen and Ivan, this time on the trumped-up charge that they had been involved in the scheme to liberate her. The two were placed in a facility known as Horserød Camp, where they remained until the following month, when Jørgen developed pneumonia. At this time, both were released.

As it happened, it was during this same month, May 1944, that Monica finally went before the court. By all accounts, it was a riveting day in occupied Denmark.

The Trial

Gestapo headquarters in Copenhagen was the setting for the tribunal, which was presided over by three judges. Dressed in SS uniforms and haughty in their demeanor, they sat at a tall, polished bench, a menacing portrait of Adolf Hitler hanging behind them.[24] Unbeknownst to Monica and the other ten defendants, the Reich had specified that four death sentences be handed down, although it was left to the judges to decide who, exactly, would die.

The proceedings got underway quickly, with Monica's case the first to be heard. Throughout it, she was forced to stand, which she did without complaint even though she had spent the better part of four months in a tiny prison cell with little food and thus was in a weakened condition. Observers noted that her attitude had not softened, however. When Jacob, her accuser, entered the room to testify against her, she studiously ignored him, just as she regarded the judges with an air of aloofness. According to Gerner Nielsen, her demeanor was truly remarkable. "[A]ll calm dignity," he said, "with just a faint suggestion that the lengthy interrogation was beginning to bore her."[25]

Once Wichfeld's case had been heard, the remaining defendants were tried, after which the principal adjudicator read the decisions to the crowded courtroom. He began with Monica's verdict, proclaiming it was the court's opinion that she was guilty of aiding the enemy. Then, with seeming relish, he revealed her punishment.

"Condemned to death!" he declared.[26]

As the judge may have hoped, his theatrical pronouncement shocked the spectators who filled the courtroom, since no woman in Denmark had received the death penalty in several centuries. The Danish people had long considered executions to be barbaric, especially for women.

Monica, on the other hand, appeared to be neither surprised nor alarmed. Unruffled, she glanced at the three judges and asked evenly, "Anything else, gentlemen?"[27]

And, indeed, there was something else: the chance for clemency. The judge said he would permit Monica to plead for leniency, which, if granted, would reduce her sentence to life imprisonment.

"Does that also apply to my companions?" she asked.[28]

"No!" he exclaimed.[29]

"Then it is of no interest!" she exclaimed in kind.[30] And with that, Monica sat down, removed a compact from her purse, and began powdering her face, according to witnesses who were present in the courtroom. Once the judges' attention shifted to the next defendant, she reached behind her chair and squeezed Viggo's hand.

As for the other defendants, three of them also received death sentences, thereby fulfilling the Reich's quota. Two of these men had been Monica's accomplices, Gerner Nielsen and Hans Christian Hovmand, both of whom, when allowed to make final statements, voiced their pride at having acted on behalf of their beloved Denmark. Their sentences were later commuted. Five other defendants received prison terms, while the charges against the two remaining men were dropped due to a lack of evidence. Of the latter, one was twenty-year-old Viggo, whose acquittal appeared to bring Monica enormous relief. All the same, she remained silent and poised, seemingly determined that the Gestapo would not see her lose control of her emotions.

The Danish people, by comparison, did not hesitate to express themselves. When Monica's death sentence became known, the nation's journalists rushed to lend her support, risking their careers in the Nazi-controlled media by reminding readers about other women the Gestapo had killed, albeit not through the judicial system. Trade unions also threatened to strike, ignoring the regime's decree forbidding them from doing so. Even the Danish Red Cross acted, warning the Reich about the volatile repercussions of placing Wichfeld before a firing squad. Most consequential to Monica, however, were the actions of Claire Buchardt-Hansen, the woman who had helped the underground stage her escape attempt and who, as a consequence, was being held in the same prison with her.

Buchardt-Hansen met with Monica shortly after the death sentence was announced and convinced her to challenge it. Buchardt-Hansen told her that Jørgen and the children needed her, that she was still the central figure in their lives. She also told Monica that Denmark, after the anticipated defeat of Germany, would need her as well, that her wartime experiences could be of value to the nation as it struggled to rebuild itself. And Buchardt-Hansen's reasoning seems to have struck a chord in Monica, evidently rousing in her feelings of maternalism and patriotism. For the love of family and country, it would appear, Wichfeld agreed to go back to Gestapo headquarters and seek a reprieve. Certainly she had nothing to lose but her dignity, which, as she had amply demonstrated, she knew quite well how to preserve even under the most intimidating of circumstances.

So it was that Monica found herself standing before a German judge just twenty-four hours later. The regime, presumably to ensure that she would not have sufficient time to put together a cogent appeal, demanded that the hearing take place at once. Yet that did not present a problem in that Monica was well-prepared, having had four months to ponder her case as she languished in a dank prison cell. To this end, she set to work presenting several logical arguments, among the more persuasive being that the court had handed down the death penalty partly because it believed she had played a key role in planning her own escape from Vester Faengsel. As she pointed out to the judge, she could not possibly have arranged it since she was locked away at the time, the guards watching her night and day.

Monica next brought up the matter of Danish law, which had long prohibited capital punishment. She argued that Denmark's fundamental legal principles, including the judiciary's opposition to the death penalty, remained intact in spite of the German occupation. This meant, she asserted, that the Danish legal system did not recognize the death sentence imposed upon her by the Germans and thus the sentence was invalid.

Most compelling of all, she reminded the judge that the court had no tangible evidence against her. Rather, its verdict had been based wholly on hearsay extracted by torture from a man known to have provided false testimony on other occasions, a desperate soul who had shown that he would say anything to save his own skin.

And so it went, with Monica, throughout the hearing, steadfastly refusing to plead for her life but rather submitting reasoned arguments as to why the death sentence should be lifted. Furthermore, the judge, in due course, concurred with her and converted the execution order to a life term in prison. It was in this way that the last days of her life commenced, with Wichfeld, shortly before D-Day in June 1944, preparing to leave Vester Faengsel for a series of penitentiaries in Germany to serve her sentence.

Darkness Falls

On the day of her departure from Vester Faengsel, a cadre of SS agents armed with submachine guns escorted Monica and a handful of other inmates to a waiting troop carrier, the regime apparently suspecting that the Danish underground might be lying in wait. Viggo later described his mother's appearance that day. Monica, he said, was dressed in a Harris tweed suit with an orchid corsage and was wearing her remaining pieces of jewelry, two rings and a Cartier watch.[31]

After pulling away from the prison, the troop carrier made its way across the country. According to Else Baastrup-Thomsen, a fellow inmate who accompanied Monica on the journey, Wichfeld's eyes welled with tears as they passed the island of Lolland where the Engstofte estate was located.[32] Monica pulled herself together, though, with Baastrup-Thomsen adding that Wichfeld remained in reasonably good spirits throughout the rest of the trip to the German city of Kiel. This could not have been easy, of course, especially when an Allied air raid disrupted the journey, a sortie during which Monica and her fellow inmates were trapped inside the train. Yet the trip did have a few bright moments, most notably Wichfeld's arrival in Kiel, where an unexpected source — a young, blond German guard — whispered to her that the Allied invasion of Normandy had just occurred. Exhausted, emaciated, and yearning for the war to end, Monica welcomed the news.

For the time being, though, the war raged on, with Wichfeld finding herself shuffled from prison to prison. After a short stay in Kiel, she was transferred to a facility in Hamburg, where she was confined to a large room spilling over with German prostitutes, along with inmates from Russia, Belgium, and France. Conditions were so congested that the fifty-year-old woman had to sleep on the cement floor.

Else Thomsen, the inmate who transferred to Kiel with her, recalled that

Monica's health continued to deteriorate. It certainly did not help that she was always hungry, had no access to toilets because German prisons did not have them, and had no contact with Jørgen and their children due to the collapse of Germany's postal service. As for sleeping arrangements, even when she was placed in a cellblock in which beds were available, the mattresses were stuffed with wood shavings and crawling with lice. To be sure, dreadful conditions prevailed in Germany's prisons during the final months of the war, the severe shortages that plagued the German nation being even more pronounced in its penitentiaries. All the same, Monica struggled to keep up her spirits, just as she was appeared to hold fast to the belief that her deeds on behalf of the Danish Resistance had been worthwhile.

After a stint in Hamburg, Monica was sent to Leipzig and placed in a barracks with over a hundred other women, following which she was transferred to a penal servitude colony in Cottbus. Here she remained for the next six months, a period that stretched into the winter of 1944 and proved to be the most detrimental to her health. Circumstances were horrid in Cottbus, where many of the female guards, staunch members of the Nazi Party, were former concentration camp officers. Among other chores, Monica and the other prisoners were required to unravel several miles of cord each day to be used in binding bales of hay. Occasionally, however, Wichfeld was observed to enjoy relatively pleasant moments. When she was not performing menial labor, for instance, she nurtured her friendships with the four Danish women who shared her cell, Else Thomsen among them. Her affection for these unfortunate women, as well as her laudable resilience during this time of tribulation, are perhaps most evident in her actions during Christmas of 1944.

At this juncture, the guards, realizing Monica had become too frail to work, ordered her to remain in lockup while sending her hardier cellmates to toil in a nearby gas-mask factory. She did not stay idle while they labored, however, but instead put together a surprise for them, a holiday treat. From a fir branch picked up in the prison yard she fashioned a makeshift Christmas tree, and from bits of tinfoil saved from food wrappers she created star-shaped ornaments to hang on it. She also made gifts for them, fashioning a pair of slippers from dried cornhusks, as well as two bracelets and a basket. She even transformed a handful of paper napkins into a tablecloth on which she served them a modest Christmas dinner, a meal made up of morsels of food and candy she had squirreled away. A motherly gesture, Monica's generosity seems to have touched the hearts of her cellmates during this demoralizing season in their lives. Little did they know that they all would be leaving Cottbus soon for a destination that would be even worse.

The final move came in January 1945, when the Germans evacuated Cottbus because Allied troops were approaching. Without warning, they transferred Monica and the other four women to the formidable Waldheim Prison near the city of Dresden, a turn of events that one these women described as "our descent into hell."[33]

The trip took nearly four days due to the constant interruptions along the way. Instead of traveling by passenger train, Monica and nearly two hundred other inmates were herded into three cattle cars that were subsequently dead-bolted from the outside. Being the middle of winter, temperatures were below freezing, yet the prisoners were not furnished with coats or blankets. They also had meager drinking water, with only one small bowl available for each car. By all accounts, theirs was an excruciating journey.

When the train finally pulled into Waldheim Station, the Nazis, rifles in hand, forced Monica and the others to trudge in the snow to a Lutheran chapel a considerable distance from the depot, a painful trek during which the prisoners were not permitted to speak. As before, they were given neither blankets nor coats even though many of them, Monica included, were visibly ill.

As to the reason they were marched to a chapel, the regime was using the building both as a refugee center for German citizens fleeing westward from advancing Soviet troops and as a holding area for foreign prisoners, like Monica, bound for nearby Waldheim Prison. According to Emil Viereck, the chapel's minister, when Wichfeld arrived she was so weak she could barely stand, and she had a severe cough and a blazing fever. Worried about her condition, he offered her a bowl of soup but she was too sick to swallow even a spoonful of it. Moments later, she collapsed and had to be carried to a pew to recover. And it was here, in a crowded chapel, that she suffered for several days until the Germans finally showed up and transported her to Waldheim Prison, where they locked her in a cell with a woman suffering from tuberculosis. And what happened next was wholly foreseeable: a week later, Monica whispered to an attendant that she needed to go to the hospital, whereupon she was admitted to the prison infirmary and diagnosed with viral pneumonia.

On February 27, 1945, Wichfeld, aware that her life was ebbing, asked that Pastor Viereck be brought to her bedside. She appeared to trust and respect this German minister who, besides being a man of compassion and integrity, was in contact with the Danish Red Cross and could convey a message to her loved ones. Prison officials, aware of her poor prognosis, decided to grant Monica's request. Later that day, she and Viereck had a talk in what proved to be the final conversation of her life. The next morning, when the minister called on her again, he discovered that Monica had passed away during the night.

Grief-stricken, Viereck remained faithful to a promise he had made to her, that of writing to her loved ones and informing them of her death. In his letter to the Wichfeld family, he expressed his dismay over her departure, and he passed along to Jørgen and the children her "final loving greetings" as she had requested.[34]

The following month, a memorial service was held for Monica in London, a stately affair attended by the Danish Foreign Minister, along with high-ranking figures in the British Foreign Office, the Special Operations Executive, and the Danish Resistance. A friend of the family, Reverend Dean John Seymour, presided over the ceremony. And the service in England was not the only remembrance. In Denmark, the Queen unveiled a monument in Monica's honor at Engestofte. Situated at the estate's church, it bore an inscription lauding her heroism during the occupation. Likewise, in a church in the Irish village of Derrylin, her name was inscribed on a plaque honoring the nation's war dead. In such ways, her noble deeds were commemorated by the nations she had loved so dearly.

Regarding her internment, Monica was buried at Waldheim Prison cemetery — or so the Germans claimed. After the war, when a Danish team arrived to exhume the body so that Monica could have a proper burial at her Engestofte estate, they unearthed an empty grave. To this day, her remains have never been found.

Postscript

The German occupation of Denmark came to an end in May 1945, following which the Danish Resistance Army, which numbered nearly forty-five thousand members, assumed a major peacekeeping role in the nation. Also at that time, Christian X, freed from virtual house arrest, appointed a new government, one uniquely composed of equal numbers of politicians and former resistance members. And the nation's Jews returned, whereupon they discovered that their homes and businesses during their lengthy absence had been protected and preserved by their gentile neighbors. At long last, the Danish people were able to come together once again and embark on a period of renewal.

As for the Wichfelds, Varinka and her superior in the resistance movement, Flemming Muus, moved back to Denmark after the occupation. For several months, the two had lived in London, where they had been forced to seek refuge after the Gestapo converged on them in Copenhagen. While in England, George VI decorated Muus for his bravery, with Varinka also receiving praise for her valor. In June, with Denmark liberated from the Nazis' grip, the couple married in Copenhagen.

In terms of the Wichfeld men, their lives diverged considerably after the war. Jørgen did not remarry but instead led a solitary existence at Engestofte until his death two decades later. With his demise, the property passed to Viggo, who had taken a job with an American oil company. He eventually sold the estate. As for Ivan, he moved to the United States and became a celebrated bridge player. It was a skill he acquired from his mother, bridge being a diversion she adored.

Lastly, on the subject of Monica's former lover, Kurt Reventlow, he remained in touch with Viggo and Ivan throughout the occupation, this being the only means by which he could stay abreast of events in Monica's life. Doing so was evidently quite important to him, this need to preserve a connection with her even if it was an indirect one. Kurt purportedly could not talk about her for any length of time without becoming besieged with emotion, his love for Monica having endured despite his emigration to the United States, two marriages, and the birth of a son and heir.

At war's end, Kurt returned to his homeland for a visit and his first act was revealing. Upon arriving in Denmark, he instructed his driver to take him directly to Engestofte, where, at its old stone chapel, he knelt beside the monument that had been erected in Monica's honor and bid her farewell.

4

Noor Inayat Khan and the Wireless Network of Paris

The summer of 1943 had just arrived and the situation in Paris was tense. The Germans occupied the city, with the Gestapo being fixated on preserving this state of affairs. To this end, its security officers, from their sumptuous headquarters in an eighteenth-century edifice near the Arc de Triomphe, toiled around the clock to identify and seize resistance agents. And topping their list was the Prosper circuit, an extensive network of British spies and French collaborators whose success in undermining the regime was stunning.

On June 23, the Nazis finally got their wish. Netting the circuit's mastermind, they also captured, killed, or otherwise put out of commission its top operatives and scores of its other agents. Except one.

A twenty-nine-year-old woman of Indian descent, her name was Noor Inayat Khan. A British agent, her job behind enemy lines was to serve as a wireless operator, a dicey role that entailed sending and receiving top-secret radio messages between resistance figures in the French capital and intelligence officials in London. Regarded as the most dangerous task an agent could perform, the life expectancy of a wireless operator was a scant four months. A sobering number, Noor was aware of it when she took the job. "I know I risk my life," she told an acquaintance, "since that is how most people end who do this work."[1]

Now, with the Gestapo having crushed the Prosper network, the stalwart agent dashed off a message to London alerting her boss to the circuit's alarming fate. She explained that she was the only wireless operator still at large and asked for instructions.

In his rushed reply, Noor's superior advised her to return at once to Britain. Pointing out that she was in grave danger, he said the Gestapo undoubtedly knew about her and would be better able to locate her since she was the only SOE member still transmitting from Paris. He offered to send a plane to collect her, his aim being to take her to safety as swiftly as possible. Noor's response, however, took him aback.

"She refused," said the *London Gazette*. "[S]he did not wish to leave her French comrades without communications and she hoped also to rebuild her group."[2] Noor knew the peril in which she was placing herself but was determined to fulfill her obligations to others.

And this was the essence of Noor Inayat Khan. A selfless woman, she possessed an abundance of courage and was wholly committed to her ideals. Yet she also was self-effacing and genuinely humble. In key respects, she was the embodiment of contradiction — durable yet vulnerable, practical yet philosophic, brave yet timid. In this regard, she evinced many of the traits that had distinguished her colorful and dynamic ancestors, men and women of conscience who grappled with the moral, social, and political issues of their day.

The Khan Legacy

In eighteenth century India, one of Noor's forefathers became renowned for leading the fiery opposition to Britain's colonization efforts in a region of that nation, a region known as Mysore. Tipu Sultan was his name, and he proved to be exceptionally adept at repelling the intruders. "So long as he lived," writes historian John Keay, "there was little chance of the British reaching an accommodation with Mysore."[3]

Years later, Tipu Sultan's sons took up arms against Britain as well, with their battles being bloody ones. As it happened, one of these men died in a clash with British forces, leaving behind a fourteen-year-old daughter by the name of Casime-bi. In due course, she would marry a Muslim nobleman, Moula Bakhsh Khan, and thereafter be addressed as Princess Casime-bi. This would be Noor's great-grandmother.

As for Noor's father, Inayat Khan, he was a dervish and a teacher of Sufism who hailed from India. He also was an accomplished singer and a player of the vina, a seven-stringed instrument. In 1910, he formed a trio known as the Royal Musicians of Hindustan and embarked on a tour of the United States, and it was while he was performing at an ashram in San Francisco that he became enchanted with the young woman who would become Noor's mother. Her name was Ora Ray Baker and she was a descendant of Mary Baker Eddy, the founder of the Christian Science movement. With her blue eyes and strawberry-blonde hair, the eighteen-year-old Ora made a striking contrast to the handsome, olive-skinned Inayat. Unfortunately, Ora's family did not share her regard for such cultural and physical contrasts and for this reason stood in the way of the pair's budding relationship. All the same, the two eventually married and settled in France.

"Parisians were fascinated by all things oriental," writes Shrabani Basu, "and soon the Royal Musicians of Hindustan were busy giving concerts, lessons and lectures."[4] Inayat and his trio also performed with the dancer — and later, the alleged spy — Mata Hari, she being a sensation of the era. And the City of Light offered Inayat the opportunity to rub shoulders with other luminaries of the period, among them Sarah Bernhardt, Claude Debussy, Auguste Rodin, and Pablo Casals. To be sure, it was an exciting, colorful time for the Khans.

A few months later, the Royal Musicians of Hindustan received an invitation to perform in Moscow, so the couple moved to Russia and settled near the Kremlin. In the age-old city with its magnificent spires and graceful domes, Inayat sang and played the vina to public acclaim, commenced work on his first book, and founded a Sufi order with the help of his friend Count Serge Tolstoy, son of the celebrated author Leo Tolstoy. Ora, for her part, took to wearing a golden sari and leading the life of a Sufi wife, a role she chose for herself and found deeply gratifying. But Ora, like Inayat, would experience her most intense satisfaction shortly after New Year's Day, 1914, when the couple brought into the world their first child, Noor-un-nisa Inayat Khan. "Light" was the meaning of her name and it was a moniker that would suit her well throughout her lifetime.[5]

Soon after Noor's birth, Inayat and Ora, worried about the growing political tensions in Russia and Western Europe, bundled up their daughter and made their way to London. Certainly their instincts were correct: World War I was declared within days of their arrival, with the family remaining in the British capital throughout the hostilities. During this period, Inayat founded the Sufi Order of England, the Sufi Publications Society, and the Eastern Musical Society. He also sang for Mohandas K. Gandhi when the dignitary visited London, a performance that brought the Indian leader to tears. But because of mounting discrimination against Indian nationals that was affecting the Khans, the family, in 1920, moved back to France and to a tolerant town near Paris. And this is where six-year-old Noor's most delightful memories would be formed.

Described as a "delicate child, dreamy and sensitive," Noor was sweet-natured, caring, and generous throughout her childhood in France.[6] She also seemed to be fond of everyone, even those girls and boys who lived in impoverished nations. As Basu recounts in her book, *Spy Princess: The Life of Noor Inayat Khan*, Noor wished to send chocolates to these underprivileged children.[7] As for her family members, Noor was purportedly closest to her father and to her brother Vilayat, the sibling to whom she was nearest in age. Eventually, she would, for all intents and purposes, rear Vilayat herself because her mother would be unable to do so. It would be a situation that would place

Noor, as the eldest child, in a premature position of responsibility. It would be a sense of liability, of duty, she would possess for the rest of her life.

It began when she was thirteen years old. Her father returned to France after a visit to England, fell ill, and died within a matter of months. Ora felt abandoned as a result and became bitter and depressed. Unable to cope, she handed over to Noor a considerable share of the responsibility for running the household and bringing up the other three children. And Noor did so conscientiously.

"If her brothers or sisters fell ill," it was observed, "she would nurse them and give them their medicine."[8] Noor also took it upon herself to secure supplies for the family and oversee the domestic chores. "Visitors were touched by her dedication to her family."[9] By all accounts, she learned to take charge and juggle numerous tasks at a very early age.

When she was seventeen, Noor graduated from the Lycée Saint Cloud, a secondary school, where her classmates remember her as being drawn to poetry and music. They also recall that she seemed inward and spiritually-inclined. "She was always smiling, very timid, spoke very little, and did not talk about her romantic family, about which her class-mates were so curious," says Fuller. Noor, she adds, "always gave an impression of being 'elsewhere.'"[10] Along these same lines, Shrabani Basu writes that Noor tended to be a solitary figure, noting that "[t]hroughout secondary school she had been rather lonely and had made few new friends."[11] As the years passed, however, Noor's reticence diminished somewhat, a gradual transformation that began when she enrolled in two schools concurrently, the Sorbonne and L'École Normale de Musique de Paris. The former she attended in order to study child psychology, and the latter, to pursue a degree in music.

At L'École Normale, Noor studied with the acclaimed composer and conductor Nadia Boulanger. "[O]ne of the great music teachers of her time," in the words of former student Aaron Copland, Boulanger would also instruct such diverse figures as Marc Blitzstein, Quincy Jones, Ástor Piazolla, and Philip Glass.[12] Being selected to study with this distinguished woman was an achievement in itself. As for Noor, Boulanger appears to have been fond of her, saying she found the younger woman delightful.[13]

From 1931 to 1938, Noor studied harp, piano, and musical composition while also pursuing her studies in child psychology at the Sorbonne. Always affectionate toward children, she often invited them to her home, where she sang to them, recited poems, and told them stories. She also enjoyed a romance with a fellow student at L'École Normale, falling in love and becoming engaged. As it stands, little is known about her fiancé other than that his last name was Goldberg, he was studying piano, and he was a Romanian Jew who lived with his mother, a laundress in Paris. We also know that although Noor loved him and felt sympathetic toward him owing to his circumstances, the

Khan family opposed the romance.[14] It seems the Khans, among them Noor's obdurate uncles, considered their family's lineage to be analogous to royalty and insisted she only marry a man from her own social echelon. "Goldberg was a rank outsider in this circle," says Basu.[15] In the end, though, Noor made her loyalties clear: she stayed true to her fiancé for the next six years, and, in so doing, evinced a newfound independence of mind and spirit. This was remarkable given that she was a traditionally-bred, dutiful Sufi daughter and niece. She would, moreover, continue expressing her autonomy in the years to come.

In revisiting Noor's young adult years in Paris — she was in her early twenties — it is evident that she enjoyed immersing herself in life and reveling in her discoveries about the world around her. It was during this period that she befriended other young Parisian women, began wearing cosmetics, and started dressing in the elegant fashions of the day. "[P]rogressively Europeanized" is how Jean Overton Fuller describes her during this time.[16] That said, it is worth noting that Noor did not disregard her religious beliefs even as she adopted certain Western customs but instead remained involved in Sufism and the Sufi movement in France. She also continued her academic studies, attending classes at the Sorbonne and L'École Normale as well as enrolling at a foreign language institute and completing a two-year course in Hindi. Despite these and other commitments, she somehow found the energy to continue tending to her brothers, sister, and ailing mother.

Not surprisingly in light of her fondness for children, Noor, after graduating from the Sorbonne in 1938, devoted her days to them. She became a contributor to the Paris-based newspaper *Le Figaro*, in which she wrote a column for children that appeared in its Sunday edition. As well, she penned colorful yarns that she read on a children's program broadcast on Radio Paris. She even published a book the following year with a British firm. Titled *Twenty Jakata Tales*, it was a labor of love in which Noor invested herself fully. In it, she drew upon a cycle of five hundred parables that existed in traditional Indian literature, all of them having to do with the Buddha's various incarnations as he progressed to enlightenment. Having a children's audience in mind, she carefully selected stories to retell in English, each of which centered on the evolving Buddha taking on the form of a forest animal. The tales' themes involved courage, compassion, and selflessness, with the animal — a gentle rabbit, for instance — typically forfeiting its belongings or even its life for the sake of others. In turn, this act would enhance the animal's spiritual development. This motif of self-sacrifice, as it turned out, would become emblematic of Noor's own existence.

In 1939, Noor decided that France would benefit from a children's newspaper, and to this end enlisted the help of an illustrator and approached a respected publisher about the venture. When the latter warned that the project might be financially prohibitive, that many families, as war loomed, might be unable to afford the luxury of such a periodical, Noor suggested that it be sold at a steep price to rich families so it could be given free of charge to poor children. Yielding to this inventive notion, the publisher began preparing the first edition of *Bel Age*, as it was to be called, but Noor soon had to cancel the project owing to the onset of World War II on the first day of September.

The War Years

It was two days later that France entered the dispute together with Britain, Canada, Nepal, and several other nations. For Noor, this signaled not only the end of her proposed newspaper, but also fewer Radio Paris broadcasts and *Le Figaro* publications. Even more consequential, it meant she would need to reflect on the moral duty of the individual in a time of war and arrive at a principled position on the matter.

Being a devout Moslem, she initially did not want to take a political stand at all but rather wished to transcend the subject entirely and proceed with her literary works for children. However, she and Vilayat, who shared her penchant for political detachment, had a change of heart after discussing the issue. They concluded that if they were to remain on the sidelines they would be tacitly permitting the Third Reich to inflict its jackbooted malevolence on the innocent. And this would amount to negligence on their part. Then, too, Noor was dismayed by anti–Semitism, a view that may have been bolstered by her respect and affection for her Jewish fiancé and his mother. "To Noor, the ideology of the Nazis and their pogrom against the Jews was fundamentally repulsive," says Basu.[17]

In the end, Noor adopted a secondary, supportive approach to the Allied war effort. More precisely, she and her sister Khair enrolled in a first-aid course, joined the French Red Cross, and started working at a local hospital. However, when enemy troops began amassing on the outskirts of Paris in June 1940, the hospital sent the two young women home for safety reasons. And it was at this juncture that Noor and her brother Vilayat decided, with considerable disappointment, to pack up their loved ones and move the family back to England. For the most part, their decision centered on the aging and unstable Ora, for whom it would be far too dangerous to remain in Paris given that the city was about to be overrun by Hitler's forces.

Deciding that her relationship with her fiance had no future, Noor called off the engagement, and with Ora, Vilayat, and Khair set off for the Cornish coast of England. Her younger brother, Hidayat, stayed behind and joined what would become the French Resistance. In a telling glimpse of Noor's character, it appears she wished to do the same, her opposition to the Nazis mounting with each passing day. But unlike the unfettered Hidayat, she, being the oldest child, considered it her overarching duty to ensure her mother's safety, and this meant relocating to England. Even so, Noor pledged to a group of townsfolk in Le Verdon-sur-Mer, the port from which she left France, that she would be back.[18] It was an oath she would honor in the fullness of time.

A few days later, after disembarking from a Belgian steamer in the English fishing village of Falmouth, Noor and her loved ones boarded a crowded train for Southampton, where, in the historic port city, they showed up unbidden at the home of the Basil Mitchell family. By his own account, Mr. Mitchell was taken aback by the exhausted, unwashed family that faced him on the doorstep.[19] It had been an arduous journey, the Khans having suffered through bombing sorties and other trials during their eleventh-hour escape from the continent.

After a brief respite, Noor and her loved ones traveled northward to Oxford, which came to serve as the family's temporary home. It seems the academic enclave was teeming with those like the Khans, forlorn families displaced by the war.

In short order, Noor joined the British Red Cross and began working at a maternity home situated between Oxford and London. The assignment was not to last, however, with political events taking a turn for the worse and upending her plans. More specifically, the Battle of Britain broke out in the summer of 1940, at which time she decided to apply to the Women's Auxiliary Air Force (WAAF). Although Noor had been born in Russia, her passport designated her a "British Protected Person" and thus qualified her to join the armed forces. By now, both she and Vilayat had cast aside any attempt to remain politically detached.

Classified as an Aircraftswoman Second Class by the WAAF — the date was November 19, 1940 — Noor was dispatched to the spa town of Harrogate to undergo training as a wireless operator. She was one of forty WAAF members to comprise this, the first group of women in Britain to be trained in such methods.

At Harrogate, she learned her craft well and a month later progressed to a more sophisticated curriculum in Edinburgh. After sailing through this advanced course, the WAAF sent her to a Royal Air Force command center near Oxford, where she worked side-by-side with a cadre of men who, like her, sent and received radio transmissions to bombers on training missions.

During the months that ensued, it became obvious that Noor possessed a bona fide talent for code work, the result being that her superiors singled her out for a special assignment in Wiltshire. At this covert facility, she was one of the first women to receive instruction in a new and highly specialized wireless method. As had been the case previously, it was a program of study she accomplished with distinction.

Distinctive, too, was her demeanor, which was at once warmhearted and highly professional. From the start, Noor was kind, friendly, and popular with those with whom she worked. Always agreeable, with a demure smile on her face, she was appreciated for her "good humour and sportsmanship" by the men and women who toiled alongside her during these early, grueling months of the war.[20]

As for her limitations, they centered on her soldierly skills, which were less than exemplary. Occasionally late for morning drills, Noor marched out of step and could be rather clumsy. Indeed, the other wireless operators affectionately nicknamed her "Bang Away Lulu" because of the loud clacking sound her fingers made as she hammered out Morse code.[21] Noor said this was because the chilly English winter caused her fingers to swell. Whatever the case, she nevertheless was proficient at code work, even more than many of her male colleagues.

Much to her credit, Noor also managed to preserve the same independence of spirit she had shown years earlier when she refused to reject her Jewish boyfriend because her family was not impressed by his pedigree. Her autonomy burst forth, most consequentially, during an interview in August 1942, when she applied for a commission and was interviewed by an officer in Britain's intelligence community.

In the course of the meeting, the officer broached the subject of India's quest for independence from Britain. At the moment, the two nations were cooperating in the war effort, India being convinced that a Japanese victory would be even more detrimental to the Indian people than the Crown's long-standing, unwelcome presence on the subcontinent. So the officer, aware that Noor was of Indian descent, pointedly asked her opinion on this contentious topic. And Noor, as was her way, answered truthfully. She explained that she was opposed to Britain's continued presence in India, but she assured the officer that she would be loyal to the Crown throughout the course of the war. She added, though, that after the war she most likely would support India when it renewed its campaign for full independence.

When the interview concluded, Noor was crestfallen, certain she had ruined her chances of receiving a commission because of her anti–British remarks. In reality, her candor may have established her integrity and trustworthiness. Although she did not get the commission she sought, a few weeks later, in October 1943, she received an unexpected invitation from the War Office to meet with the novelist Selwyn Jepson at the Hotel Victoria in London. A well-known mystery writer, Jepson's works eventually would be adapted for the screen by Alfred Hitchcock. Unbeknownst to the public, however, Jepson at this point was also a recruiter for the top-secret organization, the Special Operations Executive (SOE), and it was for this reason that he wished to speak with Noor Inayat Khan.

As it happened, a few months earlier the British government had secretly granted permission for the SOE to begin sending female agents into occupied France. As we noted in Chapter One, the assumption was that the Germans would be less likely to suspect women of being undercover operatives. On this premise, Jepson thought Noor might be an ideal choice to work covertly in France not only because she was a woman but also a delicate-looking one with exotic features. A German officer probably would not suspect her of being a British agent. Then, too, she spoke French fluently with no trace of an accent, thus appearing to be a native Frenchwoman. Noor's other advantages included her superb skills as a wireless operator, particularly at a moment when the SOE was in urgent need of those who had acquired this specialized set of abilities. And she possessed poise, composure, and mental focus. For the chaotic, nerve-wracking job an underground wireless operator was expected to perform, one that required the person to move continually among secret locations while being error-free in their work, Noor possessed precisely those characteristics that could be predicted to lead to success.

As to the interview, Jepson conducted it in French, since this allowed him to gauge Noor's abilities in the tongue in which she would passing herself off while undercover. During their talk, he inquired about her family background, religious beliefs, education, and attraction to children's literature. Being an author himself, he seems to have felt an affinity with her because of their shared love of the writing life. The pair also discussed the political situation in France, and they spoke about the role of the British military in opposing Germany. Finally, as the recruiter became satisfied he could trust Noor, he shifted to the real reason for their unusual tête-à-tête at the Victoria Hotel.

Jepson asked Noor to serve as an undercover wireless operator behind enemy lines. As always, his presentation was thorough; he was making a life-altering proposal. Accordingly, he took pains to explain the requirements of the assignment, including the extreme hazards it presented, not the least being the prospect of being captured, interrogated, and executed by the Gestapo. In addition, he explained that she would receive no special pay, and, further, that her salary would be held in Britain until she returned from France. Lastly, he pointed out that Noor would have no legal protections if arrested. Because she would not be in uniform, she would have no rights under the international rules of warfare. For that matter, the British government would disavow any knowledge of her, a common practice in intelligence communities. Noor would, in essence, be volunteering for a perilous mission intended to subvert fascism through covert activities, with her only reward being the awareness that she was a part of the fight for freedom.

Noor pondered the offer and agreed on the spot to take the assignment. Her only request was that her earnings not be held until her return but rather sent to her mother on a quarterly basis. Now it was simply a matter of preparation. While Noor waited to commence her intelligence training, the military, for bureaucratic reasons, transferred her from the Women's Auxiliary Air Force to the First Aid Nursing Yeomanry (FANY). Subsequent to this, she received orders to report to Wanborough Manor, a sprawling country home in Surrey, to begin preparation as a covert agent. Of course, neither her friends nor family members knew she was on the road to becoming a resistance agent behind enemy lines in France.

One of the SOE's many training facilities dotted across England and Scotland — there were forty-one in all — Wanborough consisted of an enormous Tudor-style house and a private park. At this estate, Noor enhanced her physical condition by participating in the early morning runs and other exercises that comprised the curriculum. She also became proficient at map reading and gained experience in the use of firearms and explosives, including handguns, submachine guns, and grenades. For the placid twenty-nine-year-old, it was a startling change of direction.

As for her success, the appraisals of those who taught her turned out to be mixed. "Pretty scared of weapons but tries hard to get over it," read one report.[22] The same document notes that she also had difficulty jumping, a shortcoming that could be problematic in that SOE agents were usually parachuted into France. Then, too, Noor was observed to have less-than-perfect coordination. Balancing out the scales, however, were her numerous assets, first and foremost her unique amalgam of personality traits. Her instructors described her as humble, self-controlled, creative, adaptable, and conscientious. Her skills as a wireless operator were judged to be excellent, too. And she could run well, a life-saving skill if she ever needed to escape from a dangerous situation behind enemy lines. The report concluded by stating that Noor was developing self-confidence as the training progressed, and that, as a whole, her abilities thus far were satisfactory for a woman who would be serving as a wireless operator in occupied France.

In the ensuing months, Noor underwent further instruction at other SOE sites, training designed to enhance her abilities in Morse code, field security, and related areas. And, as before, she received contradictory ratings. While some praised her personality characteristics, wireless skills, and devotion to the cause, occasionally an instructor would disparage her. In one case, Colonel Frank Spooner, a man who was opposed on principle to women being sent into enemy territory, penned a string of nasty remarks in an effort to discourage the SOE from dispatching her into France. "Not over-burdened with brains," Spooner wrote about her, adding that Noor seemed sensitive, jumpy, and a bit unstable.[23] When the head of the SOE's French Section, Maurice

Buckmaster, read these comments, he dismissed them, scribbling the word "nonsense" across the sentence suggesting that Noor was overly emotional.[24] Although Spooner later admitted he was trying to prevent Noor from being sent into a deadly situation because of her gender, apparently he did harbor doubts about her ability to cope with the horrors of war. And he was not alone.

During the final stage of Noor's preparation, this time at a country estate called Chorleywood, two female operatives wrote to Vera Atkins, the top female official at SOE headquarters in London, to express their concern about the wisdom of dispatching Noor behind enemy lines. The pair wondered if the novice agent would be able to handle the situation emotionally, and, if not, whether she might unwittingly place her comrades at risk. Troubled by the prospect, Atkins made a trip to Chorleywood, where she took Noor to lunch and divulged the content of the women's letter. Although stung by their doubts, Noor said she was sure that she could manage the emotional demands of the assignment, explaining that she had merely been upset in recent days because she had told her family goodbye perhaps for the last time. With this clarification, Atkins decided that Noor's emotional reaction had been altogether normal and she should proceed with the mission. Accordingly, a few nights later Atkins bid farewell to her at an airstrip in Tangmere, England, an occasion during which the SOE official gave the new agent, for good luck, a silver brooch in the form of a little bird.

Under Paris Skies

It was Henri Déricourt who orchestrated Noor's transport into occupied France. As noted in Chapter One, Déricourt, after the war, was accused of having revealed the identities of several SOE agents to the Gestapo in Paris in order to win the latter's trust. In the summer of 1943, however, he was not yet suspected of being such a deadly double-dealer.

On the night of June 16, 1943, Noor boarded a single-engine Lysander aircraft for the flight across the English Channel and into the Loire Valley. A cloudless, moonlit evening, conditions were perfect for the fledgling agent to launch her assignment.

Awaiting her in a farmer's field was a small reception committee made up of fellow resistance members. They greeted Noor when she touched down and furnished her with a bicycle, which she rode seven miles to the nearest village before boarding a train for Paris. Soon, the SOE, adhering to its customary procedure, would airdrop a new wireless kit into France and arrange for it to be handed over to her in the capital city. It was far too chancy for her to carry it to Paris herself, the device being the size of a small valise and recognizable to those having knowledge of radio equipment.

In terms of her cover story, Noor, when in public, would go by the name Jeanne-Marie Regnier. This was the name the SOE had written into the counterfeit identification papers it had forged for her, the documents she would carry with her in case she were captured. Vera Atkins dreamed up the name, along with a carefully tailored tale that centered on Jeanne-Marie being a child psychology major at the Sorbonne who had become a children's nurse for a wealthy Parisian family. On the other hand, when Noor communicated with the SOE or the French Resistance she would use the Christian name Madeleine or the operational name Nurse. In effect, she would be juggling four names and two distinct identities. Upon arriving in Paris, Noor promptly established contact with Cinema, the code name of the underground circuit with whom she would be serving. She learned that she would be a member of a standard three-person cell to be composed of an organizer, a courier, and herself as the wireless operator. Cinema was a part of the SOE's vast Prosper network. If Noor's cell were to run into trouble, she was to get in touch with a Parisian gentleman by the name of Henri Garry, who, as it happened, was the same person as her cell's organizer. Although this was a bit baffling to Noor, she accepted it without question. Presumably, Garry's double duty reflected the shortage of SOE agents currently serving in France, the situation being dire owing to a recent Nazi sweep.

The next morning, Garry took Noor to L'École Nationale d'Agriculture in Grignon. A renowned agricultural institute, the facility also served as a front for certain underground networks, among them the Prosper operation. It was at the institute, situated west of Paris near Versailles, that Noor met a handful of fellow SOE agents and section chiefs. Among them was Professor Alfred Balachowsky, who would soon play an important role in her life. It also was here that she sent her first radio transmission to London confirming that she had arrived safely and was starting her work as a wireless operator. Noor then returned to Paris and settled into her flat, little suspecting that within a matter of days her new circumstances would collapse.

Noor was at L'École Nationale d'Agriculture when it happened: Professor Balachowsky rushed into the room and announced that his wife had just received a phone call from an acquaintance saying the Gestapo was rounding up members of the Prosper network in and around Paris. The SOE's biggest and most important spy network in France, Prosper was composed of hundreds of British and French operatives and collaborators, and its eradication could be disastrous for the Allied cause in France. Making matters worse, L'École Nationale, because it was one of Prosper's principal façades, was believed to be in the Gestapo's sights. As she had been trained to do, Noor disposed of her wireless device on the spot and fled the building. Bicycling back to Paris, she notified along the way a fellow agent about the Gestapo's crackdown, possibly saving his life. When she arrived in the capital, she told Garry about the Prosper crisis and the two set out to warn as many agents as possible. A couple of days later—it was a deceptively peaceful Sunday morning—the SOE radioed Noor and instructed her to return to the agricultural institute. Officials in London needed her to obtain from Madame Balachowsky the name of the acquaintance who had phoned about the arrests. Noor obliged at once, but when she reached her destination the intrepid agent spotted a team of Gestapo officers rushing into the complex. Not wasting a moment, she traveled back to Paris, packed her belongings, and moved into another SOE flat, one owned by a sympathetic shopkeeper. A modest, out-of-the-way apartment, it was unlikely to attract the attention of the enemy.

Notwithstanding Noor's hasty efforts to lose herself in the sprawling city, it quickly became apparent that the Gestapo knew that a small number of SOE operatives had evaded their grasp. This is because Henri Déricourt had dutifully kept the Nazis abreast of all incoming SOE agents, Noor among them. Unfortunately, this made her a hunted woman, a fugitive. It was during this time that she sent an urgent message to London informing the SOE that the Gestapo had overwhelmed the Prosper network and that she was the sole wireless operator still in the city. As recounted at the outset of this chapter, the chief of the SOE's French Section advised Noor to return to London immediately and proposed sending a plane to collect her. She turned down the offer, however, and instead stayed on the job so as to continue keeping Britain informed of developments in the French capital. Then, too, she wished to ensure that communication remained intact among her colleagues in the SOE in Paris and the French Resistance. It was with this key decision that the neophyte agent entered an exceptionally dangerous period, "the most perilous and lonely part of her work," writes Beryl Escott.[25]

Unfortunately, we know comparatively little about Noor's covert activities between June and October of 1943, when she ran afoul of the Gestapo. The nature of her work was, of course, secret, with written records seldom being kept since they could be incriminating if the enemy were to get its hands on them. We do know, however, that Noor, throughout the month of July, sent scores of wireless messages to London on behalf of that handful of SOE agents who had managed to elude the Gestapo. In special instances, she dispatched written messages to London on secret Lysander flights as well. Such deeds were exceedingly precarious, of course, especially since the Gestapo was now on her trail.

"They put a high price on her head and advertised widely for information," writes Escott.[26] In keeping with her training, Noor chose this moment to alter her appearance, dying her hair, changing her hairstyle, and donning a pair of sunglasses. She kept on the move, too, staying briefly in one flat, then another. This meant, of course, that she sometimes had to travel with her wireless kit, an act that was fraught with danger since the Gestapo possessed a van with a signal detector attached to its roof and was roaming the streets of Paris searching for her radio signal. It seemed only a matter of time before the feisty agent would run into trouble while carrying her wireless device in public.

The first time this is known to have occurred, Noor was on the Métro and a pair of German soldiers entered the car in which she was traveling. Noticing that she was carrying a case, they asked what was inside of it and she nonchalantly replied that it was a movie projector. Unconvinced, they ordered her to open it. Unable to flee because she was in a closed subway car, Noor complied, breaching the case just enough so the soldiers could glimpse the outer layer of the wireless device. Since the two men were members of the German military rather than specially trained Gestapo officers, they did not recognize the apparatus but instead seemed puzzled by it. So Noor neatly capitalized on their ignorance. "There are the little bulbs," she explained to them. "Haven't you seen one before?"[27] To save face, the confused soldiers engaged in a bit of pretense themselves, declaring that, of course, they could see it was a movie projector. And with this untruth, they apologized and went about their business.

Another hair-raising confrontation occurred when Noor found herself needing to send an urgent message one night. Because it was late and Paris was quiet — not an unusual state of affairs given the ubiquitous presence of the enemy — she decided to hang the radio antenna from a tree limb outside of her apartment. As it happened, the aerial fell to the ground, with the panicked agent hurrying down to the sidewalk to retrieve it. It was at precisely this moment that a German soldier showed up on the scene and offered to help re-hang the antenna. Evidently, he assumed that Noor was a local Frenchwoman who merely wished to listen to music on a warm summer's evening. Because of such close calls, she redoubled her efforts to ensure her safety while performing her tasks, even to the point of keeping her wireless device in a violin case so it would be less conspicuous in public.

In July, Noor rented another apartment, a small one near the Seine, but to her distress discovered that SS officers were living in the surrounding flats. Within days, she moved to another one far beyond the river. In fact, Noor, from this point onward, remained more or less in constant motion, changing dwellings ever more frequently and sometimes staying overnight in the homes of friends from her prewar days. Isolated and alone much of the time, she was largely on her own and relying on her training and instincts. Even though her circumstances were harrowing, though, she never wavered in her commitment to her duties. Throughout July and August, the devoted agent persisted in sending messages to London even as the Gestapo continued hunting down and arresting members of the decimated Prosper network. By all accounts, her communiqués were crucial to the functioning of what remained of the

SOE in Paris. As to the nature of her transmissions to London, many of them conveyed the locations of downed pilots so they could be retrieved. A transcript of an August message, for instance, reveals that Noor furnished British authorities with the whereabouts of two American pilots in Paris whose plane had been shot down. Other records suggest that she was involved in a much larger number of rescue operations, possibly helping up to thirty Allied pilots escape from occupied France, according to Marcus Binney.[28]

And Noor did more: she aided the SOE's complement, the French Resistance, in numerous ways. Befriending one of its operatives who had access to a car, she arranged for him to drive her to the suburbs each Wednesday and Friday so she could send radio messages to London. In exchange for this high-risk favor, Noor relayed messages for the operative himself, communiqués she sent to Charles de Gaulle's team whose center of operations was also situated in London during the war. Through the de Gaulle group, Noor also helped arrange for an impressive amount of money — one million francs — to be smuggled to the French Resistance, and she assisted in acquiring explosives to be used in a bombing mission. Regarding the latter, the resistance discovered that the Germans were storing torpedoes in the sewers of Paris before transferring the missiles to a U-boat facility in Brest, with the disruption of this process being regarded as a vital undertaking.

During this period, the conscientious Noor also attempted to stay in touch with her SOE colleagues in England when it seemed safe to do so. She sent a message to Vera Atkins, for instance, thanking her for the parting gift of a silver brooch. She said the pin brightened her spirits during difficult hours. As well, she radioed a hearty message to her boss, Maurice Buckmaster, saying she enjoyed working with him.[29] And being a dutiful daughter, she checked with the organization to make that sure her mother was in good health and that her needs were being met.

Rather disconcertingly, it was at this juncture, in August, that Noor's old friends began recognizing her on the street because of her growing mobility on the job. In one case, she was bicycling along the Champs Élysées when an acquaintance from her prewar days shouted Noor's name. Startled, Noor led the woman onto a side street and explained that she was now called Jeanne-Marie. In another unsettling incident, Noor encountered the former *Paris Soir* staffer who had planned to publish her children's newspaper. Although their eyes met, the two did not speak. The man later recalled that Noor doubled back, stopped near a bookstore window, and shot him a glance that said it all. He grasped her situation at once.

Perhaps Noor's most important meeting that month came when her wireless device malfunctioned. While it was undergoing repair, a fellow operative introduced her to a man by the name of Monsieur Viennot, a vibrant, if dubious, character. Although outwardly he looked as if he were a distinguished gentleman, in fact Viennot was well-connected to Paris' underworld of brigands, prostitutes, and other unconventional sorts, and he used his associations to exploit the Nazis in his midst.[30]

Politically astute, Viennot made it a point to stay on friendly terms with the enemy, most notably the male Gestapo officers at their command center on the Avenue Foch. To these men, he furnished women to suit their diverse tastes, his motive being to gain the officers' trust, and, ultimately, inside information about the Gestapo's plans. At the same time, he employed members of the French Resistance in his legitimate businesses so as to provide them with cover. Even more audaciously, he hired bands of thugs to rescue resistance fighters who had been captured. So it was that he and Noor, in short order, became comrades-in-arms, with Viennot sharing with her the intelligence he obtained from the Nazis, and she, in turn, transmitting it to London. Viennot was perhaps most helpful, however, when he saved Noor from walking into a trap the Gestapo had laid for her.

"Noor," writes Basu, "received instructions from London to go to the Café Colisée on the Champs Élysées, meet the cloakroom attendant and give a password, which would get her in touch with two Canadian agents of the French section."[31] Always diligent, Noor followed the directions to the letter, conversing with the two Canadians and in due course agreeing to help them assemble an underground network in northern France. What the SOE in London, and thus Noor, did not know is that the Gestapo had captured the original two SOE agents and replaced them with a pair of imposters. So Noor, in effect, was meeting face to face with the enemy. Predictably, the Nazis used the information she gave them to seize more SOE agents and compel them to work for the Gestapo. In fact, it forced one of these captured operatives to arrange another rendezvous with Noor, under false pretenses of course, near the Arc de Triomphe. And it was immediately prior to this meeting that Viennot wisely decided to inspect the neighborhood to make sure it was safe for her. As it turned out, he did not like what he saw. "He returned to Noor and told her it was definitely a trap," says Basu.[32] Heeding his advice, she narrowly escaped, but from this point onward the Gestapo, because of her conversation with its agents, knew what she looked like and could recognize the sound of her voice.

As swiftly as possible, Viennot set about transforming Noor's appearance. Deciding she would benefit from a look that was more conventionally French, he bought her a navy blue suit with a matching hat and arranged for her hair to be dyed auburn and styled in a more Parisian manner. In terms of her living arrangements, Henri Garry secured another apartment for her. Situated near Gestapo headquarters on Avenue Foch, it was presumably the last place the enemy would think to look for her. As for Noor during this time, she continued performing her duties with her characteristic diligence, often working into the middle of the night sending, receiving, and delivering secret messages.

It was at this point that Noor may have become involved in a shadowy incident as well — a shooting in Paris — although little is known about the specifics of the episode, including the target.[33] It also was during these tense September days that she furnished her superiors in London with a cache of information they were needing, intelligence she sent by Lysander aircraft perhaps because the packet contained illustrations. Among other materials, it consisted of details relating to Orly Airport, which was under consideration for an Allied air strike, as well as a notice to the SOE leaders that certain automobile plants, namely Renault and BMW factories in occupied France, were abetting the Nazi war machine in defiance of the armistice. Presumably, Noor intended for London to determine if sabotage of the factories might be in order. To be sure, such communiqués reveal that she was supplying the SOE with crucial material without which its operation in Paris would have been more or less defunct. Yet her productivity, while invaluable to the Special Operations Executive and the French Resistance, was exacting a cost from Noor herself.

Those who had face-to-face contact with her in September were unsettled by the agent's appearance, which had become careworn. "She was thinner and began to have a hunted look," recalled a colleague.[34] Then, too, Noor was no longer as sure-footed and composed as she had been upon launching her mission, an impaired sense of security that was heightened after her close call with the Gestapo in the Canadian incident. One day at a friend's house, the beleaguered agent broke down and wept, letting it be known that she fully expected the Gestapo to capture her; that it was, in her estimation, only a matter of time. Of course, her outlook at this juncture is not surprising considering she had withstood three months of taxing days and sleepless nights during which the Nazis had seized most of her fellow agents. She was exhausted. It was for this reason, then, that her Parisian comrades decided to intercede.

On October 5, a colleague escorted Noor to the Gare Saint-Lazare station and put her on a train to Normandy, where she was to remain in seclusion in a farmhouse. But Noor, it turns out, had a different idea, one that may have reflected her immense selflessness, or, alternatively, her mental and physical fatigue and resultant impaired judgment. It seems she decided, after disembarking in Normandy, to return to Paris. And indeed, she arrived two days later back in the capital city. It was at this point that her superiors in London concluded the time had come for her to be officially "retired," in the jargon of the intelligence community. Among their concern was the fact that some of the British operatives with whom she had made contact before leaving Paris had inexplicably vanished, suggesting that the Gestapo was not only on her trail but rapidly closing in on her. The SOE therefore informed Noor that arrangements were being made to fly her to Britain in the middle of October. While her colleagues in London and Paris agreed she had performed her duties splendidly, it was obvious the time had come for her to wrap up her work. In the meantime, she would have to survive in the besieged city.

Rather than lying low during these remaining days, Noor dropped in on companions and fellow agents in and around Paris to bid them farewell. She did not want to leave without saying goodbye, fearing they might assume the worst had happened to her. Ironically, it was in this way that it became known within British and French intelligence circles — and discovered by German intelligence officials — that she would be departing shortly. And the outcome was predictable: the Nazis, eager to seize this vital agent, stepped up their surveillance efforts, keeping tabs on the numerous addresses it had accrued for her. Then, in an instance of fateful timing, the Gestapo received the final piece of information it needed when a Frenchwoman phoned the bureau out of the blue. Although the issue of the woman's identity stirred debate after the war, many people believed, as the Gestapo asserted at her trial, that it was Renée Garry, the sister of Noor's SOE coordinator in Paris, Henri Garry. Through Henri, Noor had become acquainted with Renée and even shared a flat with her.

As revealed by the testimony of former Gestapo officials and recounted in the book *Mission Improbable*, the woman known as Renée explained in her phone call to the bureau that she wished to strike a deal with the Nazis.[35] Intrigued, the Gestapo instructed her to go to a park near the Eiffel Tower and carry a flower with her. At this rendezvous, Renée was told, she would see a gentleman carrying a magazine under his arm. He would approach her and give his name as André, and she was to respond with her own name and make her offer. What Renée did not know was that André would be concealing a pistol and that another Gestapo agent, undercover and likewise armed, would be stationed in the park as well. If they became suspicious of her, they would kill her on the spot. Fortunately for Renée, her proposal was legitimate and therefore she suffered no harm.

As to the offer, she promised André that she would furnish the Gestapo with the whereabouts of an important SOE agent whose code name was Madeleine. The agent, she added, was Britain's wireless operator in Paris. In return, Renée asked the Gestapo to pay her a sum of one hundred thousand francs, which it quickly agreed to do. What she did not know is that it would have paid ten times this amount, or one million francs. Had she paid closer attention, she would have known the Gestapo had been advertising widely for information leading to Noor's arrest.

In keeping with the agreement, Renée, the next day, met again with André, this time at a café. Renée knew that Noor would be away for several hours, meaning that this would be an opportune time to conspire against her. From the café, Renée led André to Noor's flat and pointed out where the door key was hidden, after which she led him inside and showed him Noor's wireless transmitter. As he was leaving, the Gestapo official instructed Renée to notify him the next time Noor was away so the bureau could slip into the flat and await the unwitting agent's return. It was an ugly betrayal by any measure.

The ambush took place on October 13, 1943, when Renée alerted the Gestapo that Noor was about to leave for the morning. At once, a pair of plainclothes Gestapo officers hurried to the block where Noor lived just in time to spot a slender woman with a dark complexion stroll casually out of a baker's shop. Attired in a tailored dress, blue and white in color, and wearing a matching hat, she fit Noor's description perfectly. As the Gestapo approached her, however, she vanished around a corner.

Meanwhile, a French officer collaborating with the Nazis sneaked into Noor's apartment to wait for her, a scoundrel by the name of Pierre Cartaud. A handsome, twenty-something Frenchman, Cartaud had been a member of the French Resistance until the enemy nabbed him, after which he set to helping the Nazis in order to save his own skin. And he did so with relish. Taking up residence at Gestapo headquarters on Avenue Foch, he appears to have delighted in betraying Allied operatives and participating in their interrogations — until, that is, he was relieved of the latter task because of his propensity to strike or slap those he questioned. It seems his rough treatment of his fellow citizens only stoked their defiance, thereby rendering him useless as an inquisitor.

Two hours after she gave the Gestapo the slip, Noor returned to her apartment only to find the belligerent Pierre Cartaud hiding behind the door. He grabbed her hands but she fought back savagely, biting his wrists until they bled. The Frenchman next tried to handcuff her, but Noor continued fighting, all the while shouting at him. Finally, he drew his revolver and held her at gunpoint while he telephoned Gestapo headquarters for backup. It seems the impudent Cartaud was unable to handle the fierce agent by himself.

A few minutes later, Gestapo officers rushed into the apartment, where they found Cartaud quite literally backed into a corner. He was across the room from Noor and still pointing his weapon at her, afraid to go near to her. Certainly he had reason to be frightened: she was not done with him. While the arriving officers held her back, Noor, at once desperate and livid, kept trying to attack him, having transformed into an exemplar of defiance.

Noor also was exasperated, which is understandable. She had been so close to leaving France, within a hair's breath of home and hearth. Now, however, Gestapo headquarters was her destination, where she would be ushered to the notorious fifth floor, the site of interrogations. Yet even here, under the most intimidating of circumstances, she would hold her own.

Arrest and Interrogation

Seated in front of her Nazi interrogator a few minutes later, Noor insisted, when asked her name, that it was Nora Baker, this being another of the fictitious monikers the SOE had given her. Following this spurious response, she refused to answer any further questions, truthfully or otherwise. As her determination quickly became apparent, her interrogator ordered the guards to place the uncooperative agent in one of the floor's seven cells to await another round of questions the next day. Then, as Noor was being led away, she glimpsed an opportunity. Telling her captors she needed to use the restroom, they escorted her to it, and it was now that she made her move, according to Jean Overton Fuller's account.[36]

While a guard stood watch outside the door, Noor turned on a faucet, and with the sound of the coursing water masking her movements, climbed through a small window and onto a gutter. Edging alongside the building, she contemplated jumping to her death but decided instead to continue her escape attempt. Then, seemingly out of nowhere, a man's hand appeared, which she clutched instinctively and which pulled her back inside. Noor was suddenly overtaken with regret. "She accused herself passionately," writes Fuller, "for having accepted his hand," exclaiming that she should have let herself drop from the ledge.[37]

From this point forward, the Gestapo considered her an escape risk, a reputation that would make her months in captivity even more difficult. Then, too, Noor did not make matters any easier on herself. During her first few days of confinement, she refused to eat; she only drank coffee. Sadly, she also did not sleep and was sometimes heard weeping in her cell during her long nights of captivity. Clearly, her spirits were low, and they were brought down further a week later when she learned the Gestapo had seized Henri Garry and his wife, Marguerite. It seems the Gestapo had set a trap for the couple, one in which the Garrys thought they were sending supplies to Noor. They didn't know she had been apprehended but instead believed she was still in a farmhouse in Normandy awaiting her return to London.

As for Noor's reaction to the interrogation process, day after day Hans Kieffer, the head of the Gestapo in Paris, tried to pry information out of her. But while Kieffer was known as a rational, even a diplomatic, man — his interrogations could be "patient and long-drawn-out" — he eventually became so frustrated by Noor's refusal to comply that nearly struck her.[38] For this reason, another Gestapo officer took over the sessions, but the outcome was the same. Despite the second officer's composure, Noor did not provide him with any useful material but rather tossed him innocuous bits of information that could be obtained elsewhere. This included facts she correctly assumed the Gestapo already had in its possession. Of course, this annoyed the second interrogator, just as it had infuriated Kieffer. Even so, it must be said that Noor's unshakeable strength of will, while frustrating to her inquisitors, was not without its German admirers. "[T]hey all spoke with great respect of her coolness and courage," writes Escott.[39]

Six weeks after Noor was incarcerated, she devised another escape plan. She began by forming a relationship with a detainee in the adjoining cell, a French colonel by the name of Léon Faye, with whom she communicated by means of Morse code tapped on the wall that separated them. She also made contact with another SOE agent in captivity, John Starr, who was serving as a subordinate to the Gestapo in exchange for his life. Because Starr enjoyed more freedom of movement than the other prisoners, he and Noor were able to correspond by sliding rolled-up messages inside a pencil that the pair swapped when he walked past her cell. So it was that, in early November, Noor informed the two men about a bold plan she had formulated, a plan that would involve both of them. It was an arrangement Faye and Starr felt compelled to honor if for no other reason that it was cooked up by a young woman who was obviously very brave, and, as men, they felt they should measure up to her courage by sharing the risk.

In terms of the breakout itself, each of the three, late one night, removed the bars of their cells using a screwdriver Starr had pinched from the Nazis. Fashioning ropes from blankets, they climbed through a skylight and scrambled onto the roof of Gestapo headquarters, where the trio dropped onto a balcony, shattered a window, and climbed into an apartment. Making their way through the residential building, they stole onto the street only to find themselves in a cul-de-sac with German soldiers stationed at the entrance. Faye, for one, was undeterred; dead-set on freeing himself, he raced toward the entrance but, predictably enough, the Germans seized him. Noor and Starr, on the other hand, hurried back inside the apartment building and hid.

In an uncanny coincidence, the Royal Air Force chose this moment to launch a bombing sortie over Paris, with the air raid triggering a protocol at Gestapo headquarters: the guards were to check each cell to ensure that the detainees were still present. Of course, it was immediately apparent that Noor, Starr, and Faye were missing — but not for long. With Faye having just been apprehended on the adjacent street, it was merely a matter of cordoning off the cul-de-sac until Noor and Starr could be found. And this occurred a short time later. It must be said, though, that despite the plan's dispiriting outcome, it was an audacious attempt, one that earned its architect, Noor, the begrudging respect of the Gestapo. Unfortunately, it also invited its fury.

The following morning, Kieffer issued an order for Noor to be transferred to Pforzheim Prison in Germany. He later admitted that he chose this facility because it was near his hometown and would allow him to visit his family in the pretext of checking on his prisoner. As it happened, Noor would be one of the first British agents to be sent to Germany as well as the first political prisoner to be incarcerated at Pforzheim, a small penal complex located in the Black Forest. It would appear, however, that sometime between being pulled from her cell on Avenue Foch and delivered to the train station in northeastern Paris, she managed to shake off her captors a third time, turning up at the door of a comrade and blurting out that she needed to send a message. Described as harried and breathless, Noor did not have her wireless transmitter with her; evidently, she was hoping the acquaintance might be in possession of one. Then, just as suddenly, Noor was gone, presumably recaptured by her Gestapo escorts and put on the train to Germany. We do know that she arrived at Pforzheim Prison on November 27, 1943, where her days became even more daunting.[40]

The Gestapo ordered the governor of the facility, Wilhelm Krauss, to lock Noor in a cell by herself in a small jail adjacent to, but detached from, the main prison. No inmates were to be in the adjoining cells. In addition, her hands and feet were to be shackled at all times, with the manacles being drawn together behind her back and bolted to the wall. Under no circumstances was she to leave the cell, and only Krauss and the chief warden, Anton Guillet, were to attend to her. They were not to talk to her, however. As it stood, Krauss, who was seventy-two years old, was appalled by these constraints, having never before been forced to impose such extreme measures on a person, not even the most wanton murderer. Furthermore, he never fully accepted the idea, especially since Noor was suffering needlessly. When it became evident that her incarceration would be a protracted one, Krauss decided to disobey orders, not only engaging in lengthy, considerate conversations with his new detainee but also taking off her chains at mealtimes so she could eat without being burdened by the weight of their five-foot lengths. As well, he arranged for Noor to take a walk each day on the prison grounds — under guard, of course. Yet in spite of these small liberties, she still was prohibited from talking to anyone other than Krauss. The fact is, she remained a political prisoner being held under the extreme measures set forth in the *Nacht und Nebel*, the Night and Fog decree, and Krauss could only do so much to make her existence more tolerable. This does not mean, however, that she always complied with orders, most notably the injunction against communicating with others.

In fact, Noor began doing so in January 1944, when a handful of female political prisoners arrived at Pforzheim Prison. Before long, the women became curious about the inmate who was being held in solitary confinement in a separate building. They heard she was a Russian countess. Accordingly, when they saw her taking a walk one day under heavy guard, they resolved to make contact with her and to this end scratched a short message on the bottom of a soup bowl. They knew the bowl would sooner or later make its way to her cell and they hoped she would notice what they had etched on it.

"There are three Frenchwomen in cell No. 12," said their message. A few days later, the women were surprised to receive a reply from the mystery captive. "You are not alone," read Noor's response, "you have a friend in cell 1."[41]

Thus began a correspondence that lasted several months. As for Noor's messages, they expressed her unhappiness and asked for news of the outside world.

In an attempt to fulfill the latter request, one of the prisoners walked past the window of Noor's cell one afternoon and began singing a popular French song. Rather than the lyrics to the tune, however, the words the woman sang were actually current news items. Unfortunately, a French-speaking guard overheard the ruse, and, furious, used the opportunity to punish Noor. Dragging her to an underground chamber, he thrashed her so fiercely it could be heard outside. One of the female prisoners, a resident of Bordeaux, later confirmed this disturbing observation to a war crimes investigator, adding that Noor remained self-possessed and resolute throughout the ordeal.[42] Other prisoners were likewise impressed by the way in which she handled herself when confronted by the guard.

On another occasion, the spy-hole in Noor's cell door was open without the chief warden's permission. When he become aware of the situation, the other prisoners heard him yell at Noor, who responded calmly and evenly. He then slapped her loudly, and Noor reacted defiantly. She thereafter was seen to be wearing only a sackcloth garment during her walks whereas she previously had been allowed to wear her street clothes.

To be sure, Noor's captivity was rough. With severely curtailed freedom of movement and virtually no opportunity to talk to anyone other than Krauss, she spent her time alone in her cell. In keeping with the *Nacht und Nebel* treatment, she also received the lowest possible rations, namely, cabbage soup or a broth concocted from potato peels. Even so, she continued to win the respect of those who came into contact with her. "[F]rank, open, and friendly" is how a staff member at the prison described her.[43]

Finally, Noor received word that she would be leaving Pforzheim Prison after nearly a year in solitary confinement. In a nervous hand, she etched on a bowl a terse message to the other women prisoners telling them that she was leaving. And indeed, the following day Gestapo officers escorted her by train to the city of Karlsruhe.

In this town in southwestern Germany, Noor was delighted to be reunited with Yolande Beekman, a fellow SOE agent with whom she had trained in England. The next day, Noor and Beekman, together with two other SOE agents, Eliane Plewman and Madeleine Damerment, boarded a train for Munich with a pair of guards accompanying them on their journey. At this point in the war, it was a foregone conclusion that the Allies would be victorious; they had retaken

Paris, and American troops were amassing at Germany's borders. Believing the worst was behind them, Noor and her three traveling companions were cheerful, especially since they had been told they were going to a farm. Dressed in their own clothes once again and sitting by a window on a morning express train, they enjoyed tea, sausage, and English cigarettes as they recounted their experiences.

Later that evening, the locomotive pulled into Munich, where the women, now weary, were placed on another train without delay. Near midnight it arrived at its destination — Dachau — where, within a few hours, their lives would be snuffed out. They had no idea.

At the concentration camp, the guards placed the four women in separate cells. According to the initial findings of the war crimes commission, the next morning they were taken to a square beside a crematorium, where, rather ominously, fresh sand had been spread. The guards ordered the women to kneel. While the victims held hands, an executioner shot each woman in the back of the head, with one of the casualties, Madeleine Damerment, being shot twice since the first bullet failed to kill her. This account, however, may not have been entirely accurate.

Years later, author Jean Overton Fuller, who had published a book about Noor, received letters from two readers, both of them men.[44] They had been present at Dachau during this grim episode and asserted that events had transpired differently for Noor. Both men appeared to be credible witnesses, one of them being Lieutenant Colonel Wickey, who had served as a member of Canadian Intelligence during the war and been appointed Military Governor of a British-occupied zone of Germany after the war. The witnesses stated independently that the Dachau guards separated Noor from the other women as soon as the group arrived at the camp. A guard named Ruppert, a sadist known to harbor a hatred for people of other races, was then said to have abused Noor during the night evidently because her skin was darker than that of the other women. It is possible, too, that his loathing may have been intensified by the fact that Noor was known to have escaped from the Gestapo on three occasions in Paris, as well as having bloodied her original captor. Whatever his reasons, the guard used this opportunity to torment her.

As for Noor, although she was a gentle, kind-hearted woman, she also could be a sturdy, resilient one depending on the circumstances, a woman known to resist those who tried to subjugate her. She had shown her mettle at Gestapo headquarters in Paris, with her bravado being on display again at Pforzheim Prison. Not surprisingly, then, the chance encounter between her and Ruppert proved to be a volatile one. But it also turned out to be a very one-sided confrontation in that the guard was a brawny, armed man while his opponent was an emaciated, unarmed woman. And indeed, Ruppert abused Noor throughout the night in her prison cell, with his maltreatment including sexual assault, until he finally brought the torture to an end by shooting her. Still, Noor had one last moment of defiance, uttering the word "Liberté" before Ruppert pulled the trigger.[45]

As it stands, Noor, as a political prisoner, should not have been killed but rather released at the end of the war. But the powers-that-be in Berlin, knowing Germany would surrender and a war-crimes inquiry would ensue, were eager to eliminate all traces of those who had knowledge of Nazi atrocities. For this reason, they murdered hundreds of thousands of captives in the final months of the war.

After the war, Vera Atkins, as we saw in Chapter One, scoured German concentration camps in pursuit of her missing operatives, Noor being one of those for whom she searched. After retracing the agent's steps, learning of her valor, and uncovering her execution at Dachau, Atkins sought on three separate occasions to secure for Noor an official honor, but without success. Certainly her reasoning was sound: Noor had been the first female wireless operator to work behind enemy lines in France, and she had been the last to continue transmitting from Paris. This alone merited a decoration since her work had made it possible for the SOE to continue functioning in occupied France at the height of the war. But it was only when Vera divulged to British officials the appalling circumstances surrounding Noor's final hour, namely her maltreatment, including her rape, at the hands of the sadistic and perverse guard, that the decision was made to bestow upon Noor the George Cross.[46] Britain's highest honor for bravery, she surely deserved it. Like the self-sacrificing creatures in her Buddhist tales for children, it was because of her unflagging selflessness that countless men and women of the Special Operations Executive and the French Resistance were able to survive and succeed in their missions during one of the most atrocious periods in modern history. It was for them, and for the cause of freedom, that Noor Inayat Khan gave her life.

5

Yukiko Sugihara and the Escape of the Polish Jews

It was Romania, 1944, and Yukiko Sugihara, a Japanese woman, was living in a stately mansion in Bucharest with her husband Chiune and their three children. A diplomat, Chiune recently had been posted to the city during this period of political turmoil in the Central European nation. As Yukiko recounts in her stirring memoir, *Visas for Life*, she, too, was in turmoil in spite of the family's prominent standing and luxurious surroundings, although hers was of a more personal nature.[1] For one thing, her homeland, Japan, was allied with Nazi Germany, and she was adamantly opposed to the latter's devotion to an ideology of racial superiority and the practice of institutionalized discrimination. For another, the war was marching ever closer to the Sugiharas' doorstep, with this state of affairs heightening her anxieties about her family's safety. Certainly it was a justifiable fear, one that would reach its peak in the spring of that year when the Soviet Union's military force, the Red Army, launched an assault in Romania. Through sheer coincidence, Yukiko would find herself cut off from her husband and children and under armed attack. It was a crisis that not only would test her mettle but also reveal an essential feature of her character, namely, her compassion in the face of conflict.

It began when fighting erupted in Bucharest. The Sugiharas fled to a cottage a hundred miles away in Poiana Brasov, a fashionable ski resort in the Transylvanian Alps, where air raids were fewer and daily life, more predictable. As the family settled into the cottage, however, Yukiko's thoughts turned to the belongings she had left behind in her haste, some of which not only meant a great deal to her but were, in fact, irreplaceable. She therefore decided to make a dash back to the city to pick up a handful of cherished possessions, among them a signed photograph given to her by the celebrated Finnish composer Jean Sibelius.

With this aim in mind, Yukiko let her husband know she would be "back before nightfall," and asked her chauffeur to drive her to the capital city.[2] It was during this trip that the trouble began. En route, the car broke down, the result being that Yukiko found herself stranded; that is, until she spied a fleet of German vehicles in the distance. As it neared, she hitched a ride, little suspecting that her situation was about to become even worse. And, indeed, a man flagged down the convoy as it approached Bucharest and warned them that the Red Army was bombing the city. He advised them to go into a nearby forest and take cover, adding that Soviet forces were very close to them.

Heeding the man's counsel, Yukiko and the soldiers retreated into the woods amid a jumble of military vehicles and soon the crackle of gunfire. A distressing state of affairs, the thirty-two-year-old woman had difficulty accepting it as real.

Once she was settled in the forest, Yukiko became aware of another disturbing fact: the Soviets were not alone in their pursuit of them. The woodland also was swarming with Romanian partisans aiming to kill as many German soldiers as possible. So it was that the men who were protecting Yukiko were under assault by two sets of enemies from the air and from the ground.

"The mood was grim," writes Alison Gold, "since all chances of victory had faded away."[3] It was a siege that would last eight days.

Distraught, Yukiko wrote in her memoir that her thoughts turned to Chiune and her sons, who she knew would be frantic when she failed to return home. And it was now, as she fretted over them, that a tall, young officer by the name of Dürer arrived and put her mind at ease. Offering her a private car in which to live while she was trapped in the woods, he assured her that they would escape as soon as the opportunity presented itself. She would be safely reunited with her family, he told her, and all would be well again. But Yukiko was not so sure, especially during the early days of the siege when she was largely alone with her doubts.

On one point she was certain, however: Dürer was a good and gallant man, one who practiced benevolence during moments of adversity. For this reason, she quickly came to respect and even adore him. Furthermore, his kindness did not diminish, with the soldier stopping by her makeshift home in the car several times a day, furnishing her with blankets and offering her comforting conversation.

As the days accrued and the group continued hiding in the snowy woodland, Dürer spent increasing amounts of time with his new companion, who told him stories about life with her family in Japan. Before long, the young officer's enthusiasm prompted his war-weary comrades to seek out Yukiko as well. It was as if their beset group had momentarily transcended the tribulations of war, with Yukiko having now collected herself and taken to serving as a soothing, even motherly, source of strength to the fatigued soldiers. As to the friendship that was emerging between her and Dürer, it proved to be short-lived, just as Yukiko's intuition had warned her.

When the end came, it was swift. In the middle of the night, Dürer told her their group was departing. He said that he planned to drive one of the cars and asked if she would sit by his side. "I will never forget this time we had together," he said.[4] A bittersweet moment, it was now that they said their goodbyes.

Once they were on the road, their convoy was assailed by Soviet forces and Romanian partisans. Flashes of light illuminated the night sky and the sound of shelling shook the area, according to Yukiko's aforementioned account of the ordeal. Ahead on the road, they watched as German trucks became engulfed in flames, soldiers springing from them only to collapse a short distance away. Then a voice in the distance cried out that the soldiers should not remain in their vehicles, so Dürer slammed on the brakes and scurried with Yukiko to the roadside where they dropped onto the grass. During a lull in the bombing, they returned to the car and began driving again, only to be forced to reenact the same scene repeatedly. On one occasion, Yukiko injured her ankle as they leapt into a ditch, with Dürer thereafter helping her walk. Then came the final assault.

"All around were flames," writes Gold. "The sky itself was tinged with red."[5] Scuttling yet again to the side of the road, Yukiko, stumbling over maimed German soldiers, looked up to discover a partisan taking aim at her. Shocked, she retreated into her mind and for an instant saw herself once again in the company of her husband and sons. Seconds later, she found herself face-down in the grass, unharmed, with Dürer lying across her body in a noble effort to shield her from harm. As the whirr of bullets filled her ears, Yukiko passed out.

When she awoke, she spotted Dürer nearby, covered in debris. He was dead.

Once the onslaught subsided, Dürer's comrades hastily buried his remains on the site, after which they told Yukiko they planned to continue traveling on foot to the German border. Having no reason to accompany them to their homeland, she bid them farewell and set off alone for Posnia Brasov. It was to be an anguished journey made even more arduous because she was dehydrated and her foot throbbed owing to her injured ankle. All the same, she was determined to return to her loved ones. And it was now that she broke down and wept.

As she regained her composure, Yukiko was heartened to see in the distance the silhouette of a farmhouse. Expecting to be greeted by a kindhearted farmer who would offer her shelter, she instead was confronted by a rifle-wielding partisan who pulled her inside the house. Here she found herself surrounded by armed Romanian resistance fighters who did not believe she was the wife of a diplomat. They insisted that a woman of such standing would not be found stumbling, disheveled, in the countryside. Then, too, they pointed out that she was wearing a German soldier's uniform.

The fact is, the partisans suspected the diminutive Japanese woman of being an agent of the Axis powers, and for this reason held her captive for several hours until an experienced translator arrived. After interrogating her, the translator relayed to them Yukiko's account of events and assured them that she posed no threat. With this, the freedom fighters made light of their earlier suspicion that she was a Nazi spy and welcomed her into their quarters.

The next morning, they drove the intrepid Yukiko to Posnia Brasov, where Chiune and their sons, jubilant, were waiting at the door. In her memoir, Yukiko wrote that she was both laughing and crying when she was reunited with her loved ones. She added that she kept remembering the last moments of Dürer to whom she gave a final experience of wartime friendship, and who, in turn, laid down his life for her. To be sure, Yukiko had made a deep impression on the young German officer. And in the ensuing years, she would make a lasting impression on countless others around the world.

Iwate Prefecture

Yukiko was born to Tsuru and Fumio Kikuchi on December 17, 1913, in Numazu, Japan. During her childhood, she and her parents moved to Tohno, a town situated in the Iwate Prefecture in the northeastern part of the country. A region known for its deference to tradition and staunch political conservatism, the prefecture was also distinguished by its rugged coastline and harsh winters. But unlike the severe conditions in which the family lived, Yukiko's mother and father were warm and peaceful people.

In her written account, Yukiko described her parents and childhood. Her mother, Tsuru, was a well-educated, freethinking woman, one who hurried out to buy a pair of high-heeled shoes as soon as they became available in Japan. She also bought a wristwatch, another cutting-edge item for women of her day. And she met her future husband at a rather improbable event — a tennis match — tennis being an avant-garde sport in Japan at the time.

Fumio, for his part, was likewise well-educated and progressive, and he possessed common sense and compassion. An administrator in the field of education, he was regarded as innovative because he was more tolerant and inclusive than his colleagues. He refused to permit a school in which he served to expel students, for instance, convinced that banishing young men and women from the social order — in this case, the school system — was malproductive. His perspective, like that of his wife, was ahead of the times.

As could be expected perhaps, Yukiko, as the first-born daughter of such thoughtful parents, enjoyed a happy childhood. It may have been for this reason that she grew into such a confident adolescent who was, by her own account, fearless. She also was a young woman blessed with a creative streak.

The latter became evident shortly after she graduated from high school, when she decided to try her hand at poetry. Not only did she find it gratifying, but the quality of her verse was also first-rate, with some of it being published in magazines. She was especially drawn to tanka, a poetic form similar to that of haiku and composed of five lines with a set number of syllables. The inspired teen would continue writing tanka for the next several decades.

Along with poetry, Yukiko also took pleasure in the visual arts and dreamed of moving to Paris to pursue a career as an artist. What her immediate plans did not include was marriage, which, in the 1930s, continued to be one of the most revered traditions in Japan. In fact, marriage not only was obligatory, at least in the social sense, but in many cases it was still arranged by the parents. Yukiko would have none of it, however. She told her friends matter-of-factly that she did not want to rely on a man. And she might have held fast to her pledge had it not been for Chiune Sugihara, a distinctive gentleman thirteen years her senior.

Yukiko, with her pale skin, brown eyes, and dark, wavy hair, was an "idealistic, twenty-one-year-old" when she met Chiune, with his jet-black hair and warm, expressive eyes.[6] As one might predict given her keen mind, Yukiko was also an astute judge of character, a young woman who was not easily impressed. In the end, though, Chiune managed to win her hand in marriage, but only after he appealed to her sense of reason. He explained that a union with him would allow her to become a diplomat's wife, meaning that she could leave Tohno behind and travel the world with him. To the spirited Yukiko, the idea was captivating.

Besides the prospect of global adventures, however, Yukiko's decision was also influenced by Chiune's refreshing personality. A handsome man with a winning smile, he listened to, and took seriously, her ideas and opinions, a respectful style of relating that was seldom present in the other men she had known. With Chiune, she could express herself freely, secure in the knowledge that her words would be heard and valued. And, of course, she adored Chiune's charitable disposition. So it was that Yukiko and Chiune wed in 1935, and the following year celebrated the birth of their first child, a son named Hiroki.

Diplomatic Life

It was in 1937 that the Sugiharas left Japan, the Foreign Ministry notifying Chiune that he was being posted in Helsinki, Finland. As to the reason for the assignment, it was apparent, at least to those in diplomatic circles.

Finland was an "important listening post for goings-on in the Soviet Union," writes historian Hillel Levine, "and there Sugihara could take advantage of 'nordic neutrality' to spy on the Soviet Union and Nazi Germany."[7]

In the Finnish capital, a city that Yukiko came to adore, Chiune initially served as the embassy's principal translator but before long was promoted to Acting Foreign Minister. As for Yukiko, she immersed herself in the role of a diplomat's wife, taking etiquette lessons and practicing ballroom dancing, as well as brushing up on her English skills and studying German and French. She also spent a considerable amount of time with clothing designers whose creations were financed by the Japanese government. Being the spouse of an envoy and thus an unofficial co-representative of the Japanese people, she was to be well-dressed at all times, even when unwinding at the embassy. For social gatherings, she was expected to be particularly exquisite and to always wear a new gown or kimono. Since events of this type often took place on a nightly basis, it was necessary for her to have a constantly changing wardrobe.

Even more important, Yukiko was charged with organizing the embassy's receptions and galas, events on a grand scale that allowed her to rub shoulders with an array of interesting and influential men and women from around the globe. It was at one such gathering, for instance, that she became acquainted with Jean Sibelius, the composer to whom we alluded earlier in this chapter. By all accounts, Yukiko's life at the embassy was a colorful one. Even so, it could be a bit arduous at times, particularly when she became pregnant with Chiaki, her second son. Then, too, her days as a diplomat's wife sometimes clashed with her personality, with Yukiko feeling frustrated by the way in which her embassy role in the Finnish capital hampered her independence.

Like his wife, Chiune also felt constricted at times owing to his work with the diplomatic service in Helsinki. The fact is, the Sugiharas were a couple who valued their autonomy even as they respected and complied with tradition and protocol. It should come as no surprise, then, that the couple welcomed the chance to move elsewhere when the opportunity presented itself in late 1939. At this juncture, the Japanese Foreign Ministry, several weeks after the outbreak of World War II, asked Sugihara to open a small, one-man diplomatic mission in the city of Kaunas, the temporary capital of Lithuania.

From the standpoint of the Foreign Ministry, a presence in Lithuania was indispensable due to the country's location: the small Eastern European nation was adjacent to Poland as well as being situated between Germany and the Soviet Union, two military powers about which Japan had concerns. A diplomatic mission in Lithuania would thus provide Japan with an ideal observation post, with Chiune being the right person for the job because he was a self-sufficient diplomat who was fluent in both the German and Russian languages.

As the historical record reveals, Adolf Hitler, prior to the onset of the war, formed a treaty with Joseph Stalin whereby their respective nations agreed to refrain from engaging in armed conflict with one another. Yet as a secret, and certainly a devious, feature of this non-aggression pact, Germany, which was planning to invade Poland, agreed to partition and share this nation with the USSR. And, sure enough, Germany did invade Poland in September 1939, and divided it with its ally. But as we know, Hitler violated the same treaty the following year by sending troops into the Soviet Union.

It was shortly after the Germans invaded Poland that the Sugiharas relocated to Lithuania, with Chiune, as Deputy Consul General, harboring no illusions about his assignment. He knew the Japanese expected the Germans to eventually violate their non-aggression pact with the Soviets. "My consulate's main task was to rapidly and accurately determine the time of the German attack [on the USSR]," he said.[8] As it stood, Hitler's invasion of the USSR could be a boon for Japan, since it would tie up Soviet troops, heretofore a threat to Japan, and thus permit the Asian nation to pursue its own political aims in the East.

As always, the devoted Yukiko was at her husband's side in Kaunas during this time, a city whose unruffled, quiet atmosphere she appreciated. She also took pleasure in the consulate itself, the quaint, stucco edifice with wrought iron gates being situated on a hillside and offering a sweeping view of the city from its garden. And she was pleased to learn that her duties would not be as taxing as had been the case in Helsinki, according to her memoir. Yukiko believed she would now have more opportunities to relax, spend time with her loved ones, and pursue her hobbies, which included reading. As well, she wished to focus on motherhood. Indeed, it was while she was living in Kaunas that she gave birth to Haruki, their third son.

During this period, the consulate served as home to the Sugihara family and to Yukiko's sister Setsuko, while elsewhere in Kaunas lived the operation's staff. Outwardly, the consulate appear to be a minor concern — few Japanese citizens lived in Lithuania and the setup itself was a small one — but, as mentioned earlier, its location made it important. Furthermore, it soon would take on added significance, most notably for the Jewish population of its neighbor, occupied Poland.

After the German and Soviet militaries marched into Poland, the endangered Jews sought to escape to neighboring Lithuania, which did not require them to possess passports. Such lax entry requirements were truly a godsend for those refugees who faced arrest or worse, traumatized people who had been forced to flee from their homes on short notice and without proper identification. Desperate and besieged, they made their way to Kaunas by foot, automobile, or horse-drawn cart, although an intrepid few traveled by train. The railways, however, posed a grave risk because of the visibility they entailed, with soldiers waiting at train depots to arrest and in some cases execute on the spot those Jews who disembarked.

As if the situation were not dire enough, the Soviets, on June 15, 1940, moved into Lithuania and overnight its atmosphere, like that of Poland, became politically toxic. The former democracy now became known as the Lithuanian Soviet Socialist Republic, with Moscow, rather than Kaunas, as its capital. Shortly thereafter, the USSR ordered all foreign embassies and consulates in Kaunas to close their operations.

As these ominous events were unfolding, Polish Jews continued pouring into Kaunas. Prior to the war, the city was home to 120,000 Lithuanian citizens, thirty thousand of whom were Jewish. A sizable and compassionate constituency, the Lithuanian Jewish community did it utmost to help the fifteen thousand Polish Jews who now swarmed into the city in search of sanctuary. But the goal of an enduring security was questionable. It was widely suspected that the freedom enjoyed by the Jews of Lithuania — indeed, the freedom enjoyed by all people in Lithuania regardless of their religious affiliation — might well be short-lived, that the USSR might tighten its grip.

In her account of this period, Yukiko recalled that she felt an unceasing dread, waking up each morning only to find herself worrying gloomily about what misfortune the day might bring. Suffice it to say, she had reason to feel anxious: Soviet troops patrolled Kaunas around the clock, with this state of affairs cowing the citizenry and paralyzing life in the city. And then one day, Yukiko's sense of impending danger became a reality.

Incident in Kaunas

It began on July 27, 1940, a chilly morning in Kaunas in spite of the fact that it was summer. The Sugiharas arose, shared a light breakfast, and went their separate ways. Yukiko returned to her bedroom to read, but Chiune soon arrived at her side, appearing troubled.

"Take a look out the window," he said.[9]

In the street below, Yukiko spied a throng of men, women, and children, nearly two hundred strong, huddled outside the consulate's front gate. The crowd was distraught. "[F]rightened, disheveled, and very agitated," is how Yukiko described them.[10]

Chiune dispatched a young aide to bring back information about the people who had packed themselves into the entryway. He wanted to know what they were seeking. Soon, the diplomat learned they were Polish Jews trying frantically to escape from the Nazis, and they had amassed at the consulate in the hope that he would grant them transit visas. An official notation on a passport, a transit visa allows its holder to pass through another country en route to a final destination. In this case, the refugees were hoping to traverse the USSR and Japan on a vital trek eastward so as to avoid certain death. Their journey to Japan would take at least three weeks.

Upon hearing this news, Chiune walked to the gate, voiced his concern for those who had assembled there, and asked that they select a small delegation to meet with him inside the building. Here they could better discuss the dilemma and try to arrive at a solution.

Yukiko remained inside the building, peering through the curtains. It caused her anguish, she wrote in her memoir, to see so many exhausted, dispossessed people pleading for help.

A few minutes later, a group of five men entered the building. Heading it was a gentleman by the name of Zorach Warhaftig, an articulate young lawyer and ardent Zionist from Warsaw. Warhaftig confirmed that the people in the street, many without food or shelter, were newly arrived from Poland and had been waiting all night in anticipation of receiving the crucial documents. The sympathetic Chiune, in response, explained that transit visas from his consulate would only permit the refugees to pass through Japan, not to remain in Japan indefinitely. He further explained that it would be necessary for them to provide written proof of a final destination, meaning a nation or territory that would guarantee their entry upon arrival. The refugee delegation was prepared for this glitch, however. It seems that another diplomat in Kaunas, Jan Zwartendijk, the Acting Consul for the Dutch government, already had assured such a destination: Curaçao, an island in the West Indies and a Dutch possession. Unlike many nations and territories that had closed their doors to Jews, Curaçao had retained its open-door policy. Although a visa was not required, however, the governor of Curaçao's consent was necessary if one were to comply with the finer points of the entry regulations. At this critical period, though, the need for the governor's consent was disregarded by both the diplomats and the refugees themselves since they were not actually planning to travel to the island. After disembarking in Japan, most hoped to make their way to the Chinese city of Shanghai, a section of which Japan occupied at the time, since there existed in the city a sizeable community of Sephardic Jews known for helping refugees. They would claim Curaçao as their end point, however, for the sake of obtaining the Japanese transit visas.

By all accounts, Chiune genuinely wanted to aid these beleaguered people. As his old friend Tadakazu Kasai once observed, Chiune was "a generous person, eager to help and take care of others."[11] More than any assemblage Chiune had ever encountered, the Polish Jews needed his intercession.

As for Yukiko, the sole woman involved in the endeavor, she kept a watch on the families camped outside the consulate and reported back to those inside. She recalled that growing numbers of frantic men and women continued arriving at the gate, their frightened children in tow. "I was very upset by this scene," she writes, adding that it may have been in part because she had children of her own.[12] As a mother, she sympathized with the parents in the crowd.

Early the next day, Chiune, on behalf of the Polish Jews, made his request to the Soviet consul, who agreed to let the refugees pass through the USSR. The Soviet cooperation was not an instance of benevolence, however, but rather a case of profiteering: the Jews could travel across the USSR on the Trans-Siberian Railway if they were willing to pay an exorbitant fare, twice the usual amount. Accordingly, Chiune conveyed the Soviet offer to the Jewish refugees, who accepted it since there was no choice if they hoped to survive.

Now that an arrangement had been crafted among the Japanese, Dutch, and Soviet consuls, it was time for Chiune to talk to Yukiko before putting the scheme into motion. "[H]e needed Yukiko's help now in order to make a decision," says Gold.[13] Throughout their marriage, Yukiko's views had always played a role in her husband's actions. In this respect, their relationship was unique, with Yukiko enjoying a degree of influence in her marriage unknown to many Japanese wives of her day.

In terms of the distressed Jewish families that were camped outside the consulate, Yukiko's convictions were unequivocal: she and Chiune must save them. From the instant she spotted the refugees from her bedroom window to the present moment as her husband sought her advice, Yukiko felt it imperative that they make every effort to help the desperate people. And she told Chiune so. For several months, she had heard alarming rumors about the slaughter of the Jewish people, with the Polish delegation at the consulate now confirming these horrid tales. Yukiko, then, felt sure the hapless people outside her door were doomed unless she and her husband intervened. And she was right. Within months, most of those Polish Jews who did stay behind in Lithuania, like the Lithuanian Jews themselves, were slaughtered in what proved to be one of the most notorious bloodbaths of the Holocaust.

Once Yukiko and Chiune finished discussing their plans, they retired for the night, determined to get an early start the next morning. Yet this is not to suggest that they were wholly confident of their scheme. While they felt strongly that they were following a moral course of action, the potential ramifications of their deeds troubled them all the same. Yukiko later recorded in her memoir that they got very little sleep that night.

At sunrise, Chiune prepared to write the visas, but Yukiko urged him to contact his superiors in Tokyo before proceeding. She believed he would be on firmer ground if he obtained official consent to produce the hundreds or even thousands of visas that might be needed. Not only was an inordinately large number of documents being requested by a population escaping from another country, but the exodus was taking place at a time when the Soviets had already ordered the Japanese consulate to close. It was late July 1940, and the legation was slated to be vacated during the first week of August.

So it was that Yukiko and Chiune set to work securing their government's support in helping the Jews. Chiune hand-wrote a message and Yukiko typed it into diplomatic code. It stated that hundreds of distraught Jewish people were seeking transit visas and he did not wish to turn them away. He asked permission to issue the documents.

The couple sent the cable to the Ministry of Foreign Affairs in Tokyo, with Yukiko preparing two additional copies and dispatching them to the Japanese ambassadors of neighboring Latvia and Germany. Now it was just a matter of waiting for the authorities in Tokyo give their consent. In the meantime, Yukiko returned to the window to keep watch on the heartrending throng while Chiune resumed preparing the travel documents.

When the official reply came, the couple was stunned: the Foreign Ministry flatly forbade them to issue visas. "No further inquiries expected," the cable added.[14] It appears that the Japanese government, first and foremost, did not wish to risk alienating the German government, its eventual ally, by aiding the refugees. Then, too, the citizenship of Polish Jews was still up in the air at this point. "Japanese consuls throughout Europe were confounded as to what to do about issuing visas to Jewish refugees," says Levine.[15] "[T]heir plight was further complicated by new political divisions in Europe and by the changed legal status of old citizenships in annexed countries."[16]

For two more days and nights, Yukiko and Chiune fretted over the refugees' fates even as Chiune persisted in writing visas against his government's orders. Bewildered and exasperated, the couple again decided to approach the Foreign Ministry, yet, as before, the authorities responded with a brusque communiqué prohibiting them from helping the Jews. This time, the government cited trumped-up security concerns as the reason for its refusal.

Yukiko, in her written account, reveals that her health began to suffer at this time, no doubt a result of the extreme stress she was enduring. Among the problems she suffered was a diminished ability to breast-feed her youngest son. Worsening matters, the Soviet occupation of Kaunas made it unfeasible for her to purchase milk at a grocery store. In a very real sense, she was a prisoner in her own home, and the situation did not improve any time soon. The Soviets mistrusted the Sugiharas and therefore kept the family under around-the-clock surveillance while insisting they leave Lithuania. In a parallel development, the Foreign Ministry in Tokyo demanded they close the consulate and leave the country.

Still, such pressures notwithstanding, the couple was determined to help the refugees and to this end prepared a final cable. For a third time, they pleaded with the Japanese government to permit them to give travel documents to the imperiled Jews, and the Foreign Ministry again replied with a firm refusal. With this last rejection, Chiune, demoralized, asked Yukiko if she thought they should bring the project to a halt. It appears he was concerned about the consequences of his actions and about his family's future. It should be remembered that he was weighing several factors: the Soviet authorities considered him a security risk and were monitoring his movements, the Japanese authorities already had ordered him to leave Lithuania, and the Germans authorities might well execute them if it was discovered that they were aiding the Jews. For a man like Chiune for whom the safety of his wife and children was paramount, it undoubtedly was an excruciating dilemma. He never lost sight of the fact, however, that if he and Yukiko were to abandon the refugees, these defenseless people would face the unthinkable.

"No, we cannot, it would be impossible for us to leave them," Yukiko told him.[17] She later explained that she not only was telling Chiune what she felt, but also what he wanted to hear.

"You're right," he replied, settling the matter.[18]

In this way, the Sugiharas made the mindful decision to defy the Foreign Ministry's directives, thereby placing themselves in personal and political jeopardy with three different governments. The family's future suddenly became highly uncertain.

Early the next morning, the couple set to work on the daunting task that lay ahead of them, one that would consume their waking hours for weeks. Their goal was to create three hundred transit visas a day, an exceptionally tall order given that many had to be hand-inscribed with intricate Japanese symbols. Creating this number would be an unprecedented feat.

Making matters more difficult, Chiune did not want Yukiko to help him prepare the documents because she could face serious repercussions if it were ever discovered that she had done so. For that matter, the diplomat did not want any of his loved ones involved in the project, but instead wished to bear full responsibility for any adverse consequences. Ensuing reports have asserted, however, that Yukiko did, in fact, write a considerable share of the visas, perhaps up to half of them, although such claims appear to be speculative, according to Levine.[19] Certainly the Sugiharas never confirmed them, with Yukiko even stating in her written account of the incident that she did not write them. All the same, the claims remain that she did indeed take part in the preparation of the immense number of documents that the consulate created and distributed at that time.

As could be expected given the size of the task, Chiune's energy began to wane as the days wore on. An onerous chore, it was wearing him down.

"I wonder if I should stop now?" he asked Yukiko a second time.[20]

As before, however, Yukiko's passion for the undertaking remained strong and thus her answer was the same. "Many people are still waiting," she recalls telling her husband. "Let's issue some more visas and save as many lives as we can.'"[21]

In other ways, too, Yukiko encouraged and supported Chiune with the refugee project. Late each evening, for instance, a tired Yukiko would knead his hands, which were swollen from the hours of writing. "Long after Chiune had fallen asleep," writes Gold, "Yukiko continued massaging his cramped, aching palms."[22] Such thoughtfulness was characteristic of her, with Yukiko's kindness coming to the fore once again in the middle of August when the Japanese and Soviet governments renewed their pressure on her and Chiune to leave the country.

Because they needed more time to complete their altruistic mission, Chiune made an appeal to the Soviet government claiming that it was necessary to keep open the embassy a short while longer so he could conclude its business affairs. As he waited for the reply, which eventually did arrive and allowed him a few more days, he labored nonstop on the refugee project. Yukiko, as always, was by his side. Chiune also had a change of heart about his slavishness to regulations: he now began issuing visas to any Polish Jew who asked, regardless of whether the person possessed the proper documentation from the Dutch embassy. Along these same lines, he changed his mind about accepting assistance in preparing the visas, permitting others to help stamp passports and perform related duties. In one case, a remarkable effort was made by a young man named Moshe Zupnik, who was determined to save his people.

Zupnik had been a rabbi at Mir Yeshiva, one of Poland's oldest and most venerated academies. Resolute in protecting the school, he escorted the entire student body, faculty, and their families to the Japanese embassy in Kaunas, where he applied for three hundred visas. Due to the daunting size of the request, Zupnik offered to help and was allowed to do so. Because of the efforts of Sugihara, Zupnik, and others in the consulate, the yeshiva survived and relocated to present-day Israel, where it continues to thrive.

Not long after the seminarians received their documents did the Sugiharas' risky venture come to an end. It happened in late August 1940, and was quite sudden: the extension that the Soviet Union had granted the embassy expired at the same moment the Japanese Foreign Ministry insisted, once and for all, that the Sugiharas leave Lithuania. The couple could delay no longer. They could be jailed if they remained.

On their last night in Kaunas, Yukiko packed the family's belongings while Chiune burned incriminating documents in his office. Then, early the next morning, they bundled up their sons, bid farewell to the embassy staff, and with Yukiko's sister Setsuko moved temporarily into the Hotel Metropolis in the heart of the city. They planned to rest while awaiting the train to Berlin, but instead Chiune spent this time writing more visas. This was because the Sugiharas, as they left the embassy, placed a note on the door informing any Polish Jews who might arrive that the family could be found at the hotel. And sure enough, scores of refugees made their way to the hotel in search of the diplomat, who pulled up a chair in the lobby and set about issuing travel permits again. With foresight, he had brought with him a stack of blank forms and the official embassy stamp, and he persisted in creating the documents until the hour arrived for the family to travel to Germany. "Yukiko tapped him on the shoulder and told him that they had to go to the train," said Gold.[23] Yet even now, at the eleventh hour, the demand for visas did not slacken.

The dispossessed Polish Jews, pleading for travel papers, followed the family to the train station, where Chiune dispensed more documents. He even persisted in writing them once he was onboard the train, tossing them through the windows to the hands that so eagerly sought them. Hastily stamping the visas, he made use of these final moments to save as many lives as possible.

At last, as the train pulled out of the station, Chiune tossed the remaining visa forms, along with the official seal, to those running alongside the tracks. He intended for the refugees to use them to create their own documents, which, in fact, they did. Grateful for what the Sugiharas had done for them, the refugees voiced their gratitude in these last few seconds. "We'll never forget you," cried a member of the crowd as the locomotive left the station.[24] Shortly thereafter, the exhausted Chiune fell into a slumber. Yukiko, on the other hand, stayed awake, despairing for those left behind while also feeling sure that she and Chiune's actions had been the morally correct ones. "I truly believe it was our fate," Yukiko has said, referring to her and her husband's presence in Kaunas at that critical moment.[25] She added that she believed their actions had been guided by "a higher power."[26]

In September 1940, the Sugihara family and Setsuko arrived by train at a new posting in Prague, a city that somehow had managed to retain much of its magic during the early months of the war. Even so, Yukiko was not able to unwind knowing that war was underway. While the Czechoslovakian city was not yet experiencing its major effects, she found the grim reality of the conflict surrounding the city to be inescapable.

Contributing to her stress, the Foreign Ministry in Tokyo ordered Chiune to compile a list of visas the Japanese consulate in Kaunas had issued. Not surprisingly, the directive caused the couple to fear that the past had caught up with them. All the same, they set to work and in due course calculated that they had created approximately two thousand visas in their humanitarian undertaking. In reality, the number was far higher because Chiune, in his haste, had stopped numbering them early in the process, long before the bulk were written. Then, too, only one visa was required for an entire family to enter another country, meaning that the number of documents itself did not tell the whole story. The upshot is that the figure sent to Tokyo, despite being quite high, was a considerable underrepresentation of the number of men, women, and children who were able to use the documents to escape. It has been estimated that up to ten thousand Jewish lives were ultimately saved by the Sugiharas' transit visas.[27]

After submitting the list, Yukiko and Chiune nervously awaited the Foreign Ministry's response but an immediate reply was not forthcoming. Indeed, seven years would pass before they would learn the consequences of their altruism in Kaunas.

In the meantime, the Japanese government posted Chiune in Königsberg, Germany, and later in Bucharest, Romania. When the Sugiharas arrived in the latter, they found the city wet, chilly, and oppressive. As in other nations aligned with Germany, soldiers swarmed the streets and the symbols of fascism were ubiquitous. "Swastika flags flew from poles everywhere," writes Alison Gold. "[P]ortraits of Hitler were on walls in every office and house."[28] It was an unsettling sight for those, like Yukiko and Chiune, who rejected the tenets of National Socialism.

In terms of her daily life in Bucharest, Yukiko felt trapped within the walls of the mansion, according to her memoir. Fear was also her unwelcome companion. It was during this daunting period, in fact, that apprehension prompted Yukiko and Chiune to create a makeshift bomb shelter next to the mansion, although they ultimately decided to move to Poiana Brasov for safety. As recounted at the beginning of this chapter, it was during their stay in the mountain village that Yukiko tried to return to the city to salvage some of her belongings only to find herself under siege for eight days by Soviet soldiers and Romanian partisans.

It would not be until July 1945, that the Sugiharas returned to Bucharest, a city in ruins. Hitler had committed suicide and the Allies had taken control. But just when the Sugiharas thought the misery of war might finally be behind them, Soviet soldiers arrived at their door with alarming news: the family was being taken into custody.

Yukiko writes in her memoir that she, Chiune, their sons, and her sister Setsuko were placed in an internment camp on the outskirts of the city, where they lived in a room with a dirt floor and subsisted on thin soup. As for their financial condition, authorities froze the family's Swiss bank account, so they had no money. To be sure, their situation was bleak, and it would remain so for several months.

On a winter morning in 1946, Yukiko's spirits were lifted when she learned that she and her loved ones were to be released. And sure enough, a short time later as a snowstorm raged around them, the Sugiharas and Setsuko wrapped themselves in their heavy fur coats and bearing their few remaining possessions climbed into the back of a truck bound for the train station. They would be traversing the Soviet Union.

As it came to pass, their trip on the Trans-Siberian Railway would take a month. Yukiko later learned that it was the same route that had been taken years earlier by those auspicious Polish Jews to whom they had issued transit visas. Certainly it was a grueling trip by any measure, partly because the climate through which they passed was sub-arctic. And for the Sugiharas, circumstances were at their worst because the journey took place during the most frigid months, December and January. In her written account, Yukiko recalls that their train car was crowded and austere, containing only a wooden bench and an inefficient stove, and that many of the children were infested with lice.

Eventually the train pulled into Odessa, where officials removed Yukiko and her loved ones and put them in another internment camp before allowing them to continue on their railway trek across the Soviet Union. In due course, they reached the city of Nakhodka, a port on the Sea of Japan. Yet again, though, the family was taken from the train and confined in an internment facility with cramped conditions and sparse food. Imprisoned at the camp, too, were several Japanese prisoners-of-war, weary men to whom Yukiko sneaked cigarettes and morsels of food through a barbed-wire fence. Despite her travails, her compassion remained intact.

Finally, the day arrived when the Sugiharas were released from captivity. Docked in the harbor was a cargo ship, which took them to freedom in their homeland. They had been away from Japan for ten years.

Postwar Japan

Yukiko and Chiune quickly realized it was not the same country they had left behind. A lost nation, it had been devastated by war, contaminated by atomic fallout, and rendered utterly dispirited. Its economy was a shambles, and the country was under occupied control.

Worsening matters, the Sugiharas were still unable to free their money from the bank in Switzerland. And then came another blow: Chiune was not called back to work. When he inquired about his job, the Foreign Ministry said he was not needed at the moment, that it would let him know when to return. Given this brusque treatment, Yukiko feared that he may have lost his job because of their efforts helping the Polish Jews. It would not be until three months later that the Foreign Ministry would at last order the diplomat to report to its headquarters, and it turns out that her doubts had been warranted: Chiune was told to resign. Distraught, he asked why he should be deprived of his career in the foreign service, and Vice Foreign Minister Okazaki provided him with the answer. It had to do with "that incident in Lithuania," as Yukiko puts it in her memoir.[29] That is to say, Chiune was fired because he had defied the Foreign Ministry's orders, this in a society in which obedience to authority was imperative. Even the Bushido code that had guided Chiune's birth family — his mother's ancestors had been Samurai — emphasized a respect for, and a deference to, authority. Yet in the Lithuanian dilemma, the diplomat had followed his conscience and adhered to a higher ethic, a responsibility to humanity as a whole, not just to the political directives of higher-ups in the Foreign Ministry. And thus, in the eyes of his government, he had disgraced himself and his nation.

In the ensuing months, Chiune, disillusioned and struggling with depression, tried to put the past behind him. To this end, he stopped talking about his and Yukiko's valiant efforts to save the Polish Jews or about the Japanese government's termination of his career as a consequence. As for the family's financial condition, the Foreign Ministry did grant the Sugiharas a limited retirement allowance. Offended by the government's treatment of them, the couple contemplated moving their family to another country but decided to remain in Japan for the sake of their children. In her memoir, Yukiko writes that she and her husband felt that their children already had been uprooted too many times and needed more stability in their lives.

Fortunately, several months later Yukiko and Chiune were allowed to reclaim their Swiss account, yet even these assets did not provide them with nearly enough funds to meet the family's needs. With their sons to support, times were tough. While Yukiko cooked, cleaned the house, cared for their children, and gave emotional support to Chiune, he, in turn, looked for employment. Although he pondered selling rice, he ended up selling lightbulbs door-to-door.

The family's outlook eventually brightened when Chiune landed a full-time job at an American exchange shop that catered to the occupying forces. It was the first of a string of jobs through which the former diplomat would pass in the late 1940s and 1950s. He would subsequently secure a position with an American textile company, then teach Russian, and later move to the Soviet Union to work with the Science and Technology Agency. In 1960, he would take yet another job, this time with a Japanese trading firm during which he would live in a small, austere room at the Hotel Ukraine in Moscow and return to Japan once a year to visit Yukiko and their sons. To be sure, it was not a cheerful chapter in his life. In 1964, Chiune secured still another job, this one managing a Soviet factory that made sewing machines.

Yukiko's life during this same period was, by comparison, happier and more productive. For all practical purposes, she was functioning as a single mother, overseeing the household, and assuming the lion's share of responsibility for bringing up their children. By all accounts, she succeeded admirably at these tasks.

Unfortunately, her marriage would not be quite so sound, with the Sugiharas' union waning as a result of the myriad stresses that had come to define their lives. Chiune now toiled thousands of miles away in a Communist country, a state of affairs that was far from conducive to a healthy marriage. Then, too, his personality, previously characterized by optimism and enthusiasm, had been dampened by the losses he had sustained and the indignities to which he had been subjected. Surely anyone in his circumstances could be expected to become disillusioned, demoralized, and embittered. As for Yukiko's support, she tried to help the man with whom she had spent her adult life, but she had numerous obligations of her own and could do only so much to comfort him. "[S]trained" is how Levine described the couple's annual visits.[30] In due course, Chiune, age seventy-six, retired and returned to Japan. Ten years later he succumbed to a heart attack. But before he passed away, he managed to tell Yukiko how much he had enjoyed being married to her, a declaration of abiding love that moved her deeply.

As could be expected, Yukiko mourned her loss. Yet in the years that followed, she remained the same vibrant and principled person she had been since, as a young woman, she had first met him. Not only did she continue embracing her role as a mother — and now a grandmother — but she also spoke publicly from time to time about her and her husband's deeds during the Holocaust. Although reluctant to acknowledge her own actions in helping save the lives of the Polish Jews, she was always pleased to accept posthumous honors on behalf of Chiune in nations such as Israel and the United States.

At such events, Yukiko occasionally had the opportunity to meet some of the refugees who had escaped from Lithuania using the Sugiharas' visas. She discovered that most of those who had received them had temporarily settled in Shanghai, China, while a smaller number had continued on to Great Britain, Canada, the United States, and certain South American nations. Some had spent the remaining years of the war helping more Jewish people escape from Europe, while others made remarkable strides after the war. Zorach Warhaftig, for instance, one of the small delegation of men who initially met with the Sugiharas in Kaunas and convinced them to provide the visas, later became Israel's Minister of Religious Affairs. He also served as a member of the Israeli Parliament and was a founder of the National Religious Party.

In sharp contrast was the fate of the Sugiharas themselves, whose noble actions during the war, as we have seen, brought them personal difficulties for many years to come. All the same, it was a sacrifice that Yukiko and Chiune made willingly, as well as one about which they never expressed any regrets.

As the years passed, Yukiko stayed true to her convictions, spending her days voicing her opposition to war and the cruelty it begets. Her mission became that of alerting future generations to the evils of prejudice and the human costs of armed conflict. In this undertaking, she encouraged young people to be sensitive to their instincts of right and wrong and to act in accordance with them. "They should listen to their conscience and find the courage to follow the right path," she said.[31]

In her own life, Yukiko, who passed away on October 8, 2008, had surely listened to her own instincts.[32] Her compassion and her courage, like these same qualities in her husband, had helped to ensure that thousands of Jewish men, women, and children marked for murder would instead live and give life to future generations of "Sugihara Survivors."

6

Virginia Hall and the Vichy Underground

An American in Paris, the gregarious Virginia Hall, heir to a shipping and real estate fortune, neither trembled in fear nor languished in despair when World War II exploded on the continent and the Germans, in due course, advanced into France. She also did not dash home to the comfort of her family's sprawling East Coast estate, with its manor house, tennis courts, and horse stables. Rather, the hardy American rolled up her sleeves and threw herself into the war effort; this, despite the fact that it was a conflict being fought on foreign soil. By all accounts, her sense of right and wrong knew no borders. Joining a French medical corps, the Services Sanitaires de l'Armée, she underwent intensive training in first aid and a month later set to work driving an ambulance.

"Virginia helped the attending medics load the blood-caked men, some crying out in agonizing pain," writes Judith Pearson. "Then she sped off, with the patients bouncing in the back, across the rough terrain to field hospitals."[1]

As the weeks passed, Virginia found her duties physically taxing. With the fighting in France escalating, a mounting number of wounded soldiers were in need of transport and treatment, and this meant more trips and longer hours. And herein lay a problem. It seems Virginia had an impediment, a prosthetic leg, which caused her hip to throb after operating the clutch for lengthy periods of time. All the same, she was a trooper and carried on without complaint.

Ironically, it was this same impairment that had disqualified her from being promoted to a position within the U.S. Department of State three years earlier, that of an officer in its Foreign Service component. Never mind that she was well-educated — she had attended Radcliffe College, Barnard College, the Sorbonne, and the Diplomatic Academy of Vienna — or that she had served in clerical capacities with the Foreign Service in Poland and Turkey. It was solely the presence of the artificial limb that barred her from eligibility for advancement. That said, Virginia wondered if her gender may have been an unspoken concern as well, if the powers-that-be may have worried that a female officer would be ineffectual during this period of rising political tensions, particularly in Western Europe.[2]

Whatever the case, neither her synthetic leg nor the fact that she was a woman stood in the way of Virginia's life-saving actions as a battlefield ambulance driver, just as they did not impede the even more audacious deeds she would perform as a resistance agent in the years ahead. Among other feats, the "tall woman with bright red hair" would orchestrate covert missions designed to derail freight trains, blow up bridges, and ambush German soldiers.[3] Smart, adept, and focused, Virginia Hall's attention was on her abilities, not her disability, with her hands-on attitude contributing to her reputation as one of the top field agents in both the Special Operations Executive (SOE) and the Office of Strategic Services (OSS). By any definition, she was a very capable woman.

A Continental Background

By the time World War II was declared, Virginia had already spent a considerable portion of her life in Europe. Daughter of the prominent and prosperous Barbara and Edwin Lee Hall — Virginia was born on April 6, 1906, in Baltimore, Maryland — she visited Paris and other European cities with her family when she was a child. Then, several years later as a young adult, she convinced her parents that she would benefit from an education abroad, saying her studies at domestic colleges were uninspiring and that she yearned to immerse herself in European culture. Accordingly, she thereafter attended classes at the Sorbonne and L'École des Services Politiques in Paris, as well as studying French in Strasbourg, Toulouse, and Grenoble. The ambitious heiress also traveled to Austria, where she enrolled in the oldest diplomatic school in the world, the renowned Diplomatic Academy of Vienna or Konsularacademie, from which she graduated in 1929. Inquisitive and driven, Virginia did not share the blithe interests of the other young women in the Halls' social circles, instead preferring politics to parties, travel to teas. True to form, then, she promptly enrolled in the American University in Washington, DC, upon returning to the United States, which, it turned out, would be the last school she would attend. Two years later, in July 1931, she embarked on a career in the Foreign Service.

Warsaw was Virginia's first posting, where she arrived in the midst of the global economic meltdown. "Observers of contemporary Polish history refer to the period from 1931 to 1934 as the time of the Great Slump," says Ron Nowicki.[4] But while the Depression's dour effects were in evidence throughout the Central European nation, its impact, oddly enough, was subdued in the capital city itself, where the early years of the decade beheld "continued growth and cosmetic improvement."[5] It was thus a stroke of good fortune that the State Department assigned Virginia to the fairly unscathed Warsaw, and she appears to have enjoyed her stay in the historic city. Above all, she took pleasure in her work at the American Embassy.

She was twenty-five years old when she began her duties as an embassy clerk, her first job, and she performed it well. The records indicate that Virginia garnered favorable appraisals from the ambassador for her engaging personality, enthusiasm, and dedication, and was regarded as a cooperative staff member, a team player.[6] But while she was personable and well-liked and formed amiable relationships, her most meaningful one, a romantic attachment to a Polish military officer, went sour because of a petty prejudice. It seems that her lover's mother was hostile to the relationship, with the woman's antagonism stemming from the fact that Virginia was an American. Worsening matters, the maternal disapproval, in the fullness of time, loosened the couple's bond and cast a shadow over their future. As it became clear that this disheartening state of affairs was unlikely to improve, Virginia decided to bring the romance to an end, although not without regret. Shortly thereafter, she boarded a train for Turkey, where she assumed another position as a clerk, this time at the American Consulate in Izmir. The year was 1934, and Izmir was still known as Smyrna. Unfortunately, it was while she was posted in this Eurasian city by the Aegean Sea that Virginia lost her leg.

It happened during a hunting party on a December afternoon in the Turkish countryside. Lugging a twelve-gauge shotgun, she tucked it under her arm while negotiating a decrepit wire fence in the course of which she lost her footing and then lost her hold on the rifle. "Grabbing for it, she hit the trigger, discharging shot into her left foot," says former OSS agent Elizabeth McIntosh. "When gangrene set in, a surgeon was rushed from Istanbul to save her life, but he had to amputate the leg just below the knee."[7]

To recuperate, Virginia returned to her family's pastoral estate, Box Horn Farm, with its rolling hills and sweeping vistas. By any measure, the home and its surroundings were glorious. A 110-acre spread, the Maryland manor boasted a pond, riding trails, orchards, and a dairy, with tenant farmers installed at the estate as well. And it proved to be a milieu that enhanced Virginia's healing. So rapid was her recovery, in fact, that she succeeded in landing another job with the Foreign Service by year's end. "Hall never let her disability hamper her actions," notes Patrick O'Donnell.[8]

In December 1934, the resilient go-getter resumed the career she had reluctantly put on hold, traveling to the beguiling city of Venice and to the

American Consulate. Here, as before, she set to work performing clerical duties. But this time around, Virginia did even more: she substituted for the Vice Consul during those periods when he was away. It was an assignment that signaled her superiors' confidence in her demeanor, judgment, and proficiency, and it seemed to suggest that she was well on her way to becoming a Foreign Service Officer. But, unfortunately, this was not to be the case. The State Department, during her assignment in Italy, brought Virginia's career plans to a standstill when it notified her that her synthetic limb prohibited her from ascending to a position as an official.

Exasperated, she requested a review of the decision, while colleagues and friends made appeals on her behalf as well. Among the latter were associates of the esteemed Hall family who petitioned the Oval Office directly. In spite of such efforts, however, federal regulations prevailed, the effect being that Virginia watched her future as a Foreign Service Officer evaporate. And although she tried to rekindle her enthusiasm for her clerical duties, even to the point of transferring to a consulate in Estonia in the hope of reviving her interest, she ultimately tendered her resignation and thereby brought to a close her State Department career. Or so she thought. Destiny, it would seem, had other plans for her. But at this juncture, Virginia, assuming her days of government service were behind her, set off for Paris, the city on the Seine having long occupied a corner of her heart. In the month of May, she arrived at her destination.

"There is never any ending to Paris," Ernest Hemingway has written, "and the memory of each person who has lived in it differs from that of any other."[9] Certainly Virginia had warm recollections of her childhood visits to the French capital, although the memories she would henceforth form in the City of Light, and in wartime France more generally, would prove to be even more distinctive and indelible.

Underground in France

It was a distraught Paris that awaited Virginia in the late spring of 1939. Anxiety over the prospect of war was palpable and the signs of anti–Semitism, disturbingly evident. As in other parts of Europe, antiquated gripes against the Jewish people were resurfacing, with dogmatists dredging up, or inventing, scores to be settled. In Paris, among the most tolerant and progressive metropolises in Europe, Virginia found the resurgence of anti–Semitism to be particularly disappointing.

When, as feared, war did break out on the continent, she and her Parisian friends, a Left Bank café crowd, gathered each week to discuss far into the night the conflict's direction and the prospect of a German incursion into France. Her talk turned to action, however, when it became apparent that an invasion was imminent. With this unnerving news, Virginia, a gentile, and Clare de La Tour, a young Jewish woman and one of Virginia's café friends, decided to join the Service Sanitaires de l'Armée. As recounted in the opening pages of this chapter, Virginia served as an ambulance driver with the organization, a demanding task she performed until June 1940, when France surrendered. But still she did not stop. Rather, she volunteered to keep driving, the German presence notwithstanding, until all of the injured Allied soldiers who still needed conveyance to hospitals in or near Paris received it. Only at this point, weeks later, did she conclude her duties and look ahead to her own future.

Viscerally opposed to living in a country that was under the thumb of Adolf Hitler, it was at this juncture that Virginia decided to travel to England, which, as an American citizen, she was free to do. Since the United States had not yet joined the Allies, she was not subject to travel restrictions. As to the route, she booked a course that would take her by train to Spain, and thereafter by ship to England. And it was during the first leg of her journey that she had a curious, and a consequential, encounter with a stranger, an encounter that was set into motion at a Paris train station.

While preparing to board, Virginia was accosted by a long-winded gentleman, ostensibly an Englishman, who introduced himself as George Bellows, and who, for the remainder of the trip, seldom left her side. Friendly beyond custom, he asked her thoughts on the Third Reich and the occupation of France, and the forthright American, who didn't need much encouragement to sound off about such matters, set about voicing her disgust with the Nazi apparatus. As she spoke, moreover, it became apparent that she and her unsolicited companion were of a like mind. "They shared the same feelings that all the Nazis stood for was fundamentally wrong," says Pearson.[10] At last, as the two were taking leave of one another, Bellows slipped Virginia a list of names to contact in London, while also instructing her to get in touch with the American Embassy. Swayed by the chatty gentleman, she resolved to do just that.

Presenting herself to embassy officials shortly after settling in the British capital, a startled Virginia found herself being peppered with questions about conditions and developments in France in what turned out to be an intensive debriefing session. Wholly unexpected, it lasted an hour, after which American officials, in yet another twist, offered her a job as a code clerk at the embassy. If she were to accept the position, she would be assigned to a military attaché and receive a handsome salary, so Virginia seized the offer. In this way, she once again found herself in the employ of the U.S. Department of State, with her political connections proliferating overnight.

A few months later, in January 1941, an even more intriguing entrée into the world of political affairs opened up before her, the realm of espionage, when she was invited to a cocktail party at Vera Atkins' blue Victorian home, a "painted lady" as such houses are sometimes known. It was Virginia's understanding that Atkins was connected to Britain's War Office. As for the evening affair itself, it proved to be a consequential one. In the course of a discussion among the guests centering on the German incursion into France, Atkins pointedly asked Virginia to share her experiences with the group, and Virginia, being Virginia, did not hesitate to recount them. Equally important, she told the guests that she hoped to find an avenue by which she might return to France and help defeat the enemy. "Vera didn't comment," says Pearson, "but Virginia's words did not go unnoticed."[11]

The next morning, Atkins sent a note to Maurice Buckmaster, head of the French Section of the Special Operations Executive (SOE). This division of the organization, it will be recalled from Chapter One, was devoted to buttressing France's resistance networks, with Buckmaster and Atkins spearheading the operation. In regard to the note, it was titled "Prospects" and pointed out that Virginia had conveyed a desire to reenter France to help thwart the enemy.[12] "This lady," Atkins wrote, "might well be used for a mission."[13] She added that the SOE would, of course, cover the American's expenses in such a case.

Pursuing her hunch, Atkins asked Virginia to join her for a chat at the Northumberland Hotel in London, where the latter found herself escorted to a blacked-out room on an upper floor. Here, Atkins, shrouded in a cloud of cigarette smoke, revealed that she was not really with the War Office but rather with an organization known as the Special Operations Executive.[14] After she disclosed its nature and purpose, a man by the name of Jacques de Géulis joined the pair and commenced questioning Virginia about her experiences in France and her desire to return and oppose the occupying forces. Among other things, he wanted to know why a citizen of a country that was not engaged in the war was so keen on involving herself in it. Seemingly affronted by the question, Virginia replied that she had lived in Europe for many years and considered it her fight as well.

As the interview drew to a close, Atkins and Géulis agreed that the articulate American would, in fact, be well-suited to the task. "She had the wit, courage, and attention to detail that they believed would be the hallmarks of a good agent," says Pearson.[15] The prosthetic limb was not an issue. And so it was that Atkins, her intuition confirmed, offered Virginia a place with the secret organization, and, naturally, Virginia was game.

About her role in the SOE, Virginia learned that she would be a fixer, liaising with the organization in London and its operatives in France, as well as with members of France's own resistance forces and with government officials. As to specifics, she would be an initial point of contact for incoming SOE operatives in the region of France in which she would be stationed.

These men and women she would update on conditions in the area, furnish with forged francs, and ensure they received any other support they needed to embark on their assignments. In addition, she would help set up underground networks through which downed Allied pilots and prisoners-of-war could escape from enemy territory. And throughout her term in France, she would keep her eyes peeled and report back to the organization about her observations. In all, it was an assignment that would require considerable multi-tasking, one in which a single error could potentially cost human lives.

After accepting the SOE's offer to serve as a field agent, Virginia, giving a spurious reason, resigned from her job at the American Embassy. She was well aware that the United States government, if she were to seek its permission, would not consent to her serving as a covert agent for a foreign government in wartime. For this reason, she decided not to seek Washington's approval. The downside was that she could not tell her embassy employers or coworkers in London the real reason for her departure, this being the first of countless deceptions she would, by necessity, perpetrate in her new life as an espionage agent. After tendering her resignation, Virginia turned her attention to the SOE's preparatory program for undercover operatives, a course of instruction to which she gave herself wholeheartedly.

In February 1941, a month after meeting Vera Atkins, Virginia's training commenced at a rambling country estate in Wanborough, a hamlet in southeast England. The SOE program was divided into three stages, the first of which was preliminary and allowed those in command to scrutinize the fresh recruits and weed out any who seemed unsuitable for clandestine work. As it happened, a considerable number of newcomers were usually judged to be unfit during this early phase and excluded from further participation.

Regarding the Wanborough training itself, it consisted of a primer on weaponry and included hands-on exercises with submachine guns and other arms. Incorporated into the curriculum, too, were classes in map reading and related skills, along with a physical fitness component. Agents, for obvious reasons, needed to be in first-rate shape before being dropped into enemy territory. As for Virginia, who had always been the outdoorsy sort even after the ill-fated hunting party in Turkey, she had no problem with the physical fitness requirement, nor, for that matter, with any other feature of the Wanborough training. Accordingly, she completed this component of the program in the standard three weeks, subsequent to which the facility's senior officers agreed that she should proceed to the next, and more demanding, part of the training.

The second stage focused on paramilitary skills and was based in Scotland, where the Special Operations Executive had ensconced itself in large, well-appointed houses along the Highlands' blustery western coast. Being a secret program, the site did not abide unsolicited visitors, with the Admiralty prohibiting anyone from entering this region of Scotland unless they were associated with the SOE. Certainly the content of the training justified the need for such extreme measures. "Here," writes historian David Stafford, "instructors taught agents more about small arms, silent killing, demolitions, sabotage, basic infantry training, fieldcraft, and elementary Morse code."[16] The sabotage component included lessons in disrupting or destroying railroad operations, skills that Virginia would, in due course, put to good use.

It was while the recruits were secreted away in this rugged Highland setting that the staff also strove to drill into them, more generally, the gist of their reason for being sent behind enemy lines. Above all, recruits, aside from what would be their specific assignments, were made to understand that they were being readied for one overarching task, namely, "to go into occupied territory to raise hell for the enemy," according to M. R. D. Foot.[17] In this respect, Virginia was already set. As to her four weeks of paramilitary training, she sailed through it with her characteristic zeal.

Upon the favorable completion of this stage of the program — up to one-third of the participants did not succeed beyond this point — recruits were taught how to parachute in anticipation of their airdrops into France.[18] Owing to Virginia's American citizenship, however, there was no need for her to acquire this skill since she could enter France in the legal manner, passport in hand. She therefore advanced directly to the third and final stage of program. The setting would be Beaulieu, situated near the English Channel, with the training compound encompassing a manor house and several country houses.

"The jewel in the crown of the SOE training empire was Beaulieu," says Stafford.[19] Regarded as a finishing school for spies, guest instructors from Scotland Yard and MI5 played a part in the curriculum by teaching recruits how to withstand interrogation by enemy forces. In addition, in-house staff provided trainees with further information about the Third Reich and the Nazi apparatus, as well as familiarizing them with potentially lethal law enforcement practices they might encounter in those regions of France in which they would be operating. Covert agents, for obvious reasons, needed to be aware of, and wary of, local police forces that were believed to be cooperating with the Nazis. But Beaulieu's cardinal feature, the one for which it became renowned, consisted of assigning false identities and cover stories to its soon-to-be operatives and helping them absorb and perfect them.

"[A]gents had to be taught how to play a part, how to act their cover," writes Foot. "To be one person in reality, and quite another in appearance — to *live* one's cover — was unusually hard, but vitally important: survival hinged on it."[20] To help the recruits absorb their new identities, they were required to speak French throughout their waking hours and practice meticulously the local customs in the regions in which they would be serving. Failure to comply with even the most trifling convention in enemy territory — for instance, using an eating utensil in the British manner rather the French — could be sufficient to expose an agent as an imposter and bring about the operative's death. Along these same lines, recruits learned how to avoid drawing attention to themselves, since it could be dangerous for a spy to invite notice. It could lead to closer scrutiny, which, in turn, could culminate in exposure and execution. Better to assimilate. Interestingly, Foot writes that the success of the SOE in instilling in its agents a superficial "layer of diffidence," a veneer of reserve and unobtrusiveness designed to deflect attention behind enemy lines, had the untoward effect of rendering many of these same men and women "rather indifferent company in peacetime."[21] Of course, Virginia would never be perceived as shy or apathetic or humdrum in wartime or in peacetime. The presence of her prosthetic limb, however, would appear to be another matter, a thorny one. As an undercover agent tying to avoid drawing attention to herself, one might assume that her artificial leg would make her conspicuous, memorable, and readily identifiable — three effects that could lead to her undoing as a spy. Yet learning to avert notice of her gait was a task Virginia had mastered several years earlier while recovering in Maryland when she found that she could cause her impairment to become largely unnoticeable simply by taking long, graceful strides as she walked. Reconciled to the prosthetic limb, she also nicknamed it Cuthbert.

With regard to her new identities, the staff at Beaulieu assigned Virginia two fictitious names. One of them, Germaine, was an internal code name she would use when communicating with the SOE in London or with her fellow agents in France. The other, Brigitte LeContre, was the name she would use as part of her public disguise in France. In this regard, Virginia was to be in the employ of the *New York Post*, at least outwardly, as a foreign correspondent in that part of France which remained unoccupied. In this capacity, she would write articles for publication designed to keep readers in the United States abreast of the political situation in this sizable region of France that was collaborating with the Nazis. In some instances, however, she was also to imbed in her articles coded messages for the Allies.[22] As it stood, her cover was a fine fit, since Virginia spoke French fluently and was experienced in writing political text as a result of her work with the State Department. Slipping into her second skin as Brigitte LeContre, Yankee stringer for the *New York Post*, would be a cinch.

Into the Labyrinth

It would not be a cinch, on the other hand, for Virginia to bide her time in England for the next five months while waiting for her mission to commence. Passivity was not in her nature. All the same, she understood that timing was crucial when planting operatives in enemy territory, that largely uncontrollable circumstances often determined when it was safe to do so. In Virginia's case, it also was important that a seasoned SOE figure — Jacques de Guélis, the man who initially interviewed her at the Northumberland Hotel — slip into France in advance to construct the basic architecture into which to insert her. Such groundwork needed to be laid with the utmost forethought, since Virginia, to all intents and purposes, would be acting as the nucleus of a sweeping espionage system in a critical region of France. In the meantime, she had no choice but to remain in England, so she used this period to further prepare herself for the clandestine life she would be undertaking. From April to August 1941, she polished her writing skills, practiced embedding secret code in letters and other documents, and returned to Beaulieu to refresh and refine her faux identity. It was not until after the dog days of summer had arrived that she finally received the call that she had been anxiously awaiting, the call to depart.

Shortly thereafter, Virginia journeyed by sea to Portugal and by land to France and the quaint spa town of Vichy. The previous year, the famed resort had been transformed into a key administrative center when, to the mortification of countless French citizens, it became the headquarters of the Free Zone (*Zone Libré*), also referred to as "Vichy France." Encompassing a sizable swath of territory, the Free Zone spanned two-fifths of the nation from the Auvergne to the Mediterranean Sea, and its loyalties were disconcerting as was its anti–Semitism. "[R]uled from Vichy by a French collaborationist government headed by Marshal Pétain," writes Martin Gilbert, "'Vichy France' was eager to accede to German demands with regard to the isolation, and eventual deportation, of Jews, both foreign-born and French-born."[23] Although Pétain ostensibly hoped that, through his cooperation, this segment of France would be able to retain a degree of autonomy and self-governance, it is worth noting that he also shared certain ideals with the Nazis. "Pétain was above all a rightist who looked backwards," says historian Mark Mazower. "What he wanted was to purge France of Jews, communists and freemasons, police society against trouble-makers and return to the putative values of peasant France — obedience, paternalism, family and hard work."[24] Because Pétain and his puppet government did not hesitate to kowtow to Hitler, Germany, at least for the moment, found no compelling reason to formally occupy the region. As for the remainder of France, it was designated the Occupied Zone (*Zone Occupée*), and encompassed such strategic territory as the entire Atlantic seaboard and the Channel coast, along with the city of Paris.

As the SOE's first female operative to be sent into the Free Zone, Virginia spent a week in the town of Vichy before moving on to the larger city of Lyon. Two hours to the southeast, Lyon was still within the Free Zone, and it was here that she established contact with several people whose names an

Allied pilot, Flight Lieutenant Simpson, had given to her.[25] One was a woman by the name of Germaine Guérin, and she was, in the colloquial sense of the word, a madam.

It was in Guérin's salon that Virginia became acquainted with the shrewd Frenchwoman and formed an alliance that would prove beneficial to the Special Operations Executive. As the proprietor of a brothel, Guérin employed women who were in a singularly well-placed position to extract information from their clients, among them Nazis or those in partnership with the Nazis. In the world's oldest profession, it was common knowledge that a certain share of men, knocked off balance by drink and in the throes of passion or the gauzy contentment of the afterglow, sometimes let down their guard. So Guérin made a delicious offer: her women would take mental notes at such moments and share the information with the Allies. Also important to the organization, Guérin, divulging that she was on friendly terms with local black marketeers, offered to help procure for Virginia and her agents the provisions they would require during their stints in the region. And Guérin further explained that she had a prominent male friend who was eager to cooperate with the underground, a French engineer who worked in an official capacity and thus could travel freely in any part of France. To be sure, the madam was a jewel. It was she, moreover, who recommended that Virginia make contact with Jean Rousset, a local gynecologist known to be sympathetic to the resistance.

To Virginia's delight, she found Rousset to be a mannerly, amiable gentleman who was firmly anti–Nazi in his attitude and convictions. When she first met him at his office, the middle-aged doctor voiced his desire to help undermine the enemy, adding that he had come upon other trustworthy souls who likewise yearned to be brought into the fold. With her usual alacrity, Virginia met three of them at a local café, where she determined that they would, in fact, be valuable assets to the SOE.

One was a gangly gentleman, Robert Le Provost, whose father had once owned a fleet of fishing boats in the port city of Marseilles. Through this firm, the family had befriended many of their fellow boat owners along the southern coast of France, and it was in this set of circumstances that Virginia spied an opportunity. To her, the family's contacts evoked the prospect of Robert Le Provost and his companions helping Allied airmen and prisoners-of-war escape from France by sea, along with any resistance agents who might likewise need to exit. With this in mind, she recruited Le Provost.

The two other dinner companions, the Joulians, were a cheerful couple who owned a factory that manufactured metalware — pots, pans, and such. Handily, the pair, in the day-to-day operation of their plant, had reason to check with suppliers regarding the availability of those metals they needed to make their products. In their line of work, such inquires were standard procedure, but Virginia realized the procedure was also one that the SOE could exploit. The Joulians, without raising eyebrows, could use their customary method of information-gathering to keep tabs on the enemy's supply of metals that were used in the manufacture of war materials, with a shortage being news the Allies could use to their advantage. Accordingly, the forward-thinking American added the Joulians to her team.

Virginia's ingenuity as the leader of what would soon become known as HECKLER, the code name of her circuit, is epitomized by the way in which she made creative use of three of these initial recruits. When Allied pilots, escaped prisoners-of-war, or resistance fighters ran into trouble, particularly in the Lyon region, they were instructed to get in touch with her. If they were ill or injured, she would arrange for Dr. Rousset to treat them. If they needed a place to stay, she would secure lodging at Madame Guérin's brothel, a fellow agent's flat, or a safe house. And if they needed to escape, she would make plans for Le Provost and his friends to smuggle them through Marseilles to Spain. Certainly her modus operandi was a smart and successful one. Within weeks, the redoubtable American had assembled a diverse and far-reaching collection of associates with skills in multiple areas, and she worked behind the scenes with them to meet the needs of those who came to her for help. Occasionally she met face to face with the latter, but often she tried to avoid direct contact with them. Like a general on a battlefield, Virginia, as the plugged-in strategist at the heart of the HECKLER circuit, needed to stay out of the line of fire. Better to remain as invisible as possible, in the shadows or completely out of sight, since the Nazis could obliterate the intricate underground structure she had constructed in the Free Zone if they were to get their hands on her.

It also is worth noting that while Virginia's style of operation, that of an unseen puppeteer pulling the strings, was decidedly effective, her intercessions themselves were not necessarily swift or simple. Ofttimes they were measured and multifaceted. Case in point: CORSICA, the code name of an ill-starred mission in which her methodical, protracted approach led to a rescue that was, on the face of it, highly improbable.

The CORSICA Incident

On a moonlit night in October 1941, the Special Operations Executive dropped a cache of weapons and a unit of undercover agents, including a pair of much-needed wireless operators, into enemy territory. Their mission was set to take place in the Free Zone, but the landing operation failed before the CORSICA project could truly begin.

"This time it had not been a very neat operation," says a former SOE agent with knowledge of the airdrop.[26] Upon descent, one of the agents soared off course and was discovered unconscious by the Vichy police. Worse still, the local gendarmes, who were working hand in hand with the Nazis, found on him a map to a nearby SOE safe house. They raided it without delay, then lay in wait for more agents to turn up. And, sure enough, more operatives did arrive in the ensuing days and walked directly into the trap. All told, the Special Operations Executive lost fourteen operatives in the CORSICA debacle, a "bad mauling" in the words of another operative.[27]

A few months later, in December, an SOE agent by the name of Benjamin Cowburn called on Virginia. Born in Britain, Cowburn had been reared in France, where he had been employed as an oil engineer prior to the war. After the German invasion, he agreed to work undercover with the SOE because of his expertise in the oil industry and his mastery of the French language. "He had a task of strategic importance," says M. R. D. Foot, namely, "to inspect as many French oil refineries as he could reach and report on how they could be sabotaged."[28] Like Virginia, though, Cowburn performed other functions as well, and it was one such task that brought him to her door. It seems he had an important message for her from SOE headquarters in London.

"At Lyon," Cowburn writes in his memoir, "I was surprised to find a tall, blonde, charming, capable American girl."[29] The change in Virginia's hair color — it also would be red, brown, or gray at times — was yet another strategy to throw off the enemy, this being the same reason she changed her cover name occasionally. So it was that Cowburn, over a meal at a black market café, explained that the organization needed her help with the CORSICA agents who were behind bars. Since their capture, they had been held at Beleyme Prison, which was located in southwestern France between the Loire Valley and the Pyrénées and was notorious for its dearth of food, malicious treatment of inmates, and contagions. In fact, one of the circuit's members, a wireless operator who was indispensable to the Special Operations Executive, had already been tortured and executed. A dire situation, the CORSICA operatives, with their range of talents, were urgently needed if other SOE missions in the Free Zone were to succeed. For this reason, the organization was asking Virginia to consider using bribes to secure the men's release, or, alternately, to arrange their escapes. It was a tall order, but the intrepid American did not flinch.

Around this same time, the wife of one of the imprisoned CORSICA agents also approached Virginia. Her name was Marie Bloch and her husband Pierre was a French member of the hapless SOE group. Because she was a French citizen who lived nearby, the guards allowed her to bring food to her husband who was confined in a hut with the other agents. And it was through these fellow agents, the British ones, that Pierre heard about Virginia Hall. Accordingly, when Marie next brought him a meal, he instructed her to travel to

Lyon and track down a woman by the name of Brigitte LeContre, Virginia's cover name as a reporter, and tell her about his SOE circuit that desperately needed her help.

When the two women met a few days later, Marie revealed even more horrors about the prison, such as rats gnawing on frail prisoners and guards thrashing the SOE agents. With a heightened sense of urgency, Virginia set to work devising a plan of action, one in which she would make maximum use of Marie Bloch. In Virginia's strategy, the two women would work in unison, although the Frenchwoman would assume the lion's share of risk insofar as she would be dealing nose to nose with the prison staff. Virginia, by comparison, would be in a less vulnerable position. Unlike Marie, she would not go to Beleyme Prison nor would she have direct contact with anyone associated with it. Instead, she would proceed through diplomatic channels, at least initially.

Since the United States still maintained an embassy in the Free Zone, Virginia traveled to Vichy and made an appeal to U.S. Ambassador William Leahy for assistance. Her request, however, was problematical. For one thing, she was asking the American Embassy to help prisoners who were not American citizens. For another, she could not divulge, even to the diplomat, that the men were covert agents who might be executed if they were not freed from Beleyme. The question, then, was why the American Embassy would intervene on their behalf. Yet Virginia, persuasive as ever, was ready with a line of reasoning. She managed to convey to the ambassador the mens' political importance even as she protected their covers, and she further pointed out that the fight against the Axis powers was a common cause, one in which the United States had itself recently become involved as a result of the Japanese attack on Pearl Harbor. And in the end, her argument was convincing, with the ambassador agreeing to speak to his colleagues in the Vichy government about the prisoners' plight.

During the early weeks of 1942, Virginia, as the core figure in a far-reaching spy network, was called on to perform a blizzard of tasks, but she persisted all the same in her behind-the-scenes efforts to liberate the CORSICA agents. She also remained in close contact with Marie, who updated her each week on circumstances in the prison and the conditions of the men themselves. To help the Frenchwoman acquire useful information, Virginia furnished her with counterfeit francs with which to bribe the guards. Virginia also kept in touch with Ambassador Leahy, who was working on the matter through backstairs channels in the diplomatic sphere. It was just a few weeks later, moreover, that her approach began yielding benefits.

"[O]n March 14, Virginia received the telegram she'd been waiting for," writes Pearson.[30] The remaining thirteen prisoners, the ambassador notified her, were being transferred to another facility, one that was a marked improvement over Beleyme Prison. As a gauge of Beleyme's ghastliness, the more humane facility to which they were being moved was a concentration camp in the town of Mauzac. In Virginia's view, the relocation was a step in the right direction, especially since the agents' health had been deteriorating in the penitentiary. Even so, it was not her ultimate objective.

Once the SOE operatives were settled in the concentration camp, Virginia put into motion the next stage of her plan, that of orchestrating their escape. Not only was there the humanitarian imperative, but this particular assembly of agents, as noted earlier, was critical to the resistance movement in this region of France. So Virginia, acquiring a considerable sum of francs, persuaded Maria to purchase through black marketeers certain types of supplies that would fool the guards into thinking that she was trying to make her husband's existence more comfortable. In reality, they were items that would help make possible the men's escape. And thus it began, with Marie taking meals to Pierre, such as tins of fish, with the metal containers being of use in crafting makeshift keys. As well, she took him books and fresh laundry in which she slipped wire pliers and other tools. And the ploy worked. An SOE operative and inmate named Georges Bégué, a man whose background included metalwork, eventually succeeded in fashioning a key that could unlock the door of the hut.

As the time drew near for the agents' getaway, two of them decided not to flee because they believed their lawyers' optimistic claims that their releases were imminent. The remaining eleven therefore decided to leave without them. To throw the guards off-track, the men crafted figures under their blankets to make it appear they were sleeping, while Marie persuaded a mess sergeant and a guard to escort them to safety. As usual, money was the enticement.

On a midsummer's night, the CORSICA operatives broke out of the concentration camp. Sprinting to a waiting car, they and their two collaborators drove several miles to a farmhouse which Virginia had ensured was stocked with fresh food and clothing. During the next few days, the newly liberated agents bathed, dined, and relaxed while forged identity documents were readied for them. In small groups, they next traveled to Lyon, where Virginia arranged for them to leave France through Spain. As Pearson writes in her book, *Wolves at the Door*, not only was the agents' escape a coup for the SOE and the resistance movement at large, but because the men had spent months incarcerated in prisons and concentration camps operated by the enemy, they gained detailed knowledge of such facilities.[31] For the Allies, this information was priceless in that it could be used to help other incarcerated agents. As for Virginia, the CORSICA rescue demonstrates the studied manner in which she performed her job: she made use of both diplomatic channels and clandestine networks, proceeded in a measured, stepwise fashion in reaching her goal, and remained largely out of the picture throughout the project.

Throughout 1942, Virginia was at the helm of numerous projects, both large and small, and was always available to help an SOE agent, French resistance member, POW who was on the run, or downed pilot who needed her services. "She was paying the price of having a strong, reliable personality," says Cowburn. "[E]verybody brought their troubles to her."[32] The former agent adds that Virginia did not seem to mind. "She was so willing to help that when a needy visitor came she would give her ration cards away, wash clothing and make contacts for him."[33] By all accounts, her flat in Lyon was very popular in spy circles during the war years.

Most remarkable, however, was her versatility. As we have noted, Virginia helped numerous operatives flee from France by way of the sea, but in many other cases she sent them on a route that traversed the Pyrenees. Then, too, she was adept at slipping covert agents *into* enemy territory, helping to masquerade operatives as French laborers and inserting them into Nazi Germany to acquire information and help destabilize the regime. Further indicative of her flexibility is the fact that the hearty American, during the initial five months of her stint in the Free Zone, continued serving as a stringer for the *New York Post*. To preserve her cover as Brigitte LeContre, she needed to be productive as a reporter. As to the articles she penned, the first was published merely a fortnight after her arrival and focused on the crippling shortages the local population was enduring. It did not paint an attractive portrait of the Free Zone, but the *Post*, to its credit, printed it without expunging the critical content, just as it published her ensuing articles without censorship.

Then, in the summer of 1942, a noose began to tighten around her. Virginia had, by this point, acquired a solid reputation among insiders in France and England as an efficient, and an exceedingly busy, woman who at any given moment was juggling an array of tasks. Unfortunately, her deeds had come to the attention of the Gestapo, too, although the Nazis thought she was a Canadian citizen, a mix-up that no doubt worked to her advantage. One thing is clear: Virginia had no intention of being apprehended and she therefore redoubled her efforts to remain undetectable.

The Nazis were equally motivated to catch her, however. Several ominous occurrences involving the Gestapo jangled her nerves at this time, one having to do with her new wireless operator, a forty-one-year-old man by the name of Denis Rake. Born in Brussels, Rake and his mother had fled to England during World War I, where he studied Morse code and became adept as a wireless operator. Years later, when the Third Reich rose to power and the Allies were in need of people skilled in transmitting code, he applied to the SOE and the organization welcomed the vibrant, openly gay man. And certainly it is true that Rake had enjoyed an active sex life in London's theatre district prior to the war. The stage, and other men, were his two supreme passions.[34] In terms of his SOE assignment, the organization dispatched him to the city of Lyon in May 1942, where he was to join Virginia and her HECK-LER circuit. Having recently lost a wireless operator, she was eager to receive him, agents with his specialized set of skills being in short supply. So it was that Virginia collected Rake at the train station and at once sensed his unease, a disquiet that presumably sprang from his inexperience and the menacing atmosphere of the city itself. Although the Free Zone was not officially occupied at this time, the German military presence was everywhere in evidence and was an unsettling sight. To soothe Rake's nerves, then, Virginia took him to a café and soon found herself enjoying the company of the friendly, forthright gentleman. "Good men are rare," writes Geoffrey Elliott. "Denis was one, and one of a kind."[35]

At first, Rake lived in Virginia's apartment, following which he lodged in a brothel. He subsequently moved to two other apartments in Lyon, since it was essential that he stay on the move so as to elude the enemy. Within weeks, however, Virginia caught wind of the fact that the Gestapo had him in their sights, and while she could not persuade the devoted agent to close up shop and return to London, she did find him amenable to serving in Paris, and, a few weeks later, Limoges. But, alas, Rake's good fortune was not to last. The day after his arrival in the latter city, a concierge tipped off the French police about his restive, suspicious behavior, and it culminated in his arrest. And Virginia's response was typical. "Never one to hang around," says Elliott, "she took the next train to Limoges."[36] Yet here, no doubt to her frustration, the authorities stonewalled her, denying knowing of Rake and thereby rendering her unable to act on his behalf. Her hands were tied. As for Rake, the quick-witted operative could at least take comfort in the knowledge that he had spent the summer providing a vital service to the Allies, three months being a respectable stretch of time for a wireless operator to survive and function behind enemy lines.

It was on August 15, 1942, that he was locked up, approximately a year after Virginia arrived in the Free Zone. With her wireless operator now behind bars and the Gestapo on the trail of the other agents in her circuit, she knew the enemy was even closer at hand. As noted earlier, her presence in the region, while not visible to the Gestapo, was nevertheless evident by its effects. "Condemned agents escaped from prison, pilots disappeared after parachuting to earth, acts of sabotage occurred in factories and on rail lines," writes Pearson. "The trail that the Gestapo was following in their investigations led to Lyon."[37]

It was during this same period in the city of Dijon, to the north, that another potent figure arrived, but unlike Virginia he was a force of darkness. He would, moreover, relocate to Lyon in the months ahead. Chief of a Gestapo commando operation, the man was Klaus Barbie and he had a notorious appetite for tracking down and assailing his targets. Among his victims were Jewish men, women, and children, along with resistance agents, communists, and a host of others. A classic sadist, the "Butcher of Lyon," as he eventually was branded, did not so much interrogate suspects as subject them to excruciating pain, applying electroshock to them, kicking and pummeling them, and even hanging them on meat hooks. Barbie also favored a dreadful torture in which the head of his victim was "repeatedly submerged into a bathtub filled with water," according to Margaret Collins Weitz, a form of torment that brings to mind the contentious use of waterboarding in more recent years.[38] Furthermore, it was only a matter of time before Barbie would zero in on the "Limping Lady," as the Gestapo mockingly nicknamed Virginia, placing her high on his list of targets.[39] In well-trod public spots, his minions would even affix posters calling for the capture of the "Canadian" spy.

Wisely, Virginia decided to change her names at this juncture. As the Gestapo moved closer, she adopted Philomène as her new SOE code name and Marie Monin as her cover name. Furthermore, it appears to have been this same sensitivity to the mounting Gestapo threat that contributed to her skepticism in regard to a new SOE courier who unexpectedly arrived in Lyon. His name was Robert Alesh, with his SOE code name being Bishop and his cover name, Abbé Ackuin. In the French language, abbé means "abbot," the superior of a community of monks. But this man was anything but holy.

Born in Luxembourg, Alesh completed college and seminary, after which he served in a clerical capacity in parishes around the city of Paris. With the outbreak of war, the clergyman, who was in his mid-thirties, joined in the resistance activities of one of these communities even as he continued serving in the church. Then, in 1941, he applied for a new position within the diocese, and the application process itself proved to be a defining moment in his life. It seems that the priest in charge of employment decisions, a German national, made him a Faustian offer: Alesh would be awarded the new job if he was willing to change his allegiance from France to Nazi Germany. And Alesh did indeed switch his loyalties, such was the magnitude of his ambition.

The Nazis, aware of the clergyman's former role in resistance activities, subsequently presented him with an even more disturbing ultimatum: he could either infiltrate the resistance and inform on its members or be confined in a concentration camp. Evidently, Alesh did not consider a third alternative, namely, that he wash his hands of the Nazis altogether and appeal for asylum in the resistance itself. Surely the underground would have granted it; better to protect a clergyman than suffer betrayal at his hands. But Alesh chose to become a collaborator, a double agent, and it appears to have been a job he relished. Succeeding beyond expectations, he not only informed on agents and exposed their plans, including those of the SOE, but he defiled the sanctity of the confessional by relaying to his Nazi controllers the confidential admissions he heard in the booth, incriminating information from confessants who trusted him with their physical and spiritual lives. "To many," says Pearson, "it was unbelievable that the clergy would stoop to such despicable actions."[40]

So it happened that Alesh, ten days after Denis Rake was arrested, materialized in Lyon. Turning up at Rousset's office, he introduced himself as a new SOE courier and asked to speak with Virginia. It was a customary method of making contact with her, one in which the doctor, in effect, screened those who were seeking her. After Rousset sized him up, Virginia came to the office, whereupon Alesh asked for a parcel of money to take back to Paris with him. The funds, he explained, were to be used to purchase microfilm and pay off informants. But Virginia, her skepticism mounting at this point in her mission, sensed that something was amiss and for this reason decided to shelve his request until she discussed her concerns with Rousset in private. Yet it turned out that the doctor held an altogether different view of the man. Judging him to be a fine agent in whom they should put their trust, he said that Alesh had been heard to criticize National Socialism in his sermons, as if this in itself removed the agent from suspicion. It certainly was not sufficient to convince Virginia, however. Respectful of Rousset's opinions but unconvinced of the soundness in this case, she sent an inquiry to London only to receive still more assurances in response. Alesh's qualifications had been scrutinized, her superiors replied, and he was deemed reliable. They added that she should give him the money he had requested. In the end, then, she complied with the SOE's instructions, although not without misgivings.

A week later, the courier returned to Lyon, but now Virginia had even more reason to be leery, having discovered in the meantime that a handful of SOE operatives with whom he had been in contact vanished without explanation. Furthermore, he had withheld this information from her on his first visit. For such reasons, she drilled him during their second meeting and again he failed to win her trust. As she brought to a close their taut meeting, an encounter marked by cat-and-mouse sparring, she instructed Alesh to return to Paris. He did not follow her instructions, however. Instead, the double agent secretly traveled to a town in the Auvergne, where he set about penetrating GREEN HEART, another SOE circuit. Upon gaining its members' trust, he persuaded them to share with him crucial information about Virginia and the other agents in her HECKLER circuit. Her hunch about the clergyman had been correct, then, but now her cover was in jeopardy and her capture by the Gestapo, more likely.

The escalating threat to her safety notwithstanding, Virginia remained in Lyon and pushed on with her duties. Such diligence, of course, was emblematic of her. Whereas the SOE encouraged its field agents to adhere to a revolving schedule — a six-month stint behind enemy lines followed by a period of respite in England — Virginia, at her own insistence, had already served nonstop in the Free Zone for over a year. Unbeknownst to her, however, her circumstances were about to change, a dramatic shift stemming from the course of the war itself. It began on November 7, 1942, when the American Embassy in Vichy, still under the impression that Virginia was a reporter from Maryland, alerted her to an Allied offensive that was just around the corner, one that promised to be a game-changer.

And, indeed, the following day an Allied invasion of North Africa commenced, with over a thousand ships, among them hundreds of warships, streaming to the Moroccan and Algerian coasts. Dubbed Operation Torch, the United States and Great Britain were its leaders, with the invasion encountering scant opposition from Axis forces. "Somehow, curiously, the armada managed to remain almost undetected by the enemy," says Dorothy Shipley White.[41] Although the attack was inspiring to the Allies and their supporters, the fact that it placed the United States on a war footing with Germany meant that Virginia would now be more vulnerable. "With the rupture of diplomatic relations between Washington and Vichy," writes Charles Glass, "American citizens in France no longer had an embassy to represent them."[42] Furthermore, the expectation was that Germany would proceed to occupy the Free Zone out of fear that Allied troops, once they were fully installed in North Africa, would enter France by its southern coast and liberate the country. For such reasons, Virginia, upon receiving the embassy's notification of the impending invasion, decided to return at once to London rather than risk being marooned in occupied and embattled territory.

Hurrying to Rousset's office, Virginia and a handful of fellow resistance agents set about destroying reams of incriminating documents stored in the basement. Afterward, she and the doctor planned her departure, a conversation during which she voiced her desire that Rake join her. Rousset, however, reminded her that their comrade, as far as they knew, was still in prison, and that Virginia herself could ill afford to linger.[43] Conceding the point, she boarded a train later that night for a journey that would take her to the town of Perpignan near the Spanish border, the first step in her passage back to England.

What Virginia did not know is that on this same day officials had begun transporting Rake to another prison. And what Rake did not know is that the Gestapo had given orders that he was to be executed upon arrival. It was now, however, that fortune smiled on him once again. The French commandant who was accompanying Rake to his final destination was sympathetic to the beleaguered agent's plight and decided to release him. He also slipped him a train ticket to Marseilles. "[Rake] was a man one short step ahead of the Gestapo, a man who could not remember when he last soaked in a hot bath, a fastidious man plagued by fleas and lice," writes Elliott. "But he was determined to push on."[44] And push on he did, boarding the train to Marseilles, and, in due course, traveling to Perpignan. From the border town, he would make the same crossing Virginia had embarked upon a few days earlier — on November 11, 1942 — this being the same day that the Germans commenced occupying the Free Zone. It was a journey that would entail negotiating the Pyrénées into Spain.

Passage Over the Pyrénés

A tortuous path, the mountain crossing was particularly treacherous in winter, with passage being nearly impossible due to soaring snowdrifts. All the same, Virginia, the quintessential can-do American, set out with a mountain guide and a trio of resistance fighters with whom she had become acquainted in Perpignan. Although the three men were strangers to her — a Belgian military officer and two Frenchmen — she had confidence in them. They were fleeing from the Gestapo and were en route to London, where they planned to share secret information with British Intelligence before returning to France to rejoin the resistance. Because she respected their aims, Virginia covered their expenses, the men themselves lacking the funds to pay the guide.

During the next forty hours, the group tramped through the Pyrénées, a thirty-mile hike that Virginia found especially grueling owing to Cuthbert, her prosthetic leg. Yet she suffered in silence, having decided not to tell the others about the device for fear they might be averse to traveling with her. Among other revelations, her State Department career had shown her the discrimination a woman with a physical defect may face in the company of men without such a handicap. Not that the men with whom she was traversing the Pyrénées had any reason to worry. Virginia kept pace with them easily enough, and she did even more: the shrewd American furnished them with Benzedrine. Thus, rather than hinder them, she more likely sped them up. An amphetamine, the drug endowed the weary group with the stamina needed for the crossing while also curtailing their appetites, an additional benefit in that their food supply was limited.

In terms of the trek itself, it was a hazardous one and not only because of the natural challenges it presented; equally perilous were four sets of antagonists who were on the lookout for people like Virginia and her companions. Among these were the Spanish border police whose ski patrols combed the mountains, their quarry being those trying to slip into the country without documentation. Another threat was presented by Francisco Franco's national law enforcement arm, as well as by ex–Spanish Republicans who had fled Franco's military and taken to the Pyrénées. The latter were notorious for ambushing travelers for their possessions. Then, too, Germans were embedded in Spain and were hostile to members of the French underground who were in flight. All of these elements were to be avoided.

Fortunately for Virginia and the others, they did not encounter any of these forces, not while they were high in the mountains at any rate. Their journey was reasonably safe and was even crowned with a surprising opportunity. Arriving at a safe house in the foothills, they found to their delight that its owners were in possession of a wireless kit that a previous runaway had left behind. Seizing this break, Virginia radioed SOE headquarters in London and informed her superiors of her whereabouts, her eleventh-hour exit from Lyon having deprived her of the chance to notify them that she was evacuating her post.

The next morning, she and the three men, their mountain passage behind them, hurried to a railway station in a nearby village. Their intention was to hop an early train to Barcelona where they could get their hands on forged passports. To their dismay, however, they found themselves cornered at the village depot by gendarmes demanding to see their papers. When they could not produce them, the officers jailed the foursome, with Virginia, in particular, spending nearly three weeks in a dank cell before the American consulate in Barcelona could secure her release. Anxious to proceed with her journey, she traveled on to Lisbon afterward, where she boarded a ship bound for Great Britain.

In the intervening weeks, Klaus Barbie continued scouring Lyon for the clever American, unaware that she had given him the slip. He and his underlings did manage to round up some of those who had been close to her, however, among them four members of her original cadre of collaborators. These associates consisted of Madame Guérin, Jean Rousset, and Mr. and Mrs. Joulian. Admirably, not one of them, despite being subjected to fierce interrogations, admitted to knowing Virginia or working with the SOE. They were steadfastly loyal to her and the organization. Not surprisingly, then, the Nazis sent the four to prison camps, with Rousset eventually being sent on to Buchenwald to serve as a physician at the concentration camp. Much to his credit, the courageous, forward-looking Frenchman used this turn of events to stash away the medical records of scores of detainees, incriminating documents that constituted potential evidence against the Reich.

Ultimately, Rousset, Guérin, and the Joulians survived their ordeals, but all of them suffered tremendously at the hands of their persecutors. Among other abuses, the Nazis snapped Mrs. Joulian's arm and broke out her teeth, as well as looting Guérin's brothel.[45] Yet Virginia's four loyal comrades at least lived to tell their stories. The same cannot be said of Robert Alesh, the clergyman and double agent. Under false pretenses, as we have noted, he obtained secret information about Virginia and the HECKLER circuit from members of the GREEN HEART operation to whom he ingratiated himself. Because he subsequently made use of this information to expose HECKLER's agents and strategies, French authorities are believed to have put the infiltrator to death after the war despite the absence of an official record documenting his execution.[46]

Respite and Reassignment

Christmas of 1942 found Virginia enjoying a holiday gathering in London with other members of the Special Operations Executive. She would not find the ensuing months nearly as delightful, however. Unlike the solid sense of purpose and the electrifying challenges she had experienced in wartime France, Virginia told her superiors that she felt inert now that she was back in England.[47] The fact is, she was itching to return to occupied France. The SOE, however, was firmly of the opinion that she should not go back at this juncture because her presence in Lyon had become too well-known. Klaus Barbie, for one, was still hunting for her, and Lyon remained peppered with posters calling for her capture. Better to stay in England for the time being, her superiors advised.

In the late spring, after Virginia had completed a standard "cooling off" period, the SOE decided that the political situation on the continent was such that it could offer her a comparatively anonymous spot, albeit in Spain. Francisco Franco, the fascist leader, wielded power at the time and many regarded the nation's political direction as unpredictable. Spain also was teeming with undercover operators of all stripes and thus was rife with information that could be potentially useful to the Special Operations Executive. And an informal escape route — an "underground railroad" — ran through the country for those escaping from occupied France, and it was believed that Virginia's experience could be helpful in ensuring its continued success. The organization therefore inserted her into Madrid in May 1943, where her cover, as before, was that of a reporter, this time affiliated with the *Chicago Times*. While she outwardly was working as a stringer, her covert assignment was to insinuate herself into the political realm and facilitate communication between the SOE in London and those escaping from France, as well as to identify locations for safe houses. Acts of subversion were out of the question, however, with all SOE operatives in Spain being prohibited from taking part in any such activities in the neutral country.

During the ensuing weeks, Virginia found herself feeling hamstrung and ineffectual, an echo of her preceding months in England. And as she came to the realization that she would probably never find her assignment in Spain gratifying, she appealed to the SOE for a new one. She was tired of lingering in the sun-drenched country when she knew that conditions in France were worsening and that her comrades in that nation were continuing to struggle mightily to thwart the enemy. Accordingly, the SOE, sympathetic to her sentiments, returned Virginia to England and enrolled her in an advanced wireless training program in Oxfordshire. But still she yearned to go back to France even as the organization stood its ground in opposing such a move. On this point, Virginia was appreciative of the fact that the SOE had her well-being at heart, along with the safety of its agents and operations in occupied France. But she continued to hold a different opinion, perhaps because of her remarkable confidence in her abilities as an operative.

The Office of Strategic Services

In due course, Virginia learned about the Office of Strategic Services (OSS). An American creation, it was not unlike the SOE in that its purpose was to apply unconventional methods during the war, guerrilla tactics among them. Also akin to the SOE, its membership was diverse, drawn from all walks of life. "Safecrackers were sprung from prison," writes O'Donnell, "and Ivy League professors were recruited to analyze what was stolen from the safes."[48] Yet there was a crucial element the OSS lacked and it had to do with seasoned espionage agents. "Very few professional spies existed, and, because of language differences, most Americans were not ideally suited for certain aspects of secret intelligence work."[49] Virginia, however, was an exception. Not only did she know France like the back of her hand, but she also was a well-trained, veteran operative who was fluent in German, French, and English. She could be of enormous value to the OSS and she knew it. In short order, she made contact with the organization, and, with the SOE's reluctant approval, shifted to the American venture. The SOE regretted losing her services and remained concerned about her safety if she were to return to France as an OSS agent, which was expected to be the case. Virginia, on the other hand, was relieved to be returning to the besieged nation after such a long absence. As it turned out, she would be doing so under the auspices of a truly swashbuckling organization.

The Office of Strategic Services was formed in June 1942, and proved its worth during Operation Torch when it acquired information that helped steer the Allied landings in North Africa. Contributing to its effectiveness, the organization was also on friendly terms with the Special Operations Executive, with the more senior British organization being in a position to provide OSS members with essential information, training, and partnership in selected field missions. Yet there were pay-offs for the SOE as well. "The British good-naturedly envied the relative wealth of resources seemingly at the command of OSS and other American agencies and hoped to share in that bounty to expand their own operations against the Axis," reads a CIA document.[50] Being on intimate terms with both agencies, Virginia would be in the unique position of being able to share information, practices, and materials between them.

On March 10, 1944, Hall signed a contract with the OSS, with the agency arranging to send her annual salary — four thousand dollars — to her family in Maryland. As it stood, she did not appear to be all that interested in her pay, perhaps because she was independently wealthy. Whatever the case, her sole focus seemed to be on getting back into France and resuming her undercover work.

A week later, Virginia boarded a train for Portsmouth on the south coast of England, where she met a fellow OSS agent with whom she would be slipping into the occupied nation. Peter Harratt was his name and Aramis was his code name. After a brief chat that evening, Virginia, who would be working under the code name Diane during the mission, set about preparing her new cover, that of a French peasant. A dentist in Britain had already removed her fillings and restored them using the continental procedure, this being an important detail since her dental work needed to look authentically French in case the enemy were to capture and examine her. Now, on the eve of her first OSS assignment, she continued assembling her disguise, dying her hair gray, donning a set of secondhand peasant garments, and packing them with a hefty amount of stuffing. The effect: the thirty-eight-year-old American transformed herself into an elderly, stout Frenchwoman with a stooped posture and a hobbling gait. A few hour later, she and Peter, whose façade was that of an old man, boarded a motor gun boat for the trip across the English Channel. The Allies favored such vessels for drop-offs of this sort because the boats were fortified, traveled at high speeds, and were difficult targets for German E-boats, or "enemy boats."

As it happened, the Channel was far from accommodating. Blustery weather and choppy waters accosted the two OSS agents and the crew, threatening a rough crossing. And, indeed, it proved to be an onerous experience. Nearing the coast of Brittany four hours later, Virginia and Peter scrambled onto a dinghy and made their way to land only to find the chore all the more arduous owing to a lashing rainstorm along the French shoreline. And further aggravating matters, the slippery rocks on which they finally came to rest caused Peter to lose his footing and injure his leg. Even so, the stalwart agents, undeterred, slogged to a nearby farm that was known for being hospitable to resistance agents, where they caught their breath before hiking to a neighboring village. It was, by any measure, a long and grueling night. Yet their journey was far from over. Morning would find the elderly couple, as the two continued to present themselves, on a train bound for Paris. As to the afternoon, it would be one of forlorn for Virginia, her sense of anticipation about her new mission turning to disappointment as she glimpsed her beloved Paris once again.[51] A very different city than the one she had left behind, it now was disheveled, deprivation and desperation being everywhere in evidence and the populace draped in apprehension.

"The Paris air is more highly charged with menace than at any time since the French Revolution," wrote Katherine Cannel, a former *New York Times* reporter who was living in the French city during the spring of 1944. "Invasion, civil war, siege, famine, prison — whatever form the future may take—

Parisians are minutely expecting the deadliest phase of the war."[52] It truly was a precarious period, a reality to which Virginia quickly became attuned.

After spending the night at a pension in the city courtesy of an old friend and fellow resistance agent, Hall traveled to a secluded farm near an out-of-the-way village southwest of Paris. During the coming weeks, she would live in a cottage with no running water or electricity while toiling on the farm — taking the cows to pasture, making cheese, cleaning the main house, and caring for the farm's elderly matriarch. Although the setup was a bit on the earnest side, its simplicity pleased Virginia, she who hailed from Box Horn Farm in Maryland. And she was further pleased to discover that her disguise and the locale itself offered unique opportunities for covert action. When she tended the cows, for instance, she surveyed the surrounding meadows to determine if they would make suitable sites for parachute drops. Along these same lines, when peddling her homemade cheese to German soldiers in the neighboring villages, she eavesdropped on their conversations and transmitted her findings back to the OSS. The exchanges that she overheard enabled the OSS to learn about German troop movements and the locations of the enemy's regional arsenals.[53] And Virginia made it a point to become acquainted with the local villagers, her motive being to size up and enlist those people, angry or dispirited or simply patriotic, who wished to help the resistance. By all accounts, the tenacious American's stint on the farm was a productive one. Regrettably, however, her output came to a standstill on a late spring day when a knot of German soldiers showed up at her door and without explanation began rummaging through the cottage. Worse still, she discovered a few days later that they had executed four villagers. Her cover seemingly in jeopardy, Virginia packed her wireless kit and personal belongings, bid farewell to her hosts, and rushed to a safe house in Paris to await instructions from the Office of Strategic Services. As it turned out, her orders would be swift in coming.

Within twenty-four hours she was back on the move, this time settling in the town of Cosne-Cours-sur-Loire, south of Paris. Here in the countryside she experienced firsthand what was also being observed in other parts of France, namely, that the country's diverse underground factions were becoming more integrated despite the fact that conditions in the nation itself were still disintegrating. Such teamwork was most visibly the case in those areas that heretofore had not endured the brunt of German oppression. "The arrival of the Wehrmacht and the Gestapo in parts of the country previously unoccupied," says Jean Lacoutre, "radically altered the character of the Resistance and incited the various different networks to coordinate their efforts."[54] A promising state of affairs, such cooperative attitudes would make Virginia's new assignment, that of a roaming organizer behind enemy lines, all the more effective and far-reaching.

In Cosne and its surroundings, she set to work constructing a new circuit. As before, it was called HECKLER, the recycling of the code name having been decided upon before she left England to embark on this new mission. As her second-in-command, she selected the gentleman who initially received her and gave her lodging in his home, Colonel Vessereau.[55] Certainly he was the right person for the job. The well-connected Vessereau was the local chief of police and already was in the process of assembling a resistance group when Virginia arrived. To his advantage, and therefore to the benefit of Virginia and the OSS, he was acquainted with a handful of police officers who, in turn, were in contact with approximately one hundred maquisards. The latter were members of the maquis, arguably the most formidable underground strike force in occupied France.

"A maquis is a scrub-wooded upland," writes David Schoenbrun, a former intelligence agent and journalist, "but it came to mean a new form of resistance: armed camps in the woods, ready for combat."[56] The maquis, whose modus operandi entailed stunning the enemy in fierce, finely-tune maneuvers, quickly came to be fêted across occupied France as a superb guerrilla force. Owing to its reputation, moreover, its membership and number of forays rose steadily, and herein lay a problem since it was not a government-funded military organization. "As the maquis grew," writes Schoenbrun, "it needed arms, training, leadership, food."[57] And this is where Virginia entered the picture. For the maquisards in and around Cosne, she was in a position to meet such needs, which is why they were enthusiastic about her arrival and eager to cooperate with her. But while these regional members gave her a hearty welcome and deferred to her on key matters, those in other parts of the country were not always as accepting or compliant.

In the Auvergne a few weeks later, for instance, the assertive American, to her aggravation, would encounter a small number of men in the maquis who disputed her authority. These subordinates in the male-dominated guerrilla force evidently found it emasculating to take orders from a woman in a wartime situation, a form of chauvinism that reflected both the era and the battlefield mentality itself. "There was no sphere of Resistance work where women were not involved," says Margaret Collins Weitz, "although the military and the *maquis* did not welcome them readily, and few held leadership positions."[58] Virginia was no shrinking violet, however. While she was generous in furnishing the maquis with money and arms, this being a major reason for her presence in occupied France, she was not above resorting to ultimatums. And her stance was unmistakable: follow her instructions or forego OSS support. She held the purse strings and did not hesitate to make it known when the circumstances called for it.

In the Cosne venture, the first of many she would spearhead during the summer of 1944, Virginia, with Vessereau's assistance, divided the region's maquis into four branches, each composed of twenty-five members. The rationale was to make the subversive organization more manageable, the one hundred-strong guerrilla force being unwieldy as a single unit. Next, she taught Colonel Vessereau, his wife, and a band of resistance fighters how to organize a reception committee for Allied airdrops. Several steps were involved and entailed scouting the area for a secluded drop site, signaling the arriving aircraft with flashlights, retrieving the supplies or resistance agents that floated to earth, and burying the parachutes so as to conceal the enterprise itself. Last of all, Virginia set up a trial run in mid–May 1944, one composed of an actual OSS drop of a dozen containers of guns and incendiary devices for the underground. To her satisfaction, the drop went off without a hitch, with the Vessereaus and their collaborators performing their roles with aplomb. In the Cosne assignment, then, Virginia organized and armed local resistance members as well as taught them important skills, thereby enabling them to function more autonomously after she moved on to her next assignment.

Its setting, as it turned out, would be the nearby village of Sury-ès-Bois, where she would arrive at the end of May. In this instance, Virginia outfitted herself as an elderly goat herder while stealthily tracking German troop movements and organizing parachute drops. By this point, her HECKLER circuit, like a mounting number of resistance circuits in occupied France, had become a joint venture of the OSS and the SOE. Among other subversive acts, HECKLER had taken to bombing Nazi offices and destroying enemy vehicles. For HECKLER and many other such teams, the prime objective was to disrupt and thereby weaken German forces in order to better enable the Allies, in due course, to enter and liberate the country. The all-consuming question was when this would happen. And for Virginia, the answer came at precisely this moment in the form of an OSS message notifying her, if obliquely, that a new phase of Allied activity was about to commence. An allusion to the Normandy Invasion, or D-Day, the predominantly amphibian onslaught would be the most massive of its type in human history.

"On the night of 5–6 June 1944, more than 4,000 landing craft and over 1,000 warships convoyed the troops across the Channel," writes Richard J. Evans, "while three airborne divisions began parachuting down behind the German defences."[59] Fifty thousand men comprised the initial assault, a number that would rise to over two million in the course of the operation.[60] The invasion, of course, would prove to be a turning point in the war. And for Virginia, one of only thirty-three American citizens who still remained in occupied France on the eve of D-Day, it would herald a new phase of her work.[61] Henceforth, her task would focus on facilitating, in two ways, the Allies' expansion into occupied territory. First, she and her circuit would protect those roads and bridges the Allied troops would need for their advancement. And second, she and her team would put out of commission those railroad lines and other elements of the infrastructure the Germans would need as they struggled to defend against the Allies' forward movement.

To this end, Virginia and her HECKLER circuit, within forty-eight hours of the Normandy Invasion, used plastic explosives to destroy four sets of railroad lines that the enemy used to transport its supplies. Success having been achieved swiftly in this undertaking, the OSS, twenty-four hours later, dispatched the intrepid American to the Auvergne to help coordinate that region's resistance activities. And true to form, Virginia immediately got down to business organizing the fighters, funding and arming them, and devising guerrilla missions. But still she did not rest.

July of 1944 would find her traveling more southward in the Auvergne to the village of Le Chambon-sur-Lignon, where she would organize and augment the local underground. A Protestant village in the predominantly Catholic nation, Le Chambon was a destination for persecuted Jews who made their way to it in search of sanctuary. And the underground helped them reach this refuge. "Resistance groups throughout France brought Jews, especially children, to Le Chambon," write Debórah Dwork and Robert Jan van Pelt.[62] Among other deeds, the villagers hid the Jews on farms, in group homes, or in their own homes, in some cases for years. As well, they enrolled them in schools, furnished them with false documents, and even helped them escape to Switzerland. On account of the residents of Le Chambon, thousands of Jews were able to elude the Nazis and their death camps. "And in the midst of all these good deeds," says Pearson, "Virginia was planning to build a formidable Resistance circuit."[63]

Bringing together the resistance members in and around Le Chambon, Virginia explained that she was setting up an operation that would be largely identical to those the OSS and SOE were putting together in other parts of the country at this same moment. She would oversee the one at Le Chambon, she added, providing it with funds, arms, and instructions. And although Virginia, as mentioned earlier, occasionally encountered pockets of defiance among some of the male members of the maquis, she knew how to deal with them. In all, she recruited fifteen hundred maquisards during this period, along with scores of resistance members from other groups, and sent these fighters on nightly raids. Their subversive deeds included downing telephone poles and severing telephone lines, damaging roads, and blowing up bridges. They also captured or killed nearly a thousand German soldiers, forcing the surrender of five hundred in a single attack. Moreover, the indefatigable Virginia, besides orchestrating such missions, coordinated nearly a dozen parachute drops during her stint in the Le Chambon region, as well as collecting and relaying vital intelligence back to the OSS and SOE.[64] To be sure, her actions were effective in helping to "soften up" this part of the Auvergne, thereby easing the Allies' entry into it.

In early September, with the liberating forces making headway in France, Virginia's OSS mission began drawing to a close. And it was at this time that the Office of Strategic Services notified her about a forthcoming drop in her area, one that would be composed of a pair of Americans. Lieutenant Paul Goillet was one of them, a Paris-born New Yorker who was eight years younger than her and possessed a razor-sharp sense of humor.[65] As it turned out, Virginia fell for him, with the two enjoying intimate moments in an abandoned chateau before returning to England a few weeks later. Here they shared a home until December 1944, at which point they decided to attempt one last mission together. Their plan, which the OSS sanctioned, was to enter Austria and help organize its resistance, their hunch being that the SS, in particular, would retreat into the Alpine nation as the Allies continued making advances on the continent. The couple was in for a surprise when they arrived at a hotel in neighboring Switzerland, however. It was May 1945, five months since they had left England, and the OSS notified them that their Austrian project had been cancelled. Yet it was for the best of reasons: Germany, they were informed, was to formally surrender within the next few days. So it was that the pair returned to Lyon, France, where Virginia reunited with her old friends and collaborators Madame Guérin, Jean Rousset, and the Joulians, before traveling on to Paris to celebrate the Allied victory in Europe.

The Central Intelligence Agency

In the course of the war, the King of England named Virginia a Member of the Most Excellent Order of the British Empire (MBE) in appreciation of her valiant deeds with the Special Operations Executive. Because the war was still in progress and she planned to return to covert service, however, she declined an audience with the monarch and instead accepted the honor privately in an office at SOE headquarters. Then, at the war's end, she learned, albeit after the fact, that France had likewise honored her, awarding her the Croix de Guerre avec Palme, its distinguished military decoration. And there was more to come. In May 1945, the United States announced its intention to bestow upon her the Distinguished Service Cross (DSC), making her its first female recipient in history. As was the case in London, though, Virginia respectfully turned down a ceremony at the White House in favor of accepting the decoration five months later in a small, informal gathering behind closed doors. And she sought such privacy from Washington for the same reason she had previously requested it in London: she hoped to continue working in the field of intelligence and thus wished to protect her identity and previous covert deeds. Although the war had ended, her fascination with the realm of intelligence had not followed suit.

In September, Virginia returned to Maryland and to her much-adored

Box Horn Farm while her lover, Paul Goillet, settled in New York City. The pair remained romantically attached, however, the difference in location notwithstanding. It was at this juncture, moreover, that Virginia completed her contract with the OSS, with President Truman disbanding the organization two days later. Yet she still had plans. In May of the following year, the forty-year-old former spy, wishing to return to political work, applied to the Department of State for a new position. In her view, her background as a Foreign Service employee, augmented by her contributions to the SOE and OSS in occupied France, had furnished her with inimitable experience the State Department would surely welcome. Certainly she was known and respected within intelligence circles, she being "the American-born 'housemother' to anxious secret agents and escapers," in the words of Geoffrey Elliot, "orchestrator of plots and plans, fixer of false papers, pay mistress, briber of Vichy police, and a virtual FedEx hub for the movement of wireless sets."[66] By any measure, her background was spectacular. Even so, the State Department, citing budget cuts, rejected her application for a position in the Foreign Service.

Undeterred, Virginia continued searching for a path that would take her back into the sphere of international politics, and in this respect she was dissimilar from other former members of the Office of Strategic Services. "Five of every six OSS veterans had gone back to their old lives," writes Tim Weiner, author of *Legacy of Ashes: The History of the CIA*.[67] Virginia did not wish to do so, however, at least not permanently, and for this reason was heartened to learn that the United States government was fashioning a new intelligence organization. Adding to its appeal, the agency had on its staff a contact from her days in the Free Zone, former ambassador William Leahy. Known as the Central Intelligence Group, the organization, to Virginia's delight, promptly accepted her as a field agent and in the course of the next two years dispatched her to Italy, France, Yugoslavia, and Switzerland. As before, it was on the pretext of being a journalist. As could be expected in light of the era, the organization was particularly attuned to what was perceived as the growing threat of Communism abroad, with Virginia's duties consisting, in part, of keeping abreast of such developments. But one development the Central Intelligence Group did not foresee was its own approaching demise. And, indeed, despite the excellent work by some of its staff, the Central Intelligence Group proved to be disappointment, a "misbegotten and short-lived organization," partly because of President Truman's lack of clarity as to its purpose, and, as a consequence, his faltering guidance.[68] Although the organization was disbanded within two years of its creation, however, this should not be taken to mean that the United States' intelligence gathering capability ended or even suffered with its dissolution. The fact is, the consensus in Washington was that the rise of Communism in the east, a development that many feared would lead to a Soviet Union offensive against the United States, made it imperative that there exist an extensive and robust intelligence service. The cold war would not wait.

"The creation of a new American clandestine service was at hand," says Weiner.[69] To this end, the United States set about constructing "the new architecture for the cold war" by enacting the National Security Act of 1947.[70] Signed in July of that year, this document, representing, as it did, a sweeping reorganization of the nation's defense and intelligence capacities, led within two months to the formation of the Central Intelligence Agency (CIA). As to the Agency's purpose, it was intended, first and foremost, "to keep the president forewarned against surprise attack, a second Pearl Harbor," writes Weiner.[71]

Virginia promptly joined the CIA and spent the next several months shuttling between New York City and various European capitals as one of the agency's first female operatives.[72] As had been the case so many times before, her cover was that of a journalist, a time-tested masquerade to be sure. Then, in late 1948, the Agency made the decision to pull her out of Europe and reassign her to one of its façades with offices in New York City, the National Committee for a Free Europe (NCFE). Co-founded by the CIA's Allen Dulles, the NCFE's board of directors included such luminaries as filmmaker Cecil B. DeMille and future president Dwight D. Eisenhower.[73] In terms of its functions, Radio Free Europe was perhaps its most well-known brainchild, a service that broadcast propaganda behind the iron curtain in response to Joseph Stalin's repressive campaign. As for Virginia, her job was to interview those men and women who had escaped from eastern bloc nations, with the material she acquired being incorporated into these broadcasts into Communist-controlled nations.

In the years that followed, Virginia increasingly found herself assigned to desk jobs within the CIA, a state of affairs she found unsatisfying. By and large, the agency was handing its field assignments to younger staff members in spite of their relative lack of experience. Then, too, Virginia's surefootedness and assertiveness, traits that had served her well behind enemy lines and no doubt saved many lives, were not always appreciated in the maledominated, buttoned-down hallways of Washington, DC. It was, after all, the 1950s, and she did not to conform to the conventional female role of the era, a role that would have been far too restrictive for her tastes. Still, her displeasure with her job responsibilities notwithstanding, she did remain at the CIA until she reached the age of sixty, at which point she had no choice but to comply with the agency's policy of mandatory retirement.

One development that did please Virginia, on the other hand, was her marriage to Paul Goillet. Since 1944, the couple had lived together intermittently, a circumstance that depended largely on the location of their job assignments. In 1950, however, the erstwhile spies tied the knot and settled comfortably on a farm in pastoral Barnesville, Maryland. And it was here, in a charming country village with a view of Sugarloaf Mountain, that Virginia Hall, sprightly as ever, passed the remaining sixteen years of her life tending to her garden, making cheese, solving crossword puzzles, and taking pleasure in the company of her husband and their beloved French poodles. By any standard, Virginia was an American original.

7

Hannah Senesh and the Palestinian Commandos

The drone of the plane made idle conversation difficult as did the gravity of the mission itself. It was not the kind of night that lent itself to small talk. Jammed into an aircraft on a cloudless, moonlit night were four Jewish commandos from Palestine, one of them a twenty-two-year-old Zionist by the name of Hannah Senesh. The Hungarian-born woman, along with her male comrade Reuven Dafne, would be the first to jump, with the duo parachuting into a Nazi-occupied region of northern Yugoslavia. From here, they would travel to neighboring Hungary. By all accounts, Hannah was keen to begin the mission. "She exuded happiness and excitement," Dafne said.[1]

As she floated to earth, Hannah could see a mantle of snow shrouding the forest beneath her. The next moment, she was drifting off-course, the gusty conditions carrying her astray. Then she was hurtling into a towering pine tree, becoming wedged in its branches and ensnared in her parachute. At once she cut the cords and plummeted to the ground, injuring her ankle on impact. Yet even though she was in pain, her spirits remained high. Shambling to a concealed knoll, she waited for her comrades to locate her. And it was now that she heard footsteps approaching in the forest.

"Halt!" a man's voice bellowed from the shadows.[2] Barefoot in the snow, he was wearing a frayed uniform and a cap bearing a red star, the Communist insignia. It was a promising sign, since his garb suggested he was a resistance fighter, a partisan. As he aimed his firearm at her, Hannah hastily explained, in a language the man did not appear to understand, that she was a friend, a Palestinian commando airdropped by the British whose assignment was to establish contact with the Yugoslavian resistance.

Moments later, more men arrived on the scene, all of them partisans.

After further attempts to converse, they concluded that Hannah was indeed a commando and they burst into laughter. They found it comical that the British would send a young woman on what they considered a man's mission. Ready to lend a hand now, they led her to their makeshift encampment where she found her three Palestinian comrades waiting for her. Gathering their gear, Hannah, the commandos, and the partisans spent the remainder of the night trudging through the snow, arriving at daybreak at a permanent command center of the Yugoslavian resistance.

The Palestinians were now ready to launch their rescue mission, one that would include helping Jews flee from Hungary before the onset of the German occupation. But a few days later, on March 19, 1944, Hannah received the jarring news that Germany had just invaded her homeland, the upshot being that her team was too late. The Hungarian border was, in effect, closed to them. So it was that Hannah wept, one of the few times she had been seen to cry in the course of the war. But she was not tearful for long. Rather, she refocused on her reasons for returning to Central Europe. Speaking to her comrades, she insisted they pursue their original aim of helping Jews flee from Hungary, even if it meant doing so in the face of the enemy. "[W]e're just sitting here, doing nothing," she protested.[3] As it turned out, Hannah would indeed enter Hungary three months later, not with her Palestinian comrades but with a ragtag group of men she met in an out-of-the-way village. It was an undertaking that would preserve her name in the chronicles of those Zionists who, at risk of life and limb, struggled to help their fellow Jews during the Holocaust. As for Hannah's life journey, one that led her to the snowy Yugoslavian woodlands, it had been both soulful and purposeful, and it began pleasantly enough in Budapest during the summer of 1921.

Privilege and Prejudice

On July 17 of that year, Hannah was born to a wealthy couple, Béla and Catherine Senesh, who already had a one-year-old son, Gyuri. A charming family, the Seneshes lived on an elegant, tree-lined street in an affluent section of Budapest, where they enjoyed the advantages that come with being well-known and highly esteemed. For many years, the family, like its forerunners, had been afforded great respect in Hungary.

Both Béla and Catherine had come from urbane, financially comfortable Jewish families that were well-assimilated into the fabric of mainstream society. Even so, Béla, in an effort to integrate more fully, changed his surname, Schlesinger, to the less Jewish-sounding Senesh (Szenes in Hungarian). Whether or not this enhanced his social acceptability, we do know that he was highly successful in his personal and professional endeavors. While still a university student, he landed a job as a newspaper reporter, and, a few years later, a position as a theatre critic. In due course, he also penned novels, poems, and newspaper columns, as well as becoming a celebrated playwright whose works were performed in Hungary and other European nations. It seems the soft-spoken, warm-hearted Béla was trying to live to the fullest because he believed his days might be cut short. Certainly he had cause to worry: during his adolescence, it was discovered he had a serious heart condition and probably would not live long. "From then on, he was a man in a hurry," writes Peter Hay.[4]

In the summer, Béla and Catherine celebrated the birth of Hannah (Chana in Hungarian), their only daughter. As was his way, Béla gave her and little Gyuri his undivided attention, intent on sharing as much time as possible with them. Being a writer, he usually worked at home, a luxury that afforded him many chances to be with his children. And he invariably seized on these opportunities. Besides holding morning and afternoon story-telling sessions with them, he also took them on strolls along the Danube and to the Budapest Zoo and other exhibitions. By all accounts, he bestowed his love on them at every turn, an embracing, heartening love that imbued the home. "From earliest childhood Hannah's environment was warm and cheerful," her mother said.[5]

Sadly, Béla did indeed pass away at an early age—he was only thirty-three—leaving behind six-year-old Hannah and her mother, brother, and maternal grandmother, who also lived in the home. As for Hannah's reaction to his death, she was hurt by it and missed him dearly. Most telling is the fact that, despite her young age, she dictated poems expressing her loss, verses her grandmother transcribed because Hannah was too young to record them herself.

Not surprisingly perhaps, Hannah wished to become a writer like her father. To this end, she created, while still a young girl, a periodical called the "Newspaper of the Little Seneshes."[6] It contained her writings as well as those of her friends. Gyuri contributed to the project, too, serving as the newspaper's illustrator, with the typewritten text being sold to neighborhood children and classmates for a youngster's currency—chocolates.

Well into her teens, Hannah remained steadfast in her plan to become a writer. "It's my constant wish," reads one of her diary entries.[7] At other times, she conveyed her belief that writing could be not only a means of expressing herself but also of helping others. Before long, she had written scores of poems and a number of plays.

A girl of many interests, Hannah also excelled as a student, a fact that became evident in elementary school when she seldom needed to study in order to achieve high marks. In due course, she tutored other students as well. Side by side with her intelligence, moreover, was her social flair and her thoughtfulness and dependability. "She was considerate, gentle, conscientious, responsible," her mother said.⁸ Adored by teachers and students alike, Hannah was a popular girl with boundless energy, a girl who was always on the go. During her high school years, she belonged to an assortment of organizations, among them literary, stenographic, and dance clubs. In addition, she was physically fit and athletically inclined, with her favorite sports including boating, swimming, snow skiing, and ice skating. A merry child full of vitality, she looked forward to a long and happy life, a sunny outlook that began to cloud in the mid–1930s as anti–Semitism mounted around her.

During this period, anti–Jewish demonstrations erupted at Hungarian universities, radio programs set about castigating the Jewish people, and anti–Semitic newspapers boasted ever larger audiences. From streetcars to cafés to schools, anti–Jewish sentiment could be heard without qualification or apology, the mainstream population blaming the Jews for the nation's ills and portraying the Jewish people as both a scourge and a threat. Such toxic regression would have been unimaginable only a few years earlier when the nation had a thriving, well-assimilated Jewish citizenry. Indeed, in the early 1930s nearly half of Hungary's lawyers and physicians were Jewish, along with sizable percentages of journalists and businessmen. Furthermore, Jewish citizens, although comprising only five percent of the total population, possessed up to twenty-five percent of the nation's wealth.⁹ To be sure, they had ascended to the point of playing critical roles in Hungarian society. But now, as anti–Semitism blazed in Germany, so it re-emerged in Hungary, whose government hoped to curry favor with Hitler in an effort to regain the territory it had lost in World War I. "Hungary had a lot to gain by co-operating with Germany," writes Anthony Masters, "but the Jews, of course, had everything to lose."¹⁰

As for Hannah, she had been brought up in a home that placed little emphasis on its religious heritage. Although the Seneshes were assimilated Jews — Béla actually considered himself a humanist — they did not participate in the life of the Jewish community other than observing the major religious holidays. Even so, society's adverse attitudes toward the Jews still impinged on them at times, Hannah included, most notably as Hungary began aligning itself with Nazi Germany.

An occurrence in 1935 is illustrative. A highly regarded Protestant high school for girls opened in the Seneshes' neighborhood and announced it would accept Catholic and Jewish students. But there was a proviso: Catholics would be required to pay double the standard tuition while Jews would be charged triple. Although Catherine was piqued by the disparity in cost, she enrolled Hannah nevertheless because she wished for her to have the best education possible. And the money was well-spent. Hannah quickly because a star student at the academically demanding school, a successful year that caused Catherine to conclude that her daughter was scholarship material. Accordingly, the elder Senesh approached the school's administrators at the beginning of the next term, called attention to her daughter's scholastic excellence, and requested that Hannah be granted financial support. But to Catherine's dismay, the administrators refused, although they did agree to charge her double, rather than triple, the tuition paid by Protestant students.

In the ensuing months, anti–Semitism continued to spread throughout Hungarian society, with Hannah becoming more and more sensitized to the intolerance and discrimination that surrounded her. "Only now am I beginning to see what it really means to be a Jew in a Christian society," the fifteen-year-old wrote in her diary.[11] She entered this comment in the spring of 1937. In the autumn, she would experience bigotry even more directly.

It was September of that year and Hannah had just returned from a summer holiday in Italy. When she started back to school, her classmates, to her delight, elected her to the position of secretary of the Literary Society, a job she knew she would relish owing to her love of writing and her plan to become an author. But events suddenly took a sour turn: it seems the older students objected to her holding the position and they did so solely because she was Jewish. The upshot was that the votes were tossed out and a new election held, one in which Hannah was not allowed to run for office. As could be expected, she was deeply hurt by this turn of events and felt angry and indignant as well. Among other consequences, she lost interest in the Literary Society, and, for that matter, appears to have lost much of her interest in school itself. Side by side with her disillusionment, however, was a burgeoning awareness and appreciation of her Jewish roots. At this revelatory moment, Hannah's attraction to Judaism intensified, as well as her interest in Jewish history and the plight of contemporary Jews in Hungary and other European nations. In addition to reading avidly about these subjects, she also embarked on a study of the Hebrew language and began attending meetings of the Maccabee Society, a Jewish organization. Clearly, she was fashioning a robust Jewish identity, the rebuff she suffered at school having served as a catalyst. Unfortunately, coinciding with her evolution in this regard was Hungary's stepped-up efforts to disempower and suppress the Jewish citizenry.

In 1938, the Hungarian government began crafting anti–Jewish laws akin to those that were in place in Germany, although in certain respects the Hungarian versions were even stricter. The legislation sought to both restrict Jews' rights to participate in national life and limit their economic influence. By all accounts, these ominous developments cast a pall over Hungarian Jews, including Hannah and her family.

The first law, which was enacted in May of that year, was titled the "Bill for the More Effective Protection of Social and Economic Life."[12] Known as the "First Jewish Bill," it was an unsightly document. "The anti–Jewish Law of 1938 set in motion the machinery that removed the Jews from Hungarian life and culture and thereby opened the door for further discrimination against them," writes Zsuzsanna Ozsváth. "It decreed that 15,000 Jewish professionals were to lose their jobs within the next five years, which meant that, including their families, 50,000 people would lose their daily bread."[13]

Hannah, always astute, could see the writing on the wall. Five months after the First Jewish Law was set into motion, she penned a striking entry in her diary. "I've become a Zionist," she wrote. "I now consciously and strongly feel I am a Jew, and am proud of it."[14] Palestine, she added, was in her future. She had decided to move to the Middle East to help forge a Jewish national homeland.

With this declaration, Hannah began letting go of Hungary. Although she still felt close to her mother and wished for Catherine, as well as Gyuri, to emigrate with her, Hannah was in the process of emancipating. Her diary reveals that she now regarded her former interests — school, sports, and socializing — as superficial. Along these same lines, she no longer felt an affinity with many of her friends, including those who were Jewish and whose families were converting to Christianity in a futile attempt avoid discrimination. Hannah disapproved of such strategies. And, most consequential, she began setting into motion her departure by applying to a school in Nahalal, Palestine, an institution known as the Girls' Agricultural School. In her heart and mind, she already had begun living in Palestine.

It was also around this time that Gyuri graduated from high school. Although he had hoped to attend college in Austria, recent political developments made this plan doubtful. In due course, he moved to France and enrolled in the University of Lyons to study textiles. Before long, he too became an avowed Zionist.

As Hannah began preparing for life in the Middle East — a move that her mother opposed but did not impede — the Hungarian government in 1939 took the oppression of the Jews to the next level by means of further legislation. "The second set of anti-Jewish laws," writes Ozsváth, "formulated harsher goals and restrictions than were in the first one. It focused on the difference between the Jews and the Hungarians, describing it in racial terms."[15] Jews were now banned from serving as teachers or attorneys or members of parliament. To further diminish their power, the government confiscated their land. It therefore is understandable why Hannah could see no future for herself in the country of her birth; it was becoming a nation she no longer recognized. According to Catherine, Hannah, deeply demoralized, described her existence in Hungary as "miserable."[16]

By the time World War II commenced in September of that year, Hannah was fully prepared to relocate to the Middle East. Accordingly, the intrepid eighteen-year-old, who had obtained an immigration certificate and been accepted by the Girls' Agricultural School in Nahalal, packed her belongings and joined a group of Slovaks on a week-long journey to Palestine. Leaving

Budapest by train, she boarded a ship two days later, and, after a pause in Istanbul, arrived at the port in Haifa. At long last, she had reached the land of her dreams. But then came the reality. "[N]othing in her preparations," writes Hay, "could have anticipated the shock of actually confronting her dreams."[17]

Palestine

Whereas the Budapest of Hannah's early years had been an old-world gem of grand palaces, lavish opera houses, and quaint cafés, the small village of Nahalal was an altogether different matter. Situated between Nazareth and Haifa, the settlement, with its scorching sun, bone-dry air, and proximity to marshes, had been the scene of a deadly spate of malaria in the early years of the twentieth century. It was an adversity that had cost the lives of many of Nahalal's pioneers, Zionists who had journeyed from Eastern Europe to construct Palestine's first cooperative agricultural community. As it turned out, those who managed to survive the outbreak were able to bring into existence a number of farms and orchards, while attracting even more residents. Among the newcomers was the Dayan family, including young Moshe Dayan, the future Defense Minister and Foreign Minister of Israel. And yet, despite the agrarian strides made by those who crafted the community, the region itself retained much of its harshness, with its uninviting conditions taking Hannah aback when she arrived.

A further adjustment involved the Girl's Agricultural School, which was poles apart from the private school she had attended in Budapest. A fraction of its size, the Palestinian school had a two-year residential program that required daily hands-on labor interspersed with classes in subjects such as chemistry and botany. The school day itself stretched from daybreak to sundown, and was, by all accounts, grueling. For Hannah, it also was ill-suited. Because of the dawn to dusk agenda and dormitory living arrangements, she seldom had the time, energy, or privacy to reflect upon her circumstances and write poems or diary entries. In fact, during her first few days at the school she wept when alone and questioned her decision to relocate to Palestine. "I made an accounting of what I had left behind," she wrote, "and I didn't know whether the move would prove worthwhile."[18]

Ultimately, the forward-looking Hannah decided, at least for the moment, that she had made the right choice, and she persevered in her classes and chores. Among other tasks, she toiled in the chicken coops, picked olives, scrubbed the milking sheds and horse stables, and worked in the school's bakery. And there was more. She also performed domestic duties, with these being rather new to her. It seems she had not swept floors or washed dishes before moving to Palestine and had to be taught the proper way to do so.

On the social front, Hannah, as the months passed by, became increasingly estranged from those around her. A familiar pattern, she had grown away from others in Budapest as well, including people her own age. In addition, her diary reveals that she felt frustrated living at the outer reaches of critical world events, being situated, as she was, in a far-flung village in the Middle East while Europe was embroiled in war. And she continued harboring doubts about whether she was using her talents wisely, whether there might be a more substantial way for her to help advance the Jewish movement in Palestine. It was a reasonable question, of course, one she could have been expected to ask herself in light of her literary talents, leadership abilities, and ideological passions.

Still, her uncertainties aside, Hannah completed the agricultural program and graduated in 1941, following which she settled at Kibbutz Sdot Yam to carry on with her work. A primitive settlement located near Haifa — it eventually would move to Caesarea on the shores of the Mediterranean Sea — the collective was comprised of a handful of huts and tents, with Hannah living in the latter. Not only was the kibbutz stark beyond any conditions she had ever encountered, but the weather in the region was truly unforgiving. So harsh were the winters that she had to wrap rags around her body to keep warm. Owing to the cold, she also had difficulty writing; her fingers were too stiff. And storms were a problem, tempests of such ferocity they blew away the tents. All the same, the tenacious twenty-one-year-old labored tirelessly at the kibbutz in the face of these and other hardships. One question that no longer preoccupied her, however, concerned the approach she had chosen to fulfill her Zionist objectives. After two years of questioning her decision to spend her days performing manual labor, Hannah had concluded that she was, in fact, failing to use her most valuable abilities in the construction of a Jewish homeland. And loneliness remained a problem for her, too, judging from her letters and personal notes. It seems she still lacked a sense of solidarity with the other kibbutzniks.

"Why do I stay on here, anyway?" an exasperated Hannah wrote in her diary in early 1943.[19] At this juncture, she was clearly ripe for change. While her struggles at the Girls' Agricultural School and Kibbutz Sdot Yam had strengthened her mind and body, as well as eliminated many of her illusions and enhanced her self-awareness, she knew the time had come to embark upon a fresh path. And it was during this period that a thought occurred to her.

"I was suddenly struck by the idea of going to Hungary," reads another of her entries. "I feel I must be there during these days in order to help organize youth emigration, and also to get my mother out."[20] Hannah added that she knew the idea, although appealing, was "absurd."[21] Certainly she had reason to think it was preposterous given that the continent of Europe was ablaze with war, with Jews being prohibited from entering many countries. Yet shortly after she formed the idea of returning to Hungary to liberate her mother and other Jewish citizens, the real-life opportunity opened up before her. "[T]he pattern of events was strangely coincidental," writes Masters.[22]

In February 1943, a Hungarian-speaking man by the name of Yonah Rosen showed up at Kibbutz Sdot Yam. He was a twenty-three-year-old Zionist from Transylvania who was living on a kibbutz near the Sea of Galilee. During a lengthy conversation with Hannah, he disclosed a secret plan that was being devised whereby a corps of Jews from Palestine would parachute into Hungary and set about arranging the escapes of endangered Jewish citizens. Three other countries were also targeted for such missions, namely, Romania, Slovakia, and Yugoslavia. Rosen asked if Hannah knew of any Hungarian-speaking Jews in Palestine who might be willing to serve as commandos in the daring operation. It was precisely the "absurd" mission she had been picturing.

"I was truly astounded," she wrote in her diary.[23] "I see the hand of destiny in this."[24]

True to form, Hannah volunteered on the spot and never looked back. Construing the opportunity as providential, she later wrote that her former experiences in Hungary and Palestine had primed her for the demanding operation.

To say the escape plan itself was audacious would be an understatement. Described as a treacherous mission, even an act of "suicide," it was one from which few volunteers, if any, could be expected to return.[25] As to its specifics, the undertaking was a joint venture of the British military in Cairo and the Palmach, an elite arm of the Haganah, which was a Palestinian paramilitary organization created for Jewish self-defense. The Palmach was a top-notch, if illicit, strike force, and its operations were covert.[26] In this instance, the Palmach found itself at the service of its British partners, which included British Intelligence, since it was the Allies who possessed the planes necessary to drop the Jewish commandos into Central Europe. Certainly the British did not hesitate to take advantage of their superior position in the proposed operation by insisting that priority be given to their own interests.

More precisely, the British military agreed to drop approximately thirty Jews from Palestine, as well as a handful of Jewish members of the British army, behind enemy lines in Central Europe. To be inconspicuous, most of the volunteers would be natives of the four countries targeted for the mission, which, as we have noted, included Hungary. Once they were in place, their immediate task would be to make contact with local resistance figures and enlist their aid in setting up escape lines. The Jewish commandos' overarching task would be to help downed Allied airmen get out of the country, as well as prisoners-of-war who had broken free from confinement. Only after they had aided as many such men as possible could they to turn their attention to plight of European Jews and help liberate them, too.

A few weeks after Hannah volunteered to take part in the mission, she was ordered to submit to an interview before a joint British-Palestinian panel. Comprised of British military officers and two high-ranking figures in the Palmach — Ben-Gurion was one of them — the atmosphere in the room was tense. This is because relations between the British and Palestinian representatives were strained owing to the undeniably lopsided, inequitable nature of the mission. All the same, Hannah handled the situation with aplomb, effectively addressing all of the questions that were put to her, and thus found herself officially accepted as a member of the clandestine project. She subsequently sought and received permission from Kibbutz Sdot Yam to enlist in the British military, in particular the Women's Auxiliary Air Force. No one at the kibbutz was allowed to know, however, that she also was signing on to a secret Palmach mission.

In the summer of 1943, the intrepid Hannah attended a series of seminars, ideological in nature, at a mansion in Haifa. They lasted a month and furnished her and the other commandos with material they could impart to the imperiled Jews they would be encountering in Europe. It consisted of information about the history of anti–Semitism, the dangers facing the Jews of Europe, and the comparative safety of the Jews of Palestine. Designed to promote Zionism, the material also was intended to offer "a Jewish message of hope in this darkest hour," writes Hay.[27]

After finishing the classroom component, Hannah, in the autumn, traveled to a site near Tel Aviv to undergo the Palmach's paramilitary training program. Having renewed her sense of purpose, she once again was inspired and enthusiastic. "Preparing for the mission," says Hay, "helped to diminish her sense of futility."[28]

At the Tel Aviv site, Hannah completed several weeks of basic training during which she learned how to parachute and, equally important, how to protect herself. Among the self-defense measures she acquired was a familiarity with martial arts, along with the use of a Thompson submachine gun, known also as a "Chicago Typewriter" or Tommy gun. In addition, she became adept in the basic techniques of guerrilla warfare, such as learning how to set up an ambush, penetrate an enemy camp, and apply intimidation methods. Intensive and pragmatic, the Palmach program taught Hannah how to kill in order to survive.

The final step in her preparation would take her to Egypt, where British Intelligence would instruct her in additional covert procedures. Before this would occur, however, she would attend a party in Tel Aviv with her fellow commandos, a going-away salute at which Golda Meir, the future Prime Minister of Israel, would be present. As it happened, this celebration, held on

Hannah's last day in Palestine, would be the same day she would see her brother once again.

It seems that Gyuri, owing to the German occupation of France, had proceeded with his long-standing plan to flee to Palestine. But it was no easy matter, with the young Hungarian being forced to escape over the Pyrénées into Spain, where he spent the ensuing year confined in a prison camp. Hannah, for her part, did not know about his impending entry into Palestine, correspondence being what it was during wartime, and for this reason found herself besieged with emotion upon learning about his arrival. She was caught entirely off-guard. Of course, this quirk of fate, the fact that he arrived just as she was leaving, was not lost on either of them. "The time they had together — a walk, a meal, and a flood of conversation — was unreal," says Masters.[29] Still, the irony notwithstanding, the occasion provided the two with a final chance to be together, a bittersweet moment they would cherish.

The next day, Hannah and the other Palestinian commandos set out for a British military compound outside of Cairo. In the sun-baked setting, the British lodged them in private houses, kept them abreast of political developments in Central Europe, and provided them with opportunities to hone their parachuting skills. As for the intelligence training, it centered on covert acts such as operating a wireless transmitter, snapping photographs surreptitiously, forging documents, and divulging misleading information if captured. The British also showed them gruesome films of Nazi torture — it was important that they know what to expect should they find themselves in such a situation — and instructed them in the use of cyanide capsules in case suicide became necessary. In all, the training was painstaking, and the commandos, well-prepared. As fate would have it, though, just as the instruction was wrapping up and the team was preparing to embark on its mission, the situation in Central Europe took a turn for the worse.

It seems that swiftly-changing political events prompted British officials to conclude that a German invasion of Hungary was in the offing. More precisely, Admiral Miklós Horthy, the Regent of Hungary since 1920, had become disenchanted with the Nazis and their efforts to strong-arm his nation into further persecuting its Jewish citizens. In addition, he had come to realize that the Allies would likely prevail in the war, and he did not want his nation to be on the losing side. For such reasons, he began courting the Allies, suggesting through an intermediary that he was amenable to an unconditional surrender. Yet while Horthy's decision to craft an armistice with the Allies was no doubt promising for Hungary, particularly for its remaining Jewish population, it risked setting into motion a radical German reaction: an invasion and occupation of the Central European nation.

Certainly it was a possibility that did not go unnoticed by British officials in Egypt. Anticipating such an incursion, they scrubbed the planned airdrop into Hungary and replaced it with a similar strategy that would dispatch Hannah's team to neighboring Yugoslavia. Of course, Hannah suspected that a Nazi incursion would doom the one million Jews of Hungary, her mother among them, and she was outraged by the British decision to cancel the original plan. In fact, the change of strategy appears to have been a turning point for her. According to a fellow commando, Hannah became "difficult" from this point onward, meaning more obstinate as well as more determined to enter Hungary to save her mother and other Jews.[30] "She no longer chatted, only complained," writes Maxine Rose Schur.[31] In the meantime, Hannah outwardly agreed to comply with the British plan, since it would, if nothing else, provide her with the means to return to Central Europe.

Commandos on the Continent

Shortly thereafter, the British military transported Hannah and her comrades to an airport in the Italian town of Brindisi, across the Adriatic Sea from Yugoslavia. The other members of her unit, all of them men, were made up of Reuven Dafne, Abba Berdichev, and Yonah Rosen, the young Transylvanian who had originally contacted her about the mission. An organizational escort, Enzo Sereni, accompanied them on the flight as well, while two other Palestinian commandos, Yoel Palgi and Peretz Goldstein, were set to join them later. And so it was that Hannah and her team climbed into a cramped airplane on the evening of March 13, 1944, armed with maps, a wireless kit, and knives sewn into their clothing. Later that night, they parachuted into a snow-covered forest in the Balkans, this being the airdrop recounted at the outset of this chapter in which the Palestinian commandos joined up with a group of Yugoslavian partisans.

Six days later, Hannah and her group received alarming news: Germany, as expected, had invaded Hungary, the consequence being that it now appeared impossible for them to cross into her homeland. Unnerved by this state of affairs, Hannah became even more fractious.[32] She already was piqued that the British had dropped her into Yugoslavia instead of Hungary, and with the Hungarian boundary now being sealed it seemed she might never be able to rescue her mother and other Jews. Yet she still yearned to enter Hungary, the enemy presence notwithstanding. And she did more than yearn. By all accounts, Hannah became single-minded, even adamant, in her quest, insisting that her fellow commandos travel to Hungary with her as they had previously planned. They refused outright, however, arguing that such an undertaking was far too risky, even foolhardy, and that they would be signing their own death warrants. So Hannah, conceding defeat if only for the moment, reluctantly agreed to remain in Yugoslavia and continue taking part in subversive operations since she knew it would be far too hazardous to travel alone to Hungary. But she was not willing to forego her true mission. She would simply bide her time.

During the spring months — March through May 1944 — Hannah, the commandos, and the partisans concocted escape routes for Allied airmen whose planes had been shot down, and they also carried out guerrilla operations against the occupying forces. The latter included waylaying German patrols and sabotaging trains, all the while dodging the enemy and seeking cover in wooded areas. Even though the resistance fighters were triumphant in these operations, Hannah did not feel that their episodic acts of subversion were sufficient. She continued arguing that the Palestinians' efforts, in particular, could be put to better use in Hungary where the situation for Jews was especially harrowing at the moment. Certainly she was right about the urgency of the situation in her home country.

"Within two weeks of the German army entering Hungary, the Jews were being forced to leave their homes in more than five hundred towns and villages and move into ghettos," writes Martin Gilbert. "Within another six weeks they were being deported to Auschwitz."[33] While Hannah and her comrades trudged through the Yugoslavian woodlands, thousands of Jews were being herded into cattle cars destined for extermination camps, a horrific fact she learned from a group of fleeing Hungarians her team encountered. And with this, her determination to help Hungarian Jews was revived. Not only was she feeling that her acts of resistance in Yugoslavia were insubstantial in relation to the magnitude of the war, but she also had lost confidence in the partisans with whom she and her comrades were collaborating. She had reason to believe the partisans did not intend to help them in their efforts to save imperiled Jews if and when the time came. And it was at this point that she became dead-set on entering Hungary even if no one came with her. "I don't know what I've done to deserve this sacred task," she told commando Yoel Palgi in an emotional conversation in the forest, "but I do know that having begun, there's no turning back for me."[34]

Ultimately, Hannah's comrades did agree to join her, although last-minute setbacks, wholly unforeseen, made it impossible. Yoel Palgi, for his part, arranged to meet up with her at a later date in front of Budapest's principal synagogue, or, if the temple was inaccessible, at the city's main cathedral. And while Hannah was agreeable to renewing contact with Palgi in the capital city, at the moment she was still itching to depart. For this reason, she decided to cross the border alone, with Reuven Dafne and a small band of partisans escorting her to a spot near the Hungarian boundary.

For the next twenty-six days, the group trudged through the woodlands. Because the area through which they were traveling was teeming with Nazis, their excursion was long, arduous, and often circuitous. "Sometimes they slept in stables," writes Atkinson, "sometimes they hid during the day and traveled only at night."[35] At last they arrived at a village near the Hungarian border, and it was at this juncture that Hannah improvised a last-ditch plan of entry that included some unforeseen cohorts.

In this final scheme, she asked three men, refugees who recently had fled from Hungary, to join in her audacious undertaking. Hannah met them, along with the smuggler who had devised their getaways, in the village shortly after she arrived. It was a chance encounter that she perceived as a timely opportunity. The three refugees included two Hungarian Jews—a Zionist named Kallós and his friend, Fleischmann—and a former French prisoner-of-war, Tissandier. The latter had found sanctuary in Hungary prior to the German invasion. Passionate and persuasive as ever, Hannah managed to convince the scruffy trio to steal back into Hungary with her notwithstanding the fact that it was crawling with enemy troops. And it was shortly thereafter, as she and these collaborators were preparing to slip into the occupied nation through an unguarded stretch of land, that Hannah handed Dafne a piece of paper on which she had written a poem, *Blessed Is the Match*. It was June 9, 1944, and it would be the last time he would ever see her.

In Hungary, during this same period, the Third Reich's program to transport the nation's Jews to Auschwitz and other extermination centers was well underway. Hundreds of thousand of men, women, and children had already met their deaths in the gas chambers, and countless more were slated for murder in the months ahead.

For days, Hannah and the three refugees moved stealthily through the Hungarian countryside, eventually coming upon a river they recognized as a branch of the Drava. Crossing would not be an easy matter, however, particularly since Hannah insisted on keeping her wireless transmitter with her. A sensitive instrument, it was not waterproof and required gentle handling. For this reason, she decided to disassemble it, wrap its components in her clothing and that of her companions, and transport it piece by piece over the tributary. The Frenchman, Tissandier, had grave concerns about this proposal, however, arguing that they would be doomed if any of them were caught with the device or any part of it. As was her way, though, Hannah was tenacious about keeping the equipment on the grounds that she would need it in Budapest in order to stay in contact with the British military and her Palestinian comrades in Yugoslavia. So each of the four, in due course, carried pieces of the wireless transmitter and other materials as they swam across the tributary until all of their clothing and paraphernalia was on the far bank. "Four times they swam back and forth," writes Hay. "When they got everything across they were so exhausted that they needed half an hour's rest."[36] Afterward, they set out to find the village of Mureska Sobatica, where sympathetic smugglers and Jewish resistance fighters were believed to be living. Hannah's strategy was to establish contact with, and gain the help of, these underground figures.

Coming upon a settlement that fit its description, Kallós and Fleischman decided to pay the village a visit. As it turned out, it was indeed the one they were seeking, although the resistance fighters they had hoped to meet were not there at the moment. In view of that, the two headed back in the direction of the woods only to find Hungarian policemen appearing out of nowhere and demanding to see their papers.

Kallós and Fleischman obliged at once, handing the policemen their forged identity documents. Although the policemen seemed to believe the papers were authentic, they asked the pair to come with them to headquarters, which was a standard request at the time even for those assumed to be innocent. Had the two complied, they almost certainly would have been released without incident. But Kallós panicked. Snatching his revolver from his pocket, he pointed the gun to his temple and squeezed the trigger, his body crumpling to the ground. The ear-piercing crack shocked Fleischman, who suddenly found himself struggling with the policemen who had now descended on him. Owing to Kallós' hasty, unprovoked suicide, they assumed Fleischman, as well as Kallós, must be guilty of a crime. Even more disturbingly, when they searched the dead Kallós' belongings and discovered in his knapsack the earpiece to a wireless transmitter, they became even more convinced that Fleischman was not only culpable but probably a member of a resistance cell. Hence, the police alerted the military, which mounted a massive search in the region, two hundred soldiers strong. In its sights was the forest where Hannah and Tissandier were hiding.

As it stood, neither Hannah nor the Frenchman had reason to suspect that anything had gone wrong until three hours later when their companions failed to return. Walking toward the village to look for them, the pair spotted soldiers in the distance. Hannah and Tissandier hurried back into the woods. "With lightening speed they buried their weapons and cast off anything that could give away their identity," says Hay.[37] The two then fell into each other's arms and began kissing. And their ruse worked, at least for the moment. When the soldiers came upon them, they believed the two were lovers who were merely seeking some privacy in the forest. All the same, they took them to headquarters for questioning, reassuring them that they could resume their tryst once they had been released, possibly within the hour.

The police drove Hannah and Tissandier, who were handcuffed, to the police station in nearby Szombathely, where the intrepid pair was confronted by a commandant who was not nearly as gullible as his underlings. Here, the couple was demoralized to see the corpse of Kallós and a badly beaten Fleischman.[38]

For the next two days, the authorities grilled Hannah and Tissandier, who were incarcerated and interrogated in separate quarters so they would not be aware of each other's answers. Even more distressing, the inquisitors tortured them. To compel Hannah to confess, they thrashed the soles of her feet and the palms of her hands until she lapsed into unconsciousness owing to the pain. Yet despite the agony being inflicted upon her, she insisted time and again that she was innocent, that she was not a resistance fighter and knew nothing about a wireless transmitter. Her denials came to an end, however, when a cunning interrogator tricked her into confessing. The man told Hannah, falsely, that a headset to a wireless device had been found in the possession of her battered comrade, Fleischman, who, as she knew, was still alive and being interrogated. Shaken by this news and hoping to shield her companion from further abuse, she grudgingly admitted that she was, in fact, the transmitter's owner and she further revealed where it was buried. Of course, if Hannah had known the truth, that the headset had been found on the deceased Kallós, not on Fleischman, she could have carried on feigning innocence and let the dead man take the blame. Instead, the confession tied Hannah, her pretend-lover Tissandier, and Fleischman to Kallós, thereby implicating the whole team in subversive activities.

Convinced of the group's guilt, the authorities loaded them onto a train bound for Budapest, where Hungarian and German officials would take up the matter. The crime, because it centered on espionage, called for the attention of higher-ups in Budapest. As for Hannah's reaction to this intimidating turn of events, her intelligence training in Palestine and Egypt had made her aware of what was to come, namely, torture even more excruciating than that which she had just endured. It was for this reason that she attempted a brash act, one that would either save her or kill her. In Hannah's view, whichever outcome transpired would deprive her enemies of the information they would try to pry out of her in Budapest, above all the code to the wireless transmitter.

As the train raced through the countryside, Hannah told her captors she needed to use the restroom. Under armed guard, she walked toward the lavatory, then lunged at a window, determined to leap from the speeding locomotive. As she struggled to climb out of the window, however, the guard seized her and dragged her back to the compartment. Hannah, it seems, was not among those commandos who had been supplied with a cyanide capsule. But although her failed attempt to escape meant she would now have to endure further torment in Budapest, she could take at least take pleasure in a last-minute success. Disembarking from the train, she left behind one of the few possessions she had brought with her from the forest: a volume of French verse. Unbeknownst to her escorts, it contained not only a selection of poems but also the code to her transmitter without which the device was useless.

In Budapest, the guards took Hannah to the headquarters of the Hungarian National Defense, where, as she had feared, she was subjected to intense interrogation measures. The only details she would surrender, though, were her name and British military number. In terms of the transmitter's code, a cipher the Germans could use to dupe the Allies into dropping unsuspecting paratroopers into their clutches, Hannah claimed to have abandoned the code book in the Yugoslavian forest. She said it was near the transmitter, the one the soldiers had unearthed. Unfortunately, the interrogators knew she was trying to fool them, since scores of soldiers had already scoured, and even excavated, entire portions of the forest and surrounding farmland and had found no such book. The inquisitors therefore carried on with their ignoble work.

Strapping Hannah to a chair, they punched her again and again until her face and neck became swollen and bruised. Among other indignities, they stripped away her clothing, yanked hair from her head by the handfuls, and struck her in the mouth, loosening her teeth and knocking out a front tooth. In an apparent effort to step up the humiliation, they decided to present her, in this ghastly condition, to her mother, who the authorities had brought to headquarters without offering the older woman an explanation.

So it was that four guards led Hannah into an interview room, where she caught sight of Catherine, a yellow Star of David affixed to her jacket, sitting in front of a Hungarian official. Hannah was thunderstruck, as was Catherine, who had no idea her daughter was back in Hungary.

"I felt as if the floor were giving way under me," Catherine later said.[39]

The pair rushed into each other's arms, with Hannah begging her mother for forgiveness. Hannah blamed herself because her mission to rescue Catherine from Nazi persecution had instead heightened the danger for both of them. But her mother would have none of it. When the guards left the room, she comforted Hannah, assuring her that no apologies were necessary. Catherine has said she knew her daughter's actions had grown from a noble desire to protect her and other Jews from harm.[40] The two also talked about Gyuri and took solace in his safety in Palestine, and they spoke about Hannah's wounds—until, that is, the guards promptly reappeared. It seems the authorities had been eavesdropping in the hope of picking up some useful information and when it was not forthcoming they decided to put a stop to the reunion. Extricating mother and daughter, they returned Hannah to her cell and sent Catherine home. But not for long.

A few hours later, Catherine heard a pounding at the door. Stealing a look out the window, she saw a sedan parked in front of her house with SS agents swarming around it. Her deepest fears were being realized. And, sure enough, she promptly found herself under arrest and en route to the *Polizeigefängnis*, a former Hungarian jail the occupying forces had turned into a German prison.[41]

In a chamber at the penitentiary, Detective Seifert, a Gestapo official, commenced questioning the forty-eight-year-old woman about Hannah. An

SS agent also searched Catherine, a dehumanizing ordeal during which he treated her cruelly. It seems the bony-faced young man — Catherine later described his visage as resembling the Death's Head insignia on his cap — slapped her face so savagely that the blow spun her completely around.[42] His pretext for such belligerence was that she had been too slow in handing over to him a small bag containing her money.

After the inquiry, which turned out to be an otherwise civilized session, was concluded, officials locked Catherine in a cell with several other Jewish women. Among them was a Countess Zichy. Although Catherine could not know it yet, the aristocrat would intercede in her life, in effect saving it.

It happened later that night while Catherine was lying in her darkened cell reliving the harrowing events of the day. She came to the realization that Hannah, being a steadfast Zionist and commando, would not cave in easily under torture. She also was certain that the Gestapo, precisely for this reason, would redouble the violence it was inflicting on Hannah as a means of compelling her to reveal sensitive information. What worried Catherine the most, though, was the prospect that the interrogators might use her, as the mother, for leverage. That is to say, they might exploit Hannah's loyalties by presenting the young Zionist with a gut-wrenching choice: either divulge secret Allied information and thereby betray her British and Palestinian comrades or refuse to divulge such information and thereby betray her mother, who the Gestapo would torture and perhaps kill in such a scenario. In effect, the Gestapo would use Catherine as a bargaining chip. Yet there was a solution to this perverse setup, a solution that was at once logical and chilling: Catherine could simply remove herself from the equation altogether, in this way freeing Hannah from having to make such a guilt-inducing choice.

With this aim in mind, Catherine pocketed a razor blade and when all of the other women in her cell appeared to be asleep for the night, she slit her wrist. The first cut was not deep enough, however, so she slashed it a second time, and it was at this moment that Countess Zichy caught sight of her. Grasping a handkerchief and fastening it around Catherine's wrist as a tourniquet, Zichy scolded her for jeopardizing not only her own life but those of the other women as well. Handing her a raincoat, the aristocrat further advised Catherine to wear it during interrogation sessions to conceal her wounds.

As it happened, the two Senesh women were not alone in their efforts to end their own lives. Like Hannah on the train and Catherine in her prison cell, Yoel Palgi had attempted to commit suicide when he, too, was arrested in Hungary.

As to how he came to be in the occupied nation, Yugoslavian resistance leader Marshal Tito dispatched a team to guide Palgi and Peretz Goldstein across the border into Hungary. A month had passed since Hannah and her band of refugees had made the same journey. Making his way to Budapest,

Palgi went the city's principal synagogue, the one where he and Hannah had agreed to reunite. When she did not appear at the temple, he tried their back-up plan: a rendezvous at the cathedral. When she still did not come into sight, he began to fear the worst. As it stood, Palgi was in considerable danger himself. He suspected that the Hungarian police knew that he and Goldstein were in the country and were allowing the two to move about freely so they could discover the pair's underground contacts. Unfortunately, he was right. Once the officials were satisfied that they had gathered this information, the Hungarian Security Police arrested the two men and placed them in the same penitentiary as Hannah and her mother. And it was during this course of these events that Palgi cut his wrist, although his suicide attempt, like that of Catherine, was discovered and his wounds bandaged. In the meantime, the interrogation sessions dragged on without respite, most of all for Hannah.

Throughout the summer months, the Hungarians, followed by the Germans, questioned her on a daily basis, but she never relented. Disgusted by the ideology and practices of National Socialism, she made her opinions known, insulting her inquisitors at every turn. In fact, within prison circles she acquired a reputation for her propensity to badmouth the Germans and their Hungarian pawns. "Even the prison warden, totalitarian in his Nazi belief, occasionally visited her cell out of curiosity, and found himself the unwilling but immovable subject of a stream of criticism," writes Masters. "He went away from her exhausted."[43]

But even as Hannah sounded off to the enemy, she devised inventive ways to convey her love to her mother. Although held in solitary confinement, Hannah persuaded sympathetic trusties to walk her past Catherine's cell, where the mother and daughter would embrace and chat briefly. On other occasions, Hannah convinced the guards to arrange for her and Catherine to meet in a bathroom or the prison yard, where they would walk side by side and converse surreptitiously. And she did not limit her interactions to her mother. In time, Hannah established contact with other inmates as well, among them a group of Zionists locked up across the yard from her cell. At first etching a Star of David in the frost on her window, in due course she cut out letters of the alphabet and used them to post news of the outside world for her fellow captives to read. It was information she acquired through the prison grapevine. Clearly, she refused to be silenced, even when held in solitary confinement.

Meanwhile, as Hannah spent her days alone in the silence of her cell, the political situation outside the prison became ever more explosive. Hungary was in a tremendous state of flux at this moment, one consequence being that the outlook for the nation's Jews was highly unpredictable.

In the spring and summer of 1944, a period during which the Germans reigned in Hungary, four hundred thousand Hungarian Jews were packed into railroad cars and deported to Auschwitz and other camps. An industrialized nightmare, the mass murder of the nation's Jewry was one of the largest slaughters of the Holocaust. Such horrors appeared to be coming to an end in the late summer and early autumn, however, as Allied troops drew nearer to Hungary. Yet this sense of hope was not to last, with circumstances soon taking a darker course. Of course, such abrupt, seismic shifts in power produced a disturbing sense of disorientation and often foreboding in Hannah and her comrades; indeed, in all of the remaining Jews in Hungary.

Finally, on September 11, 1944, the Germans began the process of transferring Hannah to another prison while entrusting Yoel Palgi and Peretz Goldstein to Hungarian military authorities. In some respects, it was a favorable development. For one thing, Palgi and Goldstein would be in comparatively safer hands. For another, it allowed Hannah and Palgi an opportunity to converse once again, initially in a prison hallway and later while being transported in a police van. The pair had not been in contact since their days in the Yugoslavian woodlands, so it was a rare and unexpected pleasure.

In the hurried flow of their fleeting exchanges, Hannah explained why she had been unable to meet Palgi at the synagogue and the cathedral, as well as recounting how she had ditched her code book and tried to leap from a speeding train. In his memoir, *Into the Inferno*, Palgi recalls that they also talked about their ambitious rescue mission and agreed it had been doomed from the start, their small commando unit having possessed no real chance of prevailing against the enormity of the evil it was to confront.[44] Palgi later said that Hannah's mood seemed sunny on this late summer's day, her circumstances notwithstanding. Although she was en route to yet another prison, he writes that she was looking forward to the war's end and a return to normalcy.

"Come and visit me at my mother's house," she told him as she climbed out of the police van.[45] Looking back at him, she gave Palgi a jolly thumbs-up gesture.

Hannah was thereafter locked away in the Conti Street Prison, while Palgi and Goldstein were confined in a facility on Margit Boulevard in Budapest. As for Catherine, two days later the authorities transferred her to a Hungarian internment camp, Kistarsca, which proved to be a considerable improvement over the German prison she had left behind. Then, on Yom Kippur at the end of September, Hungarian officials released her from Kistarsca, along with the camp's other detainees. Catherine was finally free.

Hannah, on the other hand, continued languishing in her cell, and it was at this time that a minor mystery occurred at a Budapest theatre. It seems that one of Catherine's dearest friends, an acclaimed gentile actress by the name of Margit Dayka, found awaiting in her backstage dressing room two young men with an envelope packed with money. They said the cash was to make sure that all of Hannah Senesh's needs were met. The pair mentioned, too, that it came from a man known as "Geri," who specifically requested that his regards be conveyed to the young Zionist. Unbeknownst to either Margit or Catherine, Geri was actually Hannah's comrade, Reuven Dafne.

Shortly thereafter, when Catherine visited Hannah in prison, she told her daughter about the money and about an enigmatic figure named Geri who wished her well. When Hannah heard this news, her face was said to glow because she knew his true identity.[46] It also was during this visit that Hannah asked Catherine to bring warm clothes to the cell and as many books as possible, among them a Hebrew bible. Sadly, though, Catherine could not find a single copy of the latter anywhere in Budapest, Jewish businesses having been shuttered or demolished and Hebrew texts, destroyed. Her inability to secure such a text would dismay Catherine for the rest of her days.[47]

In addition to visiting Hannah and trying to ensure that she was as comfortable as possible, Catherine also sought tirelessly to get her released from prison, albeit to no avail. Compounding her frustration was the fact that the nation itself was still on a political rollercoaster, one that directly affected her daughter's life.

Case in point: Admiral Miklós Horthy, on October 14, 1944, pledged to release Hannah and the other Palestinian parachutists who had been a part of her team.[48] Even more sweeping, the following day he announced that he was forging a peace accord with the Allies. But then came the Axis powers' swift reaction to his announcement. As could be predicted, Horthy's declaration of intent had infuriated them, but what was not foreseeable was their crude and uncompromising response: within hours, an elite German commando unit kidnapped his adult son, Miklós Horthy, Jr., rolling him in a carpet and flying him to Germany. In this way, the Axis powers strong-armed the Regent into abdicating at once. Then, on October 16, 1944, the pro–Nazi Ferenc Szálasi was installed as both Regent and Prime Minister of Hungary. "Now the parachutists, and all 170,000 Budapest Jews, were again at risk," says Gilbert.[49] As the historical record reveals, Szálasi was associated with an extremist Hungarian party, the bloodthirsty Arrow Cross, which was a homegrown national socialist movement. Reviving the anti–Semitic carnage, it took up where the Germans had left off.

Hannah, of course, was particularly vulnerable. Because Szálasi shared Hitler's contempt for the Jews, the Arrow Cross leader's ascension to high office cast a shadow over her upcoming trial, which was scheduled to take place twelve days later. As the proceedings grew near, attorneys predicted that, given the Arrow Cross' ascendancy in the halls of power, Hannah could face up to ten or even twenty years in prison. Her only hope was to be acquitted after the war when the Arrow Cross would be driven from power.

Trial and Treachery

The tribunal took place on October 28, 1944, with the charge against Hannah being treason. It was the court's contention that she had entered her homeland for the purpose of working covertly for the Allies. The three adjudicators consisted of Count Geró László, Dr. Macskás, and Captain Elemér Simon, the latter serving as Judge Advocate or military prosecutor. Present, too, were some of Hannah's former collaborators, among them Tissandier and Fleischman, who subsequently described what unfolded in the courtroom.

After the court pronounced the charge of treason, Dr. Andre Szelecsényi, Hannah's defense attorney and a gentile, proceeded to argue her case. And he did so admirably, by all accounts. It later came to light that the judges, behind closed doors, scorned him when they learned that he planned to represent a Jewish defendant, but Szelecsényi continued to act on behalf of the young Zionist all the same.

Even more remarkable was Hannah's own self-defense, according to witnesses in the courtroom.[50] When asked if she pleaded guilty, she seized the opportunity to speak for herself in a reply that was prolonged, eloquent, and, above all, defiant.

"I'm not a traitor to my country," she declared. "My country's over there, far away, in the land of my forefathers to which I returned."[51] She added, however, that although she considered herself a Palestinian — a person of Eretz Yisrael — she nevertheless remained loyal to Hungary, the country of her birth. She then proceeded to hit back at the court most damningly, telling the judges it was Hungary's leaders who had betrayed the nation by siding with the Third Reich and participating willfully in genocide.

"The traitors are those who brought disaster on the people," Hannah said bluntly. "You should not, Your Honor, add sin to crime."[52]

At this point, the judges suspended the proceedings momentarily so the guards could remove from the courtroom Fleischman, Tissandier, and the other defendants. Evidently, the arbitrators were worried that Hannah's incisive rebuttal and remarkable bravado might inspire and embolden her indicted comrades.

Although the proceedings resumed, what transpired is unknown since the official account was subsequently destroyed. What is known is that the judges could not agree on a verdict and therefore postponed it until the following week. Within days, however, the political situation in Hungary became even more volatile, with Soviet forces gathering at the periphery of Budapest. And while the Soviet presence was a promising development, it intensified hostilities and produced such chaos, including political disarray, that a verdict was not rendered in Hannah's case as scheduled. Instead, three days later she found herself transferred from the Conti Street facility to the same prison as

Palgi, Peretz, and Fleischman. As to the reason for the move, the authorities did not give her one. All the same, Hannah was said to be lighthearted after the hasty, inexplicable transfer. "She was in high spirits," writes Palgi, whose information came from one of Hannah's childhood friends who happened to encounter her in the prison that day. "[Hannah] did not sense what was going to happen."[53]

And what happened was unconscionable: Captain Simon walked into her cell and declared that she had been sentenced to death. It was a startling announcement. After all, she had harmed no one, nor had she engaged in any noteworthy covert activity. The police had taken her into custody shortly after she crossed the Hungarian border, the result being that she was unable to engage in any clandestine work on behalf of the Allies or the Jewish citizenry. Her time in occupied Hungary had been spent almost entirely behind bars.

Captain Simon next asked if Hannah wished to request a pardon, and she replied that she wished to exercise her right to an appeal. She wanted the whole matter re-examined. But Captain Simon refused to recognize her right to an appeal and Hannah refused to plead for a reprieve from an authority she did not acknowledge as such. So the death penalty remained in place. And this was an indisputable crime.

The fact is, Hannah's death sentence was not only excessive, it also was illegal. The court had not assigned the punishment; the tribunal still had not arrived at a verdict. It was Captain Simon acting alone, without the authority to do so, who had chosen Hannah's sentence, misrepresented it as the court's decision, and ordered a firing squad to be assembled to kill her.

In the hour that remained, Hannah asked to see her mother but Captain Simon refused this last request. So instead she used her final moments to write two letters, one to her mother and the other to her imprisoned comrades. Captain Simon did not deliver either message.

At ten o'clock that morning, he did, however, summon the young Zionist from her cell. Two guards led her to an area beside a brick wall on the prison grounds where a fresh sheet of sand had been spread over the snow. They bound Hannah's hands to a post behind her back while Captain Simon prepared a blindfold. When he tried to put it on her, however, Hannah nudged it away with her head. She refused for her eyes to be covered, instead lifting her face toward the sky. Moments later, a three-man firing squad shot her to death.

"We stood petrified," said Yoel Palgi.[54] Along with Hannah's other imprisoned comrades, Palgi heard the volley of gunfire but not the sounds of the ceremony that customarily accompanied an execution, such as the blast of a trumpet and the recitation of the court's judgment. He was puzzled, although later that day he learned the awful truth. Beset with grief, Palgi writes in his memoir that he was speechless, unable to articulate his sorrow, although he did in time find the words. "She was the most wonderful person I ever knew," he uttered to his cellmates.[55] Together, the men rose to their feet, and they remained standing as a sign of respect for Hannah.

Shortly thereafter, Catherine, unaware of the execution, showed up at Captain Simon's office and insisted she be allowed to see her daughter. Although the prosecutor tried to wriggle out of the matter, Catherine persisted until he brusquely informed her that Hannah had been put to death. "She was truly proud of being a Jew," Captain Simon said, his tone conveying both respect and bewilderment.

"The world went black," Catherine recalled.[57] A cloud of despair descending upon her, she made her way to her sister's apartment through the city's tumultuous streets. A violent period, the Budapest Offensive was underway, a military operation in which the Red Army was wresting control of the capital city from the grip of the Axis powers.

Dr. Szelecsényi, that same day, glimpsed a hearse leaving the prison and learned from a gatekeeper that a young woman, a British officer, had been executed. Racing up the stairs to Captain Simon's office, Szelecsényi discovered that it was in fact Hannah who had been killed. Outraged, he confronted the prosecutor, lambasting him because the court had not yet arrived at a verdict and therefore, in Szelecsényi's view, the execution constituted judicial murder.

After leaving Captain Simon's office, the distraught attorney arranged for the Jewish Burial Society to assume responsibility for Hannah's body. Unfortunately, Hungarian authorities would not tell Catherine when or where the burial would take place, since family members of Jews were no longer privy to such information. For this reason, Hannah's grave remained unmarked and Catherine's anguish deepened.

Paralyzed by her loss, Catherine took to her bed in her sister's yellow-star apartment. This is where Catherine was now living, the city's Jews having been evicted from their homes and herded into designated buildings scattered throughout the city. It was a prelude to the formal ghettoization that was to come.

During this period, Catherine, profoundly depressed over Hannah's demise, had little desire to continue living. And it was while she was in this desolate state that she found herself, merely a week later, being ordered out of the yellow-star building and onto the street. It seems that Arrow Cross troops had surrounded the building and were forcing its dispirited residents to gather outside, where they were to embark on a death march to Austria. The sadistic scheme was to deport seventy thousand Budapest Jews, ages fourteen to fifty years old, to the Alpine nation and to do so on foot. Intended in part to exhaust and destroy those compelled to take part in it, the ones who survived would be sent on to Dachau, Mauthausen, and other concentration camps in Germany and Austria.

Although brokenhearted over Hannah, Catherine trudged with the masses through rural villages, where residents lined the route and gawked or jeered at them. As for the weather, it was excruciatingly cold, with Catherine and the others being forced to sleep in snowy fields at night. Some never awakened, most often the young, the sick, and the elderly, their corpses being left behind in the pastures the next morning. Still others committed suicide. In terms of escape, it was a gamble at best and its punishment, nefarious: through loudspeakers, the Arrow Cross warned that machine-gun fire would be aimed into the crowd itself if anyone tried to flee. Thus, an escape attempt would result in the indiscriminate slaying of the much larger number of Jews who were not trying to flee. And so it was that Catherine found herself slogging through this modern-day hell until a moment, a miraculous moment, when the prospect of taking flight presented itself to her.

It happened amidst the pandemonium of an Allied air attack. She and a handful of others scurried to a house where a sympathetic family greeted them and supplied them with clothing that did not display the stigmatizing yellow star. This permitted Catherine to hitchhike back to Budapest, obtain forged identification papers, and, with the help of sympathetic friends, move into an infirmary in a convent for protection. In time, she helped provide nursing care to the growing number of wounded soldiers who were being brought into the abbey each day.

At last, when Soviet troops liberated the capital city in the Siege of Budapest — the date was February 13, 1945 — Catherine returned to her house only to find it had been damaged during the war. She was not overcome by this discovery, however. Her thoughts still on Hannah, she realized that she no longer had any desire to live in the home they had once shared. Instead, she decided to follow a suggestion from Yoel Palgi and relocate to Palestine, where she could join Gyuri, her son. As it happened, Palgi, the only one of Hannah's Palestinian comrades to enter Hungary and survive, encouraged Catherine to make the move and even offered to help her do so. Certainly it had long been Hannah's hope that the Senesh family would eventually settle in Palestine, and Catherine would be helping to bring about this dream. It also would be a fresh start for Catherine in the land that Hannah loved so dearly and helped cultivate with her own hands. But first, however, she resolved to help bring to justice Captain Elemér Simon, the man who orchestrated Hannah's murder.

As a plethora of Nazi crimes came to light in Hungary after the war, Captain Simon was among those made to stand trial. During the proceedings, it was determined that his directive to execute Hannah had indeed been unlawful, that he had acted on a personal whim rather than in accordance with the nation's judicial system. It was further revealed that he had kept Hannah's final letters, those she had written to her mother and comrades. But disturbing as well is the fact that Captain Simon, after the proceedings, managed to escape from Hungary and thereby elude justice. He is believed to have taken the letters with him.

In the summer of 1945, Catherine acquired a Romanian passport and traveled to Bucharest, where she spent the next three months waiting for a ship to Palestine. It was in October that she finally boarded the *Transylvania*, a vessel packed with Holocaust survivors bound for the Middle East. Upon arrival, she was delighted to be met by a delegation that included Yoel Palgi, who, in the years ahead, would be named ambassador to Tanzania. He also would serve as the deputy managing director of El Al Airlines and would oversee the airlift of two hundred thousand Jewish immigrants from Muslim nations. In addition, Catherine was touched to learn that a Palestinian organization had brought together a collection of Hannah's poems and other writings and was in the process of publishing them. But she found perhaps her greatest satisfaction in December, when she was reunited with Gyuri, who had provisionally returned from Western Europe, where he had been serving with the Jewish Brigade. Although both of them would remain in Palestine, Gyuri, for the moment, still had military obligations to honor. While he was away, Catherine taught children on a kibbutz near the Sea of Galilee.

In the ensuing years, Hannah's courage was honored in Hungary, where a girls' home in Budapest was named for her, one created for children whose parents had perished in Auschwitz. A ship allocated for carrying Holocaust survivors to Palestine was likewise named in her honor, as were colonies, streets, educational centers, and even woodlands in Palestine. Then, in 1951, a particularly meaningful event occurred when Hannah's remains were returned to what now had become the State of Israel. It seems that Catherine, while still in Budapest after the war, managed to track down Hannah's grave through a Christian cemetery worker who was present at the internment. Once the body had been exhumed and transported to Haifa, it lay in state with two honor guards in attendance, one comprised of paratroopers from the Israeli Defense Force, and the other, a civilian group that included David Ben-Gurion, the nation's first Prime Minister. In the end, Hannah was given a hero's burial at Mount Herzl in Jerusalem, the national cemetery named in honor of Theodor Herzl, the founder of Zionism. By any measure, she had been an exceptional young woman, a person of unwavering principle and unfailing courage.

United States Senator John McCain, a former prisoner-of-war in North Vietnam, examined Hannah's principles in his book *Why Courage Matters*.[58] "She had exposed herself to danger for the sake of others, endured torture rather than betray her mission and her ideals, and ultimately made the last and greatest sacrifice a human being can offer," he writes.[59] Drawing attention to the latter, her self-sacrifice, McCain recounts how Captain Simon, upon informing Hannah of her death sentence, offered her the opportunity to request a pardon from him. Had she done so, it would have spared her life, and it would have done so without costing any Jewish lives. But Hannah refused to ask for a reprieve evidently because she believed it would suggest that Captain Simon possessed a certain moral superiority over her, one that entitled him to make such a decision. In repudiating his offer, she was indicating to Captain Simon that he was not morally qualified to determine her fate.

"Hannah sacrificed her life for her dignity and sense of honor," McCain says.[60] "I think she wanted to live, but on the very exacting terms she had set for herself."[61] The fact is, Hannah absolutely would not negotiate with those people whose ideological systems she regarded as ethically deficient. She would not violate or otherwise compromise her values regardless of the consequences. "She made a choice to be heroic, but to be heroic in order to be true," McCain concludes.[62]

Hannah's commitment to personal honor, to upholding her principles at all costs, suffuses her most celebrated poem, *Blessed is the Match*. It is the poem she gave to her Palestinian comrade Reuven Dafne shortly before crossing the border into Hungary. Among its words, which proved to be prophetic, are those revealing Hannah's conviction that an allegiance to honor, an unyielding devotion to it, is among the most sacred of human qualities and ultimately transcends one's temporal, earthly existence. It was quintessential Hannah Senesh.

Blessed Is the Match

Blessed is the match consumed
in kindling flame.

Blessed is the flame that burns
in the secret fastness of the heart.

Blessed is the heart with strength to stop
its beating for honor's sake.

Blessed is the match consumed
in kindling flame.[63]

[Translation from Hebrew by Marie Syrkin]

8

Christine Granville and the Polish/French Resistance

On a frosty morning in February 1940, a small, delicate figure clad in a parka and bearing a backpack could be seen skiing in the Carpathian Mountains that separated Slovakia and occupied Poland. She was a countess, Christine Granville (Krystyna Skarbek), and she had a reputation that was, in some circles, regarded as a bit scandalous. It seems the thirty-one-year-old Polish aristocrat was a free spirit who cast aside the rules of polite society when they did not suit her, a woman who did not take orders from men but who did take pleasure in trysts with those she found handsome and entertaining. She also was an equestrienne as well as an avid skier, although on this occasion she was in the mountains for reasons other than recreational ones. While other Poles were struggling to escape from their besieged homeland, Christine was slipping back into it through this rugged mountain course, her aim being to rescue her mother who was living in Warsaw. While in Poland, Christine also hoped to begin assembling a network of couriers to keep the Allies supplied with the latest intelligence. She even planned to organize an escape route, one that would wind through the Carpathians and be accessible to downed Allied airmen and prisoners-of-war who had broken out of captivity. By any measure, her ambitions were grand in scope, yet she was unwavering in her determination to fulfill them. And she began by arranging this perilous trip back into occupied Poland.

Christine was fortunate in that she would not be making the trek alone. A fellow skier, Jan Marusarz, had agreed to accompany her, if reluctantly. A member of Poland's Olympic Ski Team, he was a superb choice for this dicey undertaking because he knew the Carpathians like the back of his hand. Then, too, he was employed as a courier for a military attaché and was well-versed in security measures. So it was that the irrepressible Christine and the cautious Marusarz, steeling themselves, loaded their backpacks and embarked on their mid-winter crossing through the snow-covered peaks.

"It was a slow and desperate climb upwards in the deep snow," writes journalist and historian Madeleine Masson."[1] As if the passage were not dangerous enough — the route was rife with natural hazards as well as the threat of German patrols — a blizzard struck while they were trudging through a valley and forced them to take refuge in a cabin some distance away. Collapsing into the shelter, the weary pair unloaded their belongings, drank hot tea to warm themselves, and fell into a deep slumber. But, alas, it was not to be a restful night, and not only because of the howling storm. It seems that Christine was awakened by the sounds of distant cries, calls of desperation, that were swept up into the coiling wind and could not be pinpointed. Frantic, she yearned to help the poor souls who were stranded in the raging storm, but the more circumspect Marusarz implored her to remain inside the cabin, insisting it was foolhardy to venture into a blizzard in the middle of the night.

The next morning, the couple stuffed their spare clothing into their backpacks and set off through the drifted snow. Little did they know they were about to make a discovery, and a very grim one. "[T]hey came across the frozen bodies of a man and a girl," says Masson.[2] Victims of the blizzard, twenty-eight other people had likewise perished in the storm during the night, presumably refugees trying to flee from Nazi-infested Poland. Christine had been lucky, of course, and fortune would continue to smile upon her.

During the months that followed, the spirited countess made more journeys to her homeland and the overwrought city of Warsaw. It was through her connections to the Polish underground, moreover, that she was able to send proof to the Allies that Germany was amassing troops along the border of the Soviet Union, an alarming development indicating that the former was preparing to violate its non-aggression pact with the latter. Because of such acts, Christine came to be regarded as one of the most proficient female operatives in the resistance and was awarded numerous decorations. Ironically, it was her uninhibited, adventurous approach to life, a stance that the more straitlaced members of Polish society had frowned upon prior to the war, that allowed her to perform such bold and inventive deeds for the cause of freedom and the amelioration of human suffering. To be sure, her individualism, like her determination and *joie de vivre*, were elemental features of her personality, features that began to surface during her early years when she enjoyed a privileged upbringing in a splendid estate in the Polish countryside. It also appears to have been during this formative period that her doting father, in particular, instilled in her many of the same values and attitudes that he himself possessed.

Nobility and Notoriety

Count Jerzy Skarbek, Christine's father, was a descendant of one of Poland's oldest and most august families. A prominent bloodline, it included such illustrious figures as Frederic Skarbek, a renowned economist and the godfather of composer Frederic Chopin, and Alexander Skarbek, Deputy of the Imperial Parliament and later a prominent figure in Poland's National Democratic Party. Jerzy, however, was different. Unlike his influential ancestors, he was drawn less to the artistic, economic, and political realms and more to a life of leisure. Surely it was no secret that the debonair aristocrat spent lavishly on his hobbies, which ranged from romantic interludes with exquisite women to an impressive stable of horses. It was further known, at least within close circles, that it was his self-indulgent lifestyle that had prompted him to walk down the aisle. It seems the nobleman found it difficult to continue bankrolling his pursuits and for this reason decided to marry into the wealthy Goldfeder banking family. And, sure enough, Jerzy, who was Catholic, married Stephanie Goldfeder, who was Jewish, with the couple using the bride's dowry to pay off the groom's debts and fund his future pursuits. The latter would continue to be punctuated by flings with comely women.

After settling into their life together — it was not a state of marital bliss mainly because of Jerzy's extramarital escapades — the Count and Countess Skarbek brought into the world their first child, Andrew, a son and heir. The boy was said to resemble, and eventually prefer the company of, his mother. A few years later, Christine was born, with her birth name being Krystyna Skarbek. As an adult during World War II, she would be assigned the code name Christine Granville while serving as a spy for the Allies, and she would legally adopt this *nom de guerre* after the war. Regarding the date and place of her birth, contradictory information exists, although recent reports suggest that she was born on May 1, 1908, in Warsaw.[3] In the ensuing years, she enjoyed a wonderful childhood, the only complications being those that arose from her own willfulness and mischievousness. Yet even when she misbehaved, Count Jerzy, who was known to do the same at times, would invariably come to her defense.

"[T]here was a complete *rapport* between father and daughter," says Masson.[4] Whereas Countess Stephanie was drawn to intellectual pursuits, art and literature among them, Christine, like her father, was attracted to the sporty life, an outdoorsy one in which riding was an essential component. It also was a life that caused Countess Stephanie to fret about her tomboyish daughter, her concern being that the little girl would become coarsened by consorting with the proletariat — the "commoners" — in the stables. But Count Jerzy did not entertain this conceit. "Disregarding his wife's fears that Christine might learn rough manners and hear bad language," writes Masson, "he kept her with him as much as possible, teaching her to ride astride, instead of sidesaddle."[5] The result is that Christine, during her childhood years, became an outstanding equestrienne, as well as acquiring the ability to connect with people of different social classes. Certainly it is true that she treasured her moments with the stable boys, halcyon days during which she shared in their banter and camaraderie. Along the way, and most likely because of these experiences with the third estate, she also developed a healthy worldliness, a keen sense of humor, and an affability that would serve her well in the resistance as an adult. It was during her early days as an equestrienne, moreover, that the tenyear-old Christine befriended another child, Andrew (Andrzej) Kowerski, in a horse barn. During World War II, fate would bring the two of them together again, with the pair becoming lovers, soulmates, and comrades-in-arms.

Because Countess Stephanie, over the course of time, became convinced that her suspicions were becoming a reality, that Christine was indeed becoming a raucous young lady, she enrolled her in the Sacré-Coeur Convent in western Poland. Not surprisingly, Christine was none too happy about this turn of events and before long set out to make her discontentment known to the mother superior and others. Specifically, the young aristocrat carried out pranks that invited the authorities' disdain, her most dramatic stunt being the one in which she set fire to a priest's vestment while he was celebrating Mass. Of course, such exploits were not well-received at the convent, with the authorities suggesting to the Count and Countess that their daughter might be happier somewhere else. It was in this way that Christine found herself at another convent, Jazlowiec, which was even more rigid than the first one. But although this latest development further annoyed her, she did find it within herself to tolerate the convent's strict atmosphere and even went on to achieve academic success and enjoy enormous popularity among the other girls.

Looking back at Christine's life, it is plausible that she may have decided to become less troublesome at this point because her mother and father were struggling mightily in the financial sphere and enduring numerous hardships. She may not have wished to add to their burden. The fact is, the Skarbeks' wealth, like that of the Goldfeders and other distinguished families, was diminishing rapidly, one consequence being they were were obliged to put on the market their country estate, with its manor house, parkland, and stables. Afterward, the Count and Countess took up residence in a less opulent home in Warsaw, one better suited to their diminishing fortunes. In spite of such sacrifices, though, the couple's monetary problems persisted and their standard of living continued to decline. In the end, they watched helplessly as their wealth dried up, culminating in the same trauma suffered by countless others around the world — jarring financial ruination — during the economic collapse of 1929.

As if the Skarbek family had not been dealt enough blows, Count Jerzy succumbed to tuberculosis a year later. Naturally, Christine was grief-stricken, and she also was concerned about her own financial future. Whereas her mother had been left with enough funds to live in relative comfort — Countess Stephanie was no longer affluent but she also was not strapped for cash — Christine was in a thornier position. She had no income, yet she did not wish to accept money from her widowed mother. The obvious solution, then, was for her to join the workforce, which she promptly did by securing a clerical position at a Fiat agency. Although it was not an ideal use of her talents, times were tough and it was a paycheck.

Tough, too, was the job itself, with Christine's days at the automobile firm taking a toll on her health. While on the job, she developed an unusual respiratory illness that interfered with her breathing and produced shadows on lung X-rays. Although initially it was suspected that tuberculosis might be the culprit, a reasonable assumption given her father's medical history and her proximity to him, it eventually was determined that conditions at the agency itself had caused the ailment. Christine worked in a second-floor office that was located over a garage, and, unbeknownst to her, she had been inhaling toxic vapors for weeks on end. Provided with compensation by Fiat's insurer, she took her doctor's advice and exchanged office work for outdoor activities. Fresh air, it was believed, might help heal the lung damage.

To this end, the countess passed her days in the sunshine, with a considerable number of them spent skiing in the Tatra Mountains, a range within the Carpathians. Boasting the highest peaks in the region, these were the mountains described at the outset of this chapter, the ones she would later traverse during her stint with the resistance. Situated in the mountains, too, was the enchanting village of Zakopane, where she socialized and shared the slopes with other members, or former members, of the privileged class. And she occasionally unleashed her more wayward side, sneaking cigarettes, for instance, across the border. She had no way of knowing that her playful escapades in smuggling contraband and evading the border guards would endow her with knowledge and experience that would come in useful when she later helped Allied airmen and prisoners-of-war escape from occupied Poland. In much the same way, her familiarity with Zakopane and her friendships with its villagers would also be of benefit when she organized these precarious operations.

Fortunately, Christine's outdoor frolics did indeed restore her physical health although they did nothing to restore her financial well-being. Perhaps it was partly for this reason that in 1933 she married a wealthy gentleman by the name of Charles Getlich, a fine man by all accounts. As it stands, little is known about the details of their union except that both families felt sure Christine and the good-natured, upright Charles would enjoy a peaceful and prosperous life together. Yet it was not to be. In the fullness of time, it became evident that Charles was more drawn to his career than to domestic life — not that Christine was a homebody herself. She never had been the stay-at-home type. Realizing their mistake, the couple divorced amicably, with the stunning countess enjoying romances with other men in the ensuing years; that is, until she fell, quite literally, into the arms of Jerzy Gizycki.

Headstrong and imaginative, Gizycki, at the age of fourteen, had left behind his rich Ukrainian parents and traveled to America, where he made his way westward to work as a cowboy and pursue his luck in gold mining. Next came West Africa, where he wrote a book about its culture and peoples, and before long began enjoying success as a roving journalist. Now the strapping, handsome man with strong opinions and ambition to match was skiing in Zakopane, where he encountered the vibrant Christine. In fact, it was more of an intervention, with Gizycki catching her when she began hurtling down a sheer slope, nearly taking a tumble. From this first moment in the snow, an intense, dynamic relationship began taking shape, one that culminated in their marriage in the autumn of 1938. The following year, they were slated to move to Addis Ababa, Ethiopia, where Gizycki had accepted a position at the consulate.

It was while they were in Africa that Poland came under Hitler's boot, the German offensive being an effort to reclaim territory it had lost in World War I and then to preside over the Eastern European nation itself. As to the German strategy, that of a swift, overwhelming assault — the Blitzkrieg — it was both effective and horrible, with the ensuing situation for Poland's citizenry worsening each day. And this state of affairs was not confined to the border regions. "In Warsaw itself," says historian Richard Evans, "conditions deteriorated rapidly."[6]

Christine, of course, was beside herself with worry. Not only was the whole of Poland in dire straits, but her widowed mother still lived in Warsaw, an especially alarming circumstance in that the older woman was Jewish. For this reason, Christine, averse to remaining in faraway Africa while fascists tyrannized her mother and countrymen, sailed with her husband to Britain to join the war effort. Dead-set on rescuing Countess Stephanie, she also planned to help the Polish people more generally and assumed the British would welcome her offer of assistance. Yet her intense desire to lend a hand turned out to be a hard sell to the powers-that-be. "[T]he British authorities showed little interest in employing Granville," write Rosalind Miles and Robin Cross, "until the intervention of friends secured her a mission to Hungary, whose dictator, Admiral Horthy, was not only a German sympathizer but also a distant relation."[7]

At this early stage of the conflict — it was the autumn of 1939 — the British had not yet created agencies devoted to underground strategies or "ungentlemanly warfare."[8] Given this state of affairs, Christine realized she would need to approach the country's existing intelligence apparatus if she were to accomplish what she had in mind. Accordingly, she laid out for officials a plan she had devised: basing her operation in Hungary, she would ski over the Carpathian Mountains from Slovakia into occupied Poland, where she would help establish escape routes for resistance fighters and British soldiers. An inventive scheme, it was wholly her own idea and British Intelligence took it very seriously. Officials could tell it was well thought-out, even if its execution carried substantial risks, and the fact that the spirited aristocrat already had performed a version of it before the war was a testament to its feasibility. It will be recalled that Christine had learned to enter and exit Poland through obscure mountain routes without the border guards detecting her, and she had even smuggled contraband during such escapades. Thus, her proposal appeared to be realistic and held genuine promise for Britain in extracting its downed airmen and prisoners-of-war, as well as aiding the Polish resistance movement. Officials, in the end, were eager to enlist the countess' services.

Behind Enemy Lines

The winter solstice of 1939 would find Christine traveling to Budapest to lay the groundwork for her mission. Arriving in the picturesque Hungarian city, she presented herself as a newspaper reporter married to a diplomat. Her cover story, which was true in that British Intelligence had arranged for her to be outwardly employed as a journalist, invited the respect and cooperation of the people of Budapest, along with officials of the British Embassy and Polish Consulate. And further bolstering Christine's support was a man whose presence both surprised her and changed her life.

It was during a visit to the Polish Consulate in Budapest that she spotted him, a tall, passionate man who was pontificating on the disastrous state of affairs in Poland. Andrew Kowerski was his name, and Christine had first met him when she was a ten-year-old girl. During that more innocent era, he had been the boy who visited her family's stables, but now he was a lieutenant engaged in the fight against fascism. Shortly after their unexpected reunion in the Hungarian capital, the two became lovers despite the fact that Christine was still married to her second husband. She and Andrew became collaborators as well.

As an illustration of the couple's teamwork, it was Andrew who arranged for her to travel into occupied Poland with Jan Marusarz, the Olympic skier, as her escort. The plot was for Christine and Marusarz to slip into the traumatized nation, where the aristocrat would perform those feats recounted at the outset of this chapter. And, sure enough, she did help create escape routes and smuggle Poles and their allies into France, where the Polish government-in-exile was based. She also helped prisoners-of-war escape to England by way of Greece, exfiltrated Polish resistance members to Hungary, and shared secret information with British Intelligence. The latter involved dispatching to London instructive reports she prepared in Budapest. To be sure, Christine, beginning in February of 1940, was a very busy woman who confronted danger on virtually a daily basis.

It was at this time, early 1940, that her first trip into occupied Poland took place, and it was a mission that lasted five weeks. In every respect except one, it was a success. It seems she was unable to achieve the goal that was closest to her heart, that of convincing her mother to get out of Warsaw, and, for that matter, out of Poland itself. When the moment came, Countess Stephanie simply would not leave, Christine's pleas notwithstanding. The older woman could not seem to grasp the magnitude of evil that surrounded her as a Polish Jew. A distressing experience for Christine, she would try again on future missions to persuade her mother to flee with her to Hungary, but to no avail. And the consequences would be ghastly. "Her mother refused," write Miles and Cross, "and later died in a concentration camp."[9]

Into the summer months, Christine kept up her work with the Allies and the Polish underground, stealing into the Nazi-dominated nation by the mountain route which the Germans had now taken to patrolling by air. By this time, they also had outlawed skis so as to further prevent escapes. As for Andrew, he likewise was busy, among other deeds concocting the escapes of resistance agents from occupied Poland through his own cadre of helpers. Yet even as the couple struggled tirelessly to rescue those behind enemy lines, along with amassing weapons and ammunition, they made sure to set aside moments of reprieve for themselves. And socializing in Budapest was among their favorite diversions. Although the city was teeming with German troops, the soldiers were not antagonistic, at least not yet, since Hungary was still an Axis power at this early stage of the war. The twosome therefore made the most of their days in the elegant city.

"[T]he couple led a full life," says Masson, "visiting friends and sitting in Christine's favourite café where among those she entertained were a number of English journalists."[10] During this rousing period, the pair's romance burned brightly, with their affection being genuine and long-lasting. That said, Christine did not limit her sex life to Andrew, just as she wasn't confining it to Jerzy, her second husband. She took delight in spontaneous, no-strings-attached flings, a penchant she would evince throughout her adult life and one that recalled her late father's nonchalant attitude toward such matters. And while her spur-of-the-moment encounters were numerous, one in particular is emblematic of Andrew's tolerance of them. As Christine was slipping out of occupied Poland with Count Wladyslaw Ledochowski, a young nobleman and fellow resistance agent, the two ended up spending an intimate night together.[11] As could be expected, Andrew was displeased when Christine told him about the incident but he did not hold her in contempt. With remarkable maturity, he appears to have understood and respected her independent nature even if he did not condone her actions. He even agreed with her decision to travel with the same nobleman on her next mission into occupied Poland. As it turned out, this third journey would be memorable for an altogether different reason, namely, Christine's close call with Slovakian border guards.

It was June 1940, and she was returning to Budapest. Near a checkpoint at the Slovakian border — the route required her to travel through Slovakia en route to Hungary — the guards caught sight of her and discovered she was carrying a staggering amount of money in various currencies. They realized at once that she was connected to the underground. Unable to convince them otherwise, the fast-thinking countess offered them a choice, a tempting one designed to appeal to their material needs: they could report her to their superiors and be required to turn over the money they had found on her or they could let her go and keep the money for themselves. Their superiors would never know. And, as Christine had hoped, their self-interest won out. But although she managed to avoid arrest on this occasion, the narrow escape appeared to spell the end of her days as a covert agent in occupied Poland. This is because the guards seized not only the money she was smuggling but, as she later discovered, quite possibly some incriminating documents that were in the same satchel and which had gone missing. Yet this should not be taken to mean that she would henceforth sit passively in Budapest while Andrew carried on with his resistance work. Far from it. Among other deeds, she continued her covert activities from Budapest, and at one point joined forces with Andrew to plant contact mines — explosives held in place by magnets and containing timing devices — on the hull of an enemy barge in the Danube River that was transporting fuel to Austria. It appears their operation was successful, too, since a barge blew up in Austria soon after their act of sabotage. As a result, enemy vessels on the Danube were thereafter required to be equipped with searchlights.

As conditions continued to worsen in Europe, Polish refugees flooded into Budapest, where many of them made contact with Christine and Andrew. The couple, in turn, arranged for them to settle in safer surroundings, most often in other countries. The pair also continued supplying Britain with a torrent of intelligence, with their informants and couriers ranging from priests to princes. Perhaps it was inevitable, then, that Christine and Andrew's pivotal position in such underground goings-on would attract the attention of the enemy. Surely there were signs that Gestapo officials in Budapest had begun trying to pinpoint them.

It was during this precarious period that Christine made one final, desperate trip to Warsaw. Andrew was worried, of course, since it seemed likely that the Nazi apparatus possessed identifying information about her which they had obtained through the Slovakian border guards. Regardless, Christine, sporting a new hairstyle, cover name, and falsified documents, stole into occupied Poland to retrieve nearly a score of British men, all of them escaped prisoners-of-war who had taken refuge in a mental institution. The concern was that the Nazis were on the brink of implementing their depraved program of euthanizing those who were psychiatrically or intellectually impaired, thereby placing the POWs at risk of death. When she arrived, however, Christine discovered that the Polish underground had already managed to evacuate them, meaning her life-endangering trek had been for naught. Accordingly, the countess, exhausted and suffering from a respiratory ailment, made her way back to Budapest. And it was at this juncture, the winter of 1940, that she and Andrew learned conclusively that German officials, in collaboration with Hungarian authorities, were indeed zeroing in on them. Since the time was approaching when they would need to flee to an Allied nation, the couple began making preparations, but unfortunately the enemy was one step ahead of them.

In early 1941, the Hungarian police showed up at the couple's flat and arrested them. With forethought, Catherine and Andrew already had disposed of nearly all of the incriminating evidence in their apartment, but they remained in a fix all the same. At police headquarters, authorities handed over the two patriots to the Gestapo, who interrogated them separately for hours on end but without extracting any useful information. They even struck Andrew in the face, but again without gaining his cooperation. In due course, however, the couple's predicament did come to an end, and it was Christine's quick thinking that did it.

Confined in a room with a Hungarian guard observing her movements, the sly aristocrat, deliberately and surreptitiously, bit her tongue so hard that she pierced it. Alarmed by the sight of blood trickling down the side of her mouth, the naïve guard asked about her health and the countess, with a cough, divulged that she was very ill with a lung condition. She added, pointedly, that her aunt, a relative of Admiral Miklós Horthy, the Regent of Hungary, had offered to help her find a lung specialist. She was, of course, attempting to plant in the guard's mind the fear that she was suffering from tuberculosis. To perfect the hoax, she made sure her handkerchief was speckled with blood. And her ruse worked. The guard promptly called in a physician, who ordered lung X-rays, and, inspecting the results, misdiagnosed tuberculosis. It turns out that the scans revealed what appeared to be the telltale shadows of the dread disease, although, in reality, the images were a residual product of the lung damage Christine had sustained during her term at the Fiat agency. In short order, the Gestapo released her and Andrew, restricting the "contagious" couple to their flat.

Soon after they returned to their apartment, which the Gestapo had now placed under surveillance, Andrew persuaded a friend to drive a Chevrolet into the building's courtyard. As the gate opened and the car entered, Christine and Andrew, in a compact Opel, sped out of the courtyard onto an icy street and through Budapest to the British Embassy. The Germans pursued them, but the couple lost them on their driving spree through the city streets. Moments later, the two were ensconced in the British Minister's private quarters, where they set about readying themselves to take flight from Hungary.

Since the Gestapo was thought to be aware of the identities of Christine and Andrew, the minister, Sir Owen Saint Claire O'Malley, decided to furnish the two Poles with British passports under ostensibly British names. Because Christine's legal name at this moment was Christine Gizycki and she had possessions bearing her monograms, it made sense for her new name to share the same initials. With this thought in mind, O'Malley's daughter cooked up the English-French surname, Granville, one that Christine embraced at once and used for the rest of her life. In the same way, Andrew (Andrzej) Kowerski became Andrew Kennedy.

A few hours later, Christine escaped southward to neighboring Yugoslavia in the trunk of O'Malley's embassy sedan, the Union Jack fluttering on the front, while Andrew duped the border guards and entered the country in his Opel. It was safer for them to make their way separately during this stretch of the trip since the Gestapo was on the lookout for a couple fleeing together. Then, too, they would need transportation in Yugoslavia and the Opel would serve this purpose; certainly they couldn't keep the chauffeured sedan. Reuniting after they crossed the border, Christine and Andrew drove to the capital city, Belgrade, where friends and acquaintances were awaiting them. It was here that the cheerful group spent the night on the town, celebrating in its renowned nightclubs. From Belgrade, the pair's ambitious plan was to drive the diminutive, well-worn Opel to the Middle East, where Britain retained a major presence in Egypt.

Journey to Cairo

It was while Christine was catching her breath in Belgrade that she made contact with a local agent of the Special Operations Executive (SOE), the British agency specializing in clandestine warfare, and requested his help acquiring a Yugoslavian entry visa. She did not possess one, having slipped into the Central European nation in the trunk of a car, yet she would need it when the moment came for her and Andrew to leave the country. And to her relief, the SOE agent obliged, within days procuring for her the necessary papers. Which brings us to the relationship between Christine and the British intelligence system, including the Special Operations Executive.

As we noted earlier, Granville joined British Intelligence in 1939, well before the advent of the SOE in the summer of 1940. In due course, she became a member of the latter — she would become one of its more stellar operatives — although the available records are somewhat vague as to precisely when this occurred. It appears, though, she may have become involved with the SOE in 1940 on an intermittent, informal basis, while becoming a full-time, official member in 1944.[12]

On this same topic, the relationship between Christine and the British intelligence system, it is important to note that there were Polish intelligence officials who were suspicious of the countess because she chose to work with the British government rather than with the hastily-formed Polish government-in-exile in France. The latter was quite insular and did not condone, or trust, any underground operations in occupied Poland other than its own. And providing it with a further pretext for questioning Christine's integrity was her partnership with the Musketeers, a resistance team composed of Polish patriots that functioned independently within occupied Poland and thereby earned the mistrust of the government-in-exile. Led by one of Christine's old friends, it was a formidable squad and she often collaborated with it. Thus, she had two strikes against her in the judgment of the more obdurate members of the Polish intelligence community, and the antipathy of these detractors was not benign. Soon they would act on their suspicions, undermining her bond with British Intelligence. Egypt would be the setting for this disturbing turn of events.

Continuing toward this destination, Christine and Andrew arrived in March 1941, in the Bulgarian capital of Sophia. It was here, at the British Embassy, that she handed over to officials a cylinder of microfilm she had acquired from the Musketeers. Of course, she knew what it contained and was acutely aware of its importance: evidence of German troops amassing along the Soviet border and using the railway system to convey supplies to the region. Clearly, they were preparing to violate the Molotov-Ribbentrop Pact, the "Treaty of Non-Aggression between Germany and the Soviet Union."[13] Aptly, embassy officials rushed the material to London since the information was of great significance. Certainly it is true that Christine's submission of the microfilm was instrumental in confirming the Allies' suspicions regarding the impending German invasion, with the accuracy of the film's content being corroborated by other covert sources and ultimately proven by the incursion itself. With this timely intelligence task completed, Christine and Andrew, upon the advice of embassy officials, left Bulgaria since Britain was about to sever its ties to the southeastern European nation.

The couple's next stop, after a bone-rattling drive on rutted roads, was the entrancing city of Istanbul, where they took a room in an elegant hotel that happened to be wedged precariously between the German and Soviet consulates. Christine's curiosity piqued by the legendary city with its mosques and minarets and bazaars, she set about exploring it and soon grew to adore it. As well, she continued her resistance work, procuring funds for the Musketeers and securing a new cache of microfilm for a future drop. And she met with George, her husband, when he arrived on the scene. As to the reason for his visit, he had agreed to take over her duties with the resistance in Budapest and Warsaw, and he needed to confer with her about the details of the operation. At this point, she decided not to tell him about her romance with Andrew, her concern being that George might react by refusing to assume her underground duties at a time when his help was urgently needed.

Days later, Christine and Andrew motored to Ankara, the capital city of Turkey, where the aristocrat decided to try her hand at obtaining transit visas that would allow them to travel through neighboring Syria. A transit visa is a legal permit which allows its holder to pass through one country en route to another. Since traveling directly through Syria would shorten the journey's couple to Egypt, they decided to give it a try. They faced an obstacle, however, and it was, on the face of it, an insurmountable one. It seems that Syria was Vichy-controlled, just as the French Consulate in Ankara represented Vichy France, and Vichy France was aligned with the Nazis. The result is that the consulate could not be expected to dispense transit visas to the pair because they were citizens of an enemy nation, Britain, according to their falsified passports. But Christine was a risk taker. Brushing aside her doubts, the beautiful, charismatic, and persuasive countess waltzed into the French Consulate in Ankara and walked out with the transit papers. Her success in this scheme, however, would eventually exact a cost.

Traveling onward in the Middle East, the two operatives crossed Syria, traversed Lebanon, and passed through Palestine, where they spent two weeks relaxing in the sun before finally coming to rest in Egypt. And here, to their astonishment, they discovered that their standing in the British intelligence community had changed dramatically since they left Budapest.

"Christine's intuition warned her that something was seriously amiss in their world," says Masson.[14] Certainly her hunch was right. In Cairo, she and Andrew found themselves pushed aside, kept out of resistance work, and distanced from intelligence briefings. Soon enough, the exasperated couple learned why: Christine's detractors in the Polish intelligence community, which was connected to the Polish government-in-exile in France, had told British Intelligence that she and Andrew quite likely were German spies. The dubious line of reasoning was that the couple had received transit visas from the Nazi-aligned French Consulate in Ankara and proceeded to travel freely through Vichy-controlled Syria. Only Nazi collaborators would have been allowed to do so, argued Christine's foes. "Had they known her better," write Miles and Cross, "they would have readily understood that it was Granville's remarkable charm and coolness that had extracted visas from a pro–Vichy consul."[15] In the end, British Intelligence agreed to continue paying the couple a salary but rendered them immobile in the underground movement. Finally, they were told rather bluntly that their services were no longer desired.

"Christine and Andrew were deeply depressed," says Masson. "The only redeeming feature of their life in Cairo at that moment was that they were together."[16] The situation worsened when husband George arrived in neighboring Palestine and wished to join up with his wife. Only now learning about the callous manner in which the British had treated her, he became infuriated and washed his hands of the British intelligence community, resigning his covert position. He likewise washed his hands of Christine when she broke the news to him about her affair with Andrew. Leaving the Middle East, George settled in Canada, and he and Christine eventually divorced.

In time, Christine and Andrew were vindicated as operatives, at least in the judgment of those who were unbiased, when Germany invaded the Soviet Union in June of that year. This game-changer, known as Operation Barbarossa, made it clear that Christine, in particular, was not an enemy agent since she had hand-delivered to the Allies the microfilm revealing Germany's preparations for the invasion. In the same vein, the provision of the microfilm attested to the integrity and patriotism of the Musketeers, whose courier had smuggled the cylinder to Christine for delivery. Obviously, these were not the actions of German spies. But, alas, it was not obvious to those who were determined not to see it.

Logic be damned, the more mulish corners of Polish and British Intelligence persisted in viewing the couple through a veil of suspicion. And although Christine and Andrew, after an unreasonably long stretch of time, were permitted to take part in intelligence-related operations once again, their tasks were restricted to the Middle East. In 1942, however, their prospects began to brighten when a British official arrived in Cairo, a young man who was an astute judge of character and who promptly recognized the pair's trustworthiness and potential value to covert operations on the European continent. Interceding on their behalf, he ensured that they were approved for an SOE-sponsored paratrooper course in Palestine, and, additionally, that Christine received one-on-one training in Egypt as a wireless operator. It is surely no understatement to say that Christine and Andrew were itching to resume their covert work in Europe, their skills having been wasted in the Middle East for far too long, and that the training they now received further sparked their desire to return to action. Fortunately for them, it helped that intelligence officials had, by this time, finally reached the conclusion that the seasoned and successful pair could, in fact, be trusted. It was in this way that the two found themselves on their way back to the European underground.

In 1943, Andrew traveled to England for a briefing and other preparations, after which he was stationed in Eastern Europe to serve as a liaison officer at a training facility for paratroopers. Christine, for her part, became involved on a full-time basis with the Special Operations Executive. This occurred several months later, in the summer of 1944, and it appears that the organization was delighted to count her among its ranks. Because she had become rather well-known in occupied Poland as a formidable agent of the resistance, however, the SOE decided she should not return to the embattled country. Her cover may have been compromised. Instead, the organization created a place for her in its French Section, a sensible move in that she not only spoke French fluently but also was a qualified wireless operator at a time when the SOE urgently needed one in occupied France. And there was a further advantage: Christine was an experienced agent with an impressive track record and therefore would not require extensive training. She could begin working immediately. All she needed was a briefing on political conditions in occupied France and the details of the mission itself. Accordingly, the organization arranged for Ben Cowburn, a distinguished operative, to bring her up to date on the situation in the subjugated nation, and it appointed Lieutenant Colonel Francis Cammaerts to serve as her superior behind enemy lines. Like Granville, Cammaerts was a force of nature, and the two were expected to get along famously. Certainly Christine was now in the best of hands, which was crucial owing to the importance and the hazards of the tasks she was about to undertake.

In terms of the mission, North Africa would be its staging area, with the operation targeting the European continent, France in particular. Allied forces stationed in Algeria and Morocco would parachute into southern France a month after the Normandy Invasion, the objective being to help secure the nation's lower provinces. Italy, in due course, would be brought into the scheme as well. As for Christine, she was to serve as a courier and an underground organizer working with elements of the resistance, principally the maquis, the fierce French guerrilla force.

So it was that the Special Operations Executive branch in Cairo, in the summer of 1944, relocated the countess to a site near the city of Algiers, where she received coaching for her mission. Providing her with military cover, British officials also placed her in the all-female First Aid Nursing Yeomanry (FANY). In terms of her faux identity, Christine's code name in enemy territory was to be Pauline Armand, and, in keeping with SOE procedures, her physical appearance would change; she would look like a native Frenchwoman. To make this happen, stylists from England set to work transforming her façade, fashioning her hair and clothing in the continental manner. The organization also supplied her with the usual selection of counterfeit papers. And lastly, as she steeled herself for the flight out of North Africa, her SOE coach handed her three essentials: a knife, a revolver, and a cyanide capsule. The moment had arrived.

8. Christine Granville and the Polish/French Resistance

On the night of July 7, 1944, Christine boarded an aircraft for the trip to France. Once she was airborne, she tapped out in Morse code an uncouth message to her friends on the ground, a parting salute in the form of a coarse lyric.[17] Despite her trepidation about the operation, she managed to hold onto her sense of humor. But not for long. A few hours later, the daughter of Polish nobility took on a daunting challenge, parachuting into the black of night and alighting — more precisely, crashing onto a rocky surface — four miles off-course during what turned out to be a very stormy night. She was the first female agent to be dropped from Algeria into this war-torn region, the Vercors Plateau in the French Alps.

After being retrieved by a reception committee, Christine, whose tailbone and hip were injured and whose revolver was destroyed during her landing, was taken to meet Francis Cammaerts, the SOE agent who had created and now headed an enormous underground army of resistance fighters in this Alpine region. Understanding and appreciating the strength that may emerge from unity, he had consolidated the diverse factions of the resistance in southeastern France, the maquis foremost among them, and in so doing had built a formidable fighting force. Here in the Vercors Plateau, Cammaerts and his legion had also succeeded in forging a stronghold against the Germans, with the combination of the region's rugged, stony terrain and the vast number of fighters ready to defend it keeping the enemy at bay.

In regard to Christine's general assignment, she was to work alongside Cammaert and his covert Alpine forces, who, in turn, the SOE had instructed to help lay the groundwork for the Allies' reclamation of southeastern France. As to her specific duties, she was to serve as Cammaert's courier as well as to recruit members for the resistance: men, for the most part, she was expected to draw from a variety of sources. Like those of other underground groups, the resistance fighters who already had gathered at the Vercors Plateau represented an array of personality types and an equal share of motivations, with members ranging from patriotic French farmers to disgruntled soldiers who had defected from foreign armies. Because the countess was multilingual and socially adaptable, the SOE believed she would be adroit at attracting more such men to covert work, and the organization was right. Yet even as Christine impressed the SOE with her ability to bring aboard new members, she also won its praise, as well as that of her fellow resistance members, for her disposition itself. By all accounts, she remained composed under pressure, formed friendships readily, and engaged in the type of camaraderie that fostered the group's *esprit de corps*, the latter being a throwback to her childhood days spent mingling with her family's stable boys. It should be noted, too, that the aristocrat, relishing her personal freedom as much as ever, was regarded by the other resistance members as a free thinker and a free spirit, yet also as a team player. Never a whiner or a fault-finder, "she knew how to keep her own counsel, and to carry out her work with the minimum of fuss," writes Masson.[18] It looked certain that Christine would be a boon to Cammaert's resistance community, just as it appears that she fit into it and enjoyed being a part of it. Unfortunately, violence erupted on a massive scale shortly after her arrival at the Alpine fortress, with this development threatening both the stronghold's existence and Christine's own life.

It started on July 14, 1944, when the Germans launched an attack on the Vercors Plateau. While Christine, Cammaerts, and two of their comrades were attending a ceremony in a nearby village, Swastika-emblazoned planes appeared in the sky and sprayed the crowd with bullets. More planes followed, with bombs. For days and nights on end, the assault continued and expanded, with German planes raining grenades onto the roadways to destroy the underground's transportation routes, while marauding soldiers on the ground killed resistance fighters, villagers, farmers, and their livestock. They also torched countless homes so the maquis and other guerrilla forces could not take refuge in them. And in some cases, the soldiers went so far as to rape their victims, a heinous wartime tactic designed to compound the trauma of military assault by personalizing it and thereby furthering the demoralization. Finally, nine days after the enemy commenced its offensive, Cammaert's resistance community decided to disperse since it had become evident that it was facing a no-win situation. To stay in place was to die.

Throughout this nightmare, Christine remained unruffled and levelheaded, recalled those on the scene.[19] She decided to leave the stronghold, however, when Cammaerts advised her to do so. He, too, was planning to exit, along with a handful of his top associates, the time having arrived for them to shift their subversive operations to other locales. And so it was that Granville and the weary yet resilient group scuttled down a mountainside and trudged on foot to a safe house in a village nearly seventy miles away.

Shortly thereafter, the exhausted aristocrat prepared to embark on the next stage of her mission, brushing aside Cammaert's recommendation that she remain in the village, treat her wounds, and recover her strength. True to form, Christine insisted there was still work to be done and for this reason could not allow herself to linger. "Within days of being parachuted into the Vercors," writes David Oliver, "Granville was climbing Alpine passes into Italy, despite a badly bruise hip."[20] It seems that her SOE mission now called for her to establish relations with Italy's partisans as well as to recruit Polish and Russian fighters for the underground in France.

During the ensuing fortnight in France and Italy, Christine was successful in inducing hundreds of foreign soldiers into defecting to the French underground. Among them were fellow Poles whom the occupying forces had strong-armed into serving in its military and dispatched to Italy, along with discontented Russians, among them Armenians and Tartars, who were serving in Germany's Nineteenth Army but wished to take part in guerrilla warfare on the side of the Allies. By all accounts, the ranks of the resistance in southeastern France, particularly the number of maquis, swelled considerably owing to Christine's efforts; endeavors, as one might expect, that were neither simple nor safe.

On a daily basis, the countess traveled to treacherous sites, placing herself in jeopardy as she revealed herself to be an envoy of covert forces and sought to sway soldiers into joining the resistance. Equally dangerous, she risked being captured by the Germans during her frequent trips back and forth across the border. It is worth noting, in this regard, that German soldiers did in fact stop her for questioning on two occasions, but both times she managed to give them the slip by pretending to be a simple provincial woman going about her mundane business. On a third occasion, however, she was not as lucky. It seems a squad of soldiers seized her and an Italian partisan she was ushering to a maquis camp. Ordered to place her hands on her head, Christine complied at once. But she did something else as well: in each hand she clutched a grenade, its pin pulled. Warning the Germans that unless they released her and the partisan she would drop the grenades and kill them all, she was gambling with her life. Of course, the countess knew exactly what she was doing. Not wishing to tempt fate — or, more precisely, not wishing to further provoke what appeared to be a cornered madwoman — the Germans walked away, as did Christine and the partisan. It was yet another wartime episode that revealed the aristocrat's formidable personality. "The petite, olive-skinned woman with jet-black hair was strong willed," says Oliver, who added that she was also "quick-tempered."[21] A few days after this harrowing incident, Christine's mettle was again in evidence when she returned to the French coast only find another conundrum awaiting her.

It was approximately two weeks later, on August 11, 1944, that she traveled to Seyne, a town in Provence by the Mediterranean Sea. Here she discovered that the Gestapo had captured, interrogated, and imprisoned Francis Cammaerts and two other SOE agents who were traveling with him. The Nazis had released the trio's driver, Claude Renoir, a descendant of the impressionist painter Auguste Renoir, and it was he who furnished Christine with an account of events.

Cammaerts and his two fellow operatives had traveled to a nearby town, Renoir explained, where they picked up from a French official a sizable sum of money to fund their covert missions. Each of the men hid a third of the money on his person, since it would look suspicious if one individual was carrying so much cash during this period of the war. Unfortunately, as the trio was returning to Seyne, they came to a roadblock whereupon they were searched, questioned, and ultimately detained. They were held because they claimed that they did not know each other, yet they were found to be transporting money from the same series of bills. It looked suspicious. At this point, the Gestapo entered the picture, hauling the men back to Nazi headquarters and interrogating them with their trademark brutality. Although the Gestapo could not yet prove that the three were covert agents — none of them cracked under interrogation — the men were nevertheless transferred to a dank prison in the town of Digne, where the Nazis planned to deal with them more thoroughly at a later date.

Upon learning of this sequence of events, Christine became frenzied. She knew the three men would be drilled further, the results of which could well lead to Cammaert's execution and to the exposure of his sizable network of covert agents and resistance fighters in southeastern France. Renoir tried to reassure her, explaining that SOE authorities in Algeria were aware of the incident and were in the process of addressing it. But this was not enough for Christine. "Granville's reaction was swift and decisive," write Miles and Cross.[22] Taking matters into her own hands, she set about plotting for the Cammaerts' escape from prison and that of the other two operatives. Time was of the essence.

With lightening speed, Christine arrived at the prison, where her first task was to ensure that Cammaert was still present and alive. This she accomplished by walking around the perimeter of the prison humming the melody of "Frankie and Johnny." Within minutes, Cammaert's voice joined her in the song, in this way signifying he was still inside the facility.

Next, Christine, claiming to be Cammaert's wife, navigated her way through the prison staff until she found herself nose to nose with a certain Max Waem, a notorious Gestapo figure in southern France and a man who was in a position to intercede on Cammaert's behalf and that of his two comrades. Interestingly, Christine did not attempt to appeal the Nazi's higher, more humane self; perhaps she wasn't sure if he possessed one or possibly she sensed it would be more expedient to speak directly to his lower self in a language he would understand: self-preservation and greed. Whatever her reasoning, she launched into a menacing argument, making it clear that Waem had better arrange for the escape of her husband and his two companions if he hoped to save his own skin. Asserting, again falsely, that she was also the niece of General Bernard Montgomery, the countess claimed to be in radio contact with the military legend, adding that he was well aware that his son-in-law was locked up at Digne. Furthermore, she reminded the Nazi official that Allied forces would be arriving on the south coast at any minute, and that they would no doubt storm the prison and rescue her husband and his comrades or exact revenge if any of them had been harmed or executed. She concluded by notifying Waem that he would surely be put to death for his part in the affair either by the Allies or the local maquis.

Waem was shaken. He knew the Allies would soon retake France, and he also knew they were already after his scalp. Realizing he had no time to waste, the frantic Nazi reached an agreement with Christine whereby she would pay him a sum of two million francs and ensure his safety if he would arrange for Cammaerts and the two other SOE agents to escape from prison.

Obtaining the money from British officials in Algeria by means of a parachute drop, Christine traveled back to the prison and paid off Waem as arranged. In turn, he showed up at the imprisoned men's cell in full Nazi regalia and ordered them to accompany him. Because he was holding a revolver, they assumed he was going to execute them, but instead he led them to the prison gates and to an idling Citroën in which Christine was waiting. The entire party, Max Waem included, then sped off. It was late afternoon. Hours later, Waem received the protection that Christine had promised him, being sent on to Italy where the British Field Police placed him in protective custody. As for Cammaerts, his two comrades, and Christine, late that night they celebrated their escape at a barn in the French countryside, listening as a BBC radio broadcast surreptitiously thanked Christine for her intrepid deed. For this episode, she would receive the esteemed George Medal for heroism, which was fitting considering that she risked her own life to save not only a prominent SOE agent and two other operatives, but quite possibly countless other SOE agents, along with a large contingent of the maquis in southern France.

The threat Christine had used to intimidate Waem, that of an impending Allied entry into southern France, came to pass a few days later, with a massive number of troops setting about unshackling the region from the Germans' grip. It also was a turn of events that signaled the end of Christine's assignment in occupied France. The fact is, it had always been the strategy of the SOE's French Section to phase out its clandestine operations when Allied troops arrived in the subjugated nation, the organization's covert missions to be supplanted by overt battle. It was at this juncture, then, that Christine and Francis Cammaerts took their final journey together, this one to Lyons, where they enjoyed the company of their friends and comrades who had gathered in the newly-liberated city. Then, too, it was in Lyons that Granville said goodbye to Cammaerts, a man to whom she had become quite close. And with these festivities and farewells, her most meaningful years came to an end. "This was the last time Christine would enjoy the life of action and danger that stimulated her," says Masson.[23] A life of ennui and disorganization was just around the corner.

Christine at Sea

It started in the autumn of 1944 with a blunder that emerged from the chaos of war and the indifference of the Special Operations Executive. Christine, it seems, was left high and dry when her SOE mission in France came to a close. Departing for England in October of that year, she was, quite literally, penniless, the only assets she possessed being a packet of currency she had been unable to deliver to the maquis before the Allied invasion. She also was alone. When she arrived in London after her exemplary performance behind enemy lines, she was met by no one. For lodging, she turned to a friend in London, and for moral support she stayed in touch with her lover, Andrew, who was serving at an SOE site in Italy. Most of all, though, she waited for her next assignment, the war not being over despite the Allied invasion of occupied France. Other nations were still in need of covert help, with these embattled countries including occupied Poland. Yet Christine heard nothing from her superiors in the intelligence community. It was as if she had ceased to exist.

Adding insult to injury, the Special Operations Executive kept her at arm's length on the matter of citizenship. After she returned to London, a figure in the organization petitioned for the countess to be granted British citizenship, this being a status for which she yearned, but the SOE's official position, both offhanded and cold, was that she would be required to adhere to the standard, protracted procedure if she hoped to become a citizen. That is to say, she would need to fulfill the residency requirements, file a formal application, and submit the document to a government attorney.[24] She would be treated like any other immigrant. And although the SOE's inexplicable, hard-line stance was challenged by Granville's supporters in the organization, British citizenship, or even assistance in seeking it, was not immediately forthcoming.

A few weeks later, in November, the SOE found itself in need of the countess' exceptional skills once again, so it decided to send her on another mission, this one in Nazi-occupied Poland. To facilitate her work behind enemy lines, she was furnished with an honorary commission as a flight officer in the Women's Auxiliary Air Force (WAAF). As to the particulars of the assignment, once she arrived in the occupied nation, Christine was to function as an observer with the Polish Home Army, but her overarching task was to stay abreast of political developments in her homeland and share her findings with the SOE's other operatives in the Eastern European nation. The information she provided would be intended to help them advance their own covert missions in enemy territory. As well, Christine was to transmit reports to London, thereby keeping SOE headquarters up-to-date on conditions in occupied Poland. Before she could take on this critical assignment, however, British officials insisted that she submit to a security check to make sure she could be trusted. And with remarkable equanimity, the seasoned agent and eventual George Medal recipient did indeed yield to the government's scrutiny this late in the game, and, naturally, was found to be honorable and dependable. The Polish Home Army, by comparison, did not question her integrity, even agreeing in advance that she could use her own encryption system in her communications between the various parties in England and Poland. They trusted her implicitly.

Later that month, Christine flew to Italy on the first leg of her journey to occupied Poland only to find that the mission had been aborted. It seems the Soviet Union had launched an assault on the Eastern European nation, one that rendered it impossible for her to enter it. For the moment, then, she would be remaining in Italy. Examining her circumstances at this point, the fast-thinking operative decided to take two steps, neither of which was related to the Polish assignment but both of which were significant in terms of her immediate future.

First, and for reasons unknown, she resolved to bring to an end her romance with Andrew Kennedy. Since he, too, was in Italy, she was able to do it in person. As could be expected, Andrew was both surprised and hurt by this unexpected turn of events, but he made up his mind to go his own way. Even so, the countess remained close to his heart. [25]

Second, Christine decided to settle in Cairo, at least for the time being. To this end, she traveled to the desert city and returned to the pleasures it previously had held for her, most notably sunbathing and socializing at a European-style country club. Before long, she also could be seen on the arm of Lieutenant Colonel Henry Threlfall, a handsome SOE figure she had first met during her resistance days in Europe. All the while, she looked forward to news about her next assignment, a wait, it turned out, that would be long and the news, disappointing.

It was in March 1945, that the Special Operations Executive sent word to Christine that it no longer needed her services. Caught off-guard by the notification, she did not immediately relinquish her attachment to the organization. Still eager to serve, she volunteered to travel to Germany in an effort to save imprisoned SOE agents from execution. Her offer was not acted upon, however.

Further diminishing her morale, two months later her military ties were severed as her WAAF commission came to an end. Among other losses, this removal of military status, paired with the SOE's previous departure, meant she would no longer have an income. Fortunately, the Special Operations Executive re-entered the picture at this juncture and proposed paying the aristocrat a small living allowance until the end of the year, roughly half the amount of her usual salary. And she accepted the offer. Christine knew she would be needing the money because the war would soon end and she would have to make important choices, consequential choices that would require financial resources. Of these, the most pressing centered on where she would reside. Returning to Poland was out of the question in view of the Soviet domination of the fraught nation, and it was equally apparent that she would have difficulty finding suitable employment in Egypt. In the end, then, England seemed to be the logical choice, especially since she still longed to be a British citizen. Of course, relocation would require funds, but the SOE's temporary allowance would provide them.

Returning to London, Christine's limited allowance did indeed dissipate at the year's end, at which point she fell on hard times, some of which she appears to have brought on herself. On one hand, she was more or less without basic support in that neither the Polish nor the British government offered her legal, financial, or other forms of assistance regardless of her outstanding wartime service to both countries. Yet even when she was offered help, she either did not accept it or she undercut it. For instance, the SOE, apart from the British government, located work for her in and around London, but she found none of it to her liking. Instead, she secured jobs on her own, positions for which she was overqualified and none of which worked out. The countess and war heroine worked briefly in retail sales at Harrods, only to find that its customers did not appreciate her forthright appraisal of their size requirements in clothing. As well, she worked as a switchboard operator; a job, by her own account, that made her jumpy.[26] And she served as the supervisor of a linen room at a hotel—not exactly a riveting set of duties compared to her clandestine work behind enemy lines.

Finally, in 1947, Christine was granted British citizenship, following which she applied for a job that was commensurate with her background and qualifications. It was a position in the British division of the newly-established United Nations office in Geneva, Switzerland. During the interview, however, the man conducting it turned her away, discounting her citizenship as nothing more than that of a Polish refugee with British papers. Christine became angry at his insolence, and understandably so. She also became more demoralized.

Despondent and distractible, the thirty-nine-year-old aristocrat increasingly lived an unsettled, provisional life, with her emotional state causing concern to those who cared about her. Among these people were Francis Cammaerts from her SOE days, and Andrew Kennedy, with whom she once again was becoming friendly. Perhaps she was experiencing a longing for the war years, particularly since she appeared to be trying to reconnect with those with whom she had served in enemy territory.

The fact is, Christine seems to have become a lost soul after the excitement and sense of purpose she experienced during her five years with the resistance. Thriving on danger and intrigue, along with the heartening knowledge that her deeds were both life-saving and consistent with her fundamental values, she appears to have found the postwar era drab and pointless by comparison. Certainly this was known to occur in those who served in the resistance, with a postwar adjustment period often being necessary. In Christine's case, she seems to have had an unusually thorny readjustment, appearing to be mired in the gloom. "[T]he reality of ordinary life was so unsupportable and the battle-fatigue she felt so intense, that for a time she seemed to have lost the will to struggle back to the light," writes Masson.[27]

Perhaps Christine was trying to fashion a more vibrant, gratifying existence for herself when she subsequently exchanged the overcast skies and humdrum routine of London for the sun and pulse of Nairobi, Kenya. Besides Nairobi being a city in which she had an acquaintance, Michael Dunford, Kenya was a country that she had enjoyed when she visited it with her second husband before the war. So it was that Granville settled in for a lengthy stay in the East African nation, but only after a protracted tussle over the right to do so. Inexplicably, the British colony was reluctant to accept her as a long-term resident, leaving her little choice but to use her political connections in London to obtain consent.

Once Christine had established herself in Kenya, she wrote to Andrew Kennedy and invited him to join her. He declined, however. He did not wish to live in Africa, or at least this was the reason he gave to her. So as before, the countess found herself in a country that did not welcome her and with only an acquaintance to keep her company. Soon, though, her life would take a fateful turn and Africa would be but a memory.

In a startling incident, Andrew Kennedy was in a car wreck in England and rendered unconscious for quite some time. A distraught Christine left Kenya, never to return, and rushed back to be at his side. And it was while the two were together during his recovery that a tempting offer fell into her lap, a prospect the couple believed might rescue them from the financial deficiencies they had endured since the war's end.

This glimmer of hope arrived in the form of a letter to Christine, a message from a Soviet friend who had served with the Allies during the war and thereafter settled in Australia. In the South Pacific nation, he and a partner were laying the groundwork for an enterprise whereby they would market expensive European cars. Sensing a legitimate business opportunity, Christine and Andrew were eager to be a part of the venture. Because the countess had no money, however, Andrew stepped in for the two of them and invested his entire capital. He risked everything in the hope that his gamble would culminate in their prosperity.

A period of optimism, Christine finally appeared to be emerging from her despondency and planning realistically for her future. By all accounts, she was enthusiastic about the business deal. But as with other episodes in her postwar life, this upturn was followed by a downturn when the two partners in Australia had a falling out a few months later, a dispute that threatened to torpedo the whole arrangement. A startling development, Christine and Andrew became deeply concerned since it was to have been their way back, financially.

In an effort to salvage the deal, Christine decided to travel to Australia and meet personally with the estranged partners. As to how she would get there given her dearth of funds, the resourceful Granville secured a position as a stewardess on an ocean linter, the *Rauhine*, bound for New Zealand and Australia. Shortly thereafter, in the spring of 1951, she sailed to the South Pacific on the ship's maiden voyage, a state of affairs that made it a special occasion for everyone on board, Christine included. Once again, though, what appeared to be a promising turn of events carried with it a darkness that would grow over the course of time and eventually overshadow this intimation of hope. And it began, innocently enough, when she befriended a restroom steward, Dennis Muldowney, aboard the ship.

A small, diffident, and insecure man who came from a background lacking in stability and family togetherness — he grew up in an orphanage — it was Muldowney who came to Christine's defense when other employees on the ocean liner began criticizing her. Evidently, the women on the crew were envious of her beauty while the men resented her impressive deeds with the resistance, deeds that became well-known on the ship. Grateful for Muldowney's support in the face of these detractors, Christine took the eccentric steward under her wing, never expecting the emotionally needy man to become besotted with her and to focus his full attention on her.

Christine's attention, in contrast, was still focused on the defunct business arrangement, and upon arriving in Australia she set about trying to repair it. Despite having traveled halfway around the world to save the deal, however, she made no progress, the ex-partners wishing to remain that way. She therefore sailed back to England empty-handed, with her and Andrew's prospects of financial security appearing to be dashed for good. All the same, the pair remained on affectionate terms. Having begun as friends in wartime and progressed to comrades-in-arms and eventually lovers, they now had come full circle, enjoying a durable companionship that was warmed by their romantic history. As for Christine's future, she continued working as a stewardess even though the job took her away from London for weeks on end. When she returned, however, she and Andrew took delight in spending their days together, a pleasure that would become increasingly difficult owing to Dennis Muldowney and his growing invasiveness. It seems the steward's infatuation with Christine had progressed to an obsession, and he was determined to make known his adoration at every turn.

Indeed, the peculiar steward, well into 1952, tagged along when Christine went on social outings, and he could sometimes be seen pacing the sidewalk outside of the London hotel in which she lived. A stalker he had become, and Christine told her friends that she was very uncomfortable with him. Worsening matters, his jealousy and possessiveness intensified to the point that he began flying into rages, with his flare-ups occasionally occurring in front of her friends and acquaintances and spoiling her social life. Naturally, she and Andrew wished to be rid of Muldowney, but it seems they were unwilling to push him too hard, whether out of pity or a fear of retaliation. Meanwhile, he became steadily more deranged.

It was at this point in time that Christine, at wit's end, signed on for a voyage to Capetown, South Africa, thinking the long stretch at sea would pry him loose. Although he would be on the same ship, its rules about staff fraternization were quite rigorous and would, in effect, keep them apart. During the crossing, however, it became evident that the circumstances were doing nothing to quell his obsession. And it was now, during the return voyage, that Christine realized he would never leave her side voluntarily and that she must therefore come up with a way to make it happen involuntarily. So it was that the countess sent a message to Andrew, who was in Germany at the moment, explaining that she had finally arrived at a course of action that promised to distance Muldowney forever: she would leave the country. She would escape to a land where he could not find her. And Andrew applauded the idea, proposing that she meet with him in Liège, Belgium, as soon as she returned so they could plan her next move.

Arriving in London and at the Shelbourne Hotel where she often lived between voyages, Christine began packing some of her belongings into a trunk, which she aimed to put into long-term storage at the hotel. Suddenly, Muldowney arrived at her door and demanded to know where she was going. When Christine explained that she was traveling abroad and would be away for two years, the steward became furious. "He raved on about her relationship with Andrew," says Masson, "and with a score of other men."[28] After Muldowney stormed out of the room, Christine continued preparing her garments for storage. Moments later, she began walking down the staircase leading down to the lobby.

And then it happened. Clutching the wooden handle of a dagger, Muldowney lunged at her. Christine cried out for help, but for an eternal moment she remained alone on the staircase with her assailant. In an instant, he plunged the dagger into her heart. Crumpling to the ground, Christine was bleeding so profusely that she went into shock and was dead by the time authorities arrived at the hotel.

The murder of Christine Granville was a tragedy, the killing of a heroine distinguished by her "courage, strength, and flair," in the words of Rosalind Miles and Robin Cross.[29] It truly was a horrible and senseless end to her life, this woman who had given so much to the cause of freedom in the course of the war. Yet its dreadfulness notwithstanding, the crime brings up the troubling matter of her relationship with the murderer.

Madeleine Masson, Granville's biographer, has written that Muldowney's obsession with the countess "pandered both to her power complex, and to her feelings of deep compassion for the little steward."³⁰ And indeed, it is entirely plausible, as Masson submits, that Christine may have found a sense of reassurance and personal worth in Muldowney's devotion to her, especially at the outset of their relationship when other crew aboard the *Rauhine* were disparaging her. Then, too, it appears that she genuinely pitied the needy, self-conscious man in much the same way that she had shown sympathy for underdogs and the downtrodden throughout her lifetime. So Masson may well be correct in suggesting that two of Christine's emotional needs — notably dissimilar ones, at that — found fulfillment in Muldowney's fawning and clinging. But the question remains: why did Granville permit him to hang about once she realized he was becoming unhinged and potentially dangerous?

As we have seen, Christine's eventual assailant, for over a year, clung to her with mounting desperation, even to the point of stalking her, yet she was never known to have told him, point-blank, to leave her alone. Even when he deteriorated to the point of exploding into rages and making threats to her, there is no account of her having reported the situation to the police or otherwise solicited their help; this, despite telling friends that she feared for her life and hinting that she might never see them again. Instead, she permitted the pathological association to continue while concocting cat-and-mouse strategies to prevail over her pursuer.

The answer to this puzzle may lie in her personality and background. Christine, having not only survived but triumphed for five years in the resistance, may have felt confident that she could handle Muldowney. If she could outmaneuver the Nazis, she may have thought, she could surely manage an eccentric restroom steward. Alternately, she may had found in the high-stakes match with Muldowney the sense of intrigue and danger on which she had thrived during the war years. If this were the case, she may have been reluctant to put an end to this peculiar form of excitement while she was still able to do so, inadvertently allowing the toxic situation to progress until it culminated in tragedy.

In the end, it is doubtful we will ever know why Christine did not put a stop to the relationship or secure protection from the authorities. What we do know is that after she lost this final struggle, Muldowney lost his own life as well, being found guilty of murder and hanged on September 30, 1952. On the eve of his execution, the deranged little man told authorities that by slaying Christine he had finally taken complete possession of her.

Fact and Fiction

"Her hair was very black and she wore it cut square and low on the nape of the neck, framing her face to below the clear and beautiful line of her jaw," writes Ian Fleming, the assistant to the Director of Naval Intelligence during

World War II and author of the James Bond novels.[31] "Her skin was lightly sun-tanned and bore no trace of make-up except on her mouth which was wide and sensual."[32] Fleming is describing Vesper Lynd, a double agent in his inaugural book of the series, *Casino Royale*, and a character who had a curious effect on the priapic spy. The British writer continues,

> Bond was excited by her beauty and intrigued by her composure. The prospect of working with her stimulated him. At the same time he felt a vague disquiet. On an impulse he touched wood.[33]

It is widely believed that Fleming based the character of Vesper Lynd on Christine Granville, especially since the two women, real and fictional, shared certain physical characteristics and both had Polish lovers. As to the name, it was a cunning play on "West Berlin."

John Pearson, a Fleming biographer, writes that Vesper Lynd was the first of the long line of James Bond's nubile, eager and ultimately disposable bed-mates ... [who] seems to embody most of Fleming's own somewhat grudging view of female dignity formed during those hit-and-run affairs of his early thirties." He adds, "Vesper Lynd is essentially a passive girl who, like all these heroines ... never answers back."[33]

Like another Bond character, the coy secretary Miss Moneypenny who was modeled on the tough-as-nails spy mistress Vera Atkins, the purring Vesper Lynd is nowhere near as commanding and robust as Christine Granville. The latter was anything but a submissive woman who never talked back. As to whether Fleming was acquainted with Granville in real life, the whole matter remains rather murky. We do know that the novelist was aware of her deeds with the resistance if for no other reason than he mentioned her by name in his nonfiction book, *The Diamond Smugglers*.[34] He praised her in the context of notable female operatives. But more open to question is a claim by Donald McCormick, another writer, that Granville and Fleming were lovers for a year.[35] As it stands, this claim has never been confirmed, the purported sources remaining sketchy, unavailable, or otherwise unverifiable. All the same, the fanciful 1994 assertion caught fire with the public, with magazine articles, books, and feature films continuing to repeat the delicious story to this day. Ultimately, we may never know if Fleming and Granville ever met, yet alone engaged in a romance. For that matter, we may not learn if Vesper Lynd was indeed based on the countess or if she was a composite of female SOE agents Fleming had heard about, or known, during the war years. What is obvious, however, is that the real woman, Christine Granville, was more multifaceted, commanding, and ultimately more fascinating than any of those subservient and dispensable females who comprised the notches on James Bond's bedpost.

On a more somber note, the passing of the extraordinary Christine was devastating to those who cared for her. Unfortunately, this seems to have been a rather small number of people judging by the way in which so many of her former superiors, comrades-in-arms, friends, and acquaintances disregarded the countess during her years of personal struggle after the war. Yet at her funeral in northwestern London, two hundred mourners showed up, among them members of the British and Polish governments, along with former agents of the French and Polish resistance. At the burial, Polish soil was sprinkled on her grave so that Christine could rest beneath a blanket of earth from her homeland.

It should come as no surprise, of course, that Andrew Kennedy was crushed by her death. At her service, he served as a pallbearer, and he remained close to Christine in memory for the rest of his days. He never stopped loving her, settling in Germany and eschewing marriage.

For her astonishing valor, Christine was awarded the George Medal (Britain) and the Croix de Guerre (France), and was decorated by both the Polish Resistance and the French Pioneers of the Resistance. In addition, she was named to the Order of the British Empire (OBE). As to her place of rest, her remains were interred at Saint Mary's Roman Catholic Cemetery in Kensal Green, England, where, at the foot of her grave, the ashes of Andrew Kennedy were also buried. Passing away thirty-six years later, it was his wish to remain with his adored Christine into eternity.

Notes

Introduction

1. Higonnet, et al. (1987).
2. Ibid., p. 150.
3. Ibid.
4. Pattinson (2007).
5. Ibid., p. 165.
6. Ibid., p. 166.
7. Ibid.
8. Jacques Abtey, in Baker and Chase (1993, p. 235).
9. Spoto (2006, p. 25).
10. Hepburn, in Spoto (2006, p. 23).

Chapter 1

1. Millar (1979, pp. 324–325).
2. Helm (2005).
3. Ibid.
4. Ibid, p. 133.
5. Helm (2005).
6. Ibid.
7. Fussell (1975/2000, p. 3).
8. Helm (2005, p. 121).
9. Ibid., p. 171.
10. Stevenson (2007, p. viii).
11. Helm (2005).
12. Casey (1988, p. 26).
13. Millar (1979, p. 316).
14. Brown (1987, pp. 550–551).
15. Foot (1984, p. 9).
16. Dalton, in Binney (2009, p. xiii).
17. Foot (1984).
18. Churchill, in Foot (1984, p. 48).
19. Foot (1984).
20. Kramer (1995, p. 24).
21. Hastings (1981, p. 37).
22. Binney (2009, p. 96).
23. Ibid., p. 323.
24. Hasting (1981, p. 37).
25. Foot (1984, p. 60).
26. Ibid.
27. Basu (2006/2007).
28. Hilda Atkins, in Hastings (1981, pp. 37–38).
29. Millar, 1979, p. 319.
30. Operative, in Hastings (1981, p. 38).
31. Ibid.
32. Basu (2006, p. 63).
33. Binney (2009, p. 4).
34. Hastings, 1981, p. 37).
35. Millar (1981, p. 327).
36. Hastings (1981, p. 31).
37. Helm (2005).
38. Ibid., p. 222.
39. Lifton (1986).
40. Gilbert (1998).
41. Ibid., p. 287.
42. Helm (2005).
43. Douglas (June 2, 2000).
44. Helm (2005).
45. Hoess, in Helm (2005, p. 224).
46. Fuller (1989, p. 6).
47. Vera Atkins, in Fuller (1989, p. 287).
48. Atkins, in Millar (1970, p. 401).
49. Helm (2005).
50. Ibid.
51. Ibid.
52. Ibid., p. 436.
53. Helm (2005).
54. Millar (1970, p. 317).

55. Douglas (June 2, 2000).
56. Atkins, in Kramer (1995, p. 283).
57. Ibid.

Chapter 2

1. White Rose Leaflet #1, in Scholl (1970, p. 73).
2. Ibid., p. 74.
3. Ibid.
4. McDonough (2009/2010, p. 97).
5. Ibid.
6. Inge Scholl, in Vinke (1980, p. 12).
7. Robert Scholl, Hanser (1979, p. 42).
8. Dumbach and Newborn (1986/2006, p. 14).
9. Ibid.
10. Ibid., p. 37.
11. McDonough (2009/2010).
12. Ibid., p. 15.
13. Inge Scholl, in Vinke (1980, p. 39).
14. Kater (2004, p. 104).
15. Ibid., p. 103.
16. McDonough (2009/2010, p. 31).
17. Scholl (1970, p. 13).
18. Ibid.
19. Plant (1986, p. 111).
20. Ibid.
21. Newborn (2006).
22. Vinke (1980).
23. Jens (1984).
24. Ibid.
25. Newborn (2006, p. 10).
26. McDonough (2009/2010, p. 93).
27. Ibid., p. 95.
28. Sophie Scholl, in Jens (1984, p. 207).
29. Mueller, in Axelrod (2001, p 62–63).
30. Ibid., p. 60.
31. McDonough (2009/2010).
32. Sophie Scholl, in Jens (1984, p. 211).
33. Robert Scholl, in Hanser (1979, p. 197).
34. Jens (1984).
35. Dumbach and Newborn (1986/2006, p. 114).
36. Sophie Scholl, in Axelrod (2001, p. 77).
37. McDonough (2009/2010).
38. Hitchcock (2008, p. 139).
39. Ibid.
40. McDonough (2009/2010).
41. Dumbach and Newborn (1986/2006, p. 135).
42. Sophie Scholl, in Jens (1984, p. 267).
43. Ibid., p. 267.
44. Axelrod (2001, p. 79).
45. Sophie Scholl, in McDonough (2009/2010, p. 119).
46. McDonough (2009/2010).
47. Ibid.
48. Ibid.
49. Dumbach and Newborn (1986/2006, p. 145).
50. Ibid., p. 146.
51. McDonough (2009/2010).
52. Shirer (1960, p. 269).
53. Ibid., p. 1023.
54. Ibid.
55. Ibid.
56. Sophie Scholl, in Dumbach and Newborn (1986/2006, p. 157).
57. McDonough (2009/2010).
58. Sophie Scholl, in Hanser (1979, p. 279).
59. McDonough (2009/2010).
60. Hans Scholl, in Dubach and Newborn (1986/2006, p. 161).
61. Rothfels (1961, p. 13).
62. Halpern (August 17, 1986).
63. Mommsen (1986/2000, p. 11).

Chapter 3

1. Muus and Muus (1955, p. 28).
2. Sutherland (1990, p. 53).
3. Sutherland (1990).
4. Adolf Hitler, in Shirer (1960, p. 681).
5. Jacobsen (1986, p. 108).
6. Muus and Muus (1955).
7. Ibid., p. 122.
8. Sutherland (1990).
9. Muus (1956, p. 106).
10. Muus and Muus (1955, p. 128).
11. Muus and Muus (1955).
12. Levine (2000, p. 18).
13. Hitler, in Sutherland (1990, p. 129).
14. Freedom Council of Denmark, in Muus (1956, p. 107).
15. Levine (2000, p. 55).
16. Hilmar Wolff, in Muus and Muus (1955, p. 129).
17. Thune Jacobsen, in Levine (2000, p. 27).
18. Adolf Hitler, in Levine (2000, p. 65).
19. Monica Wichfeld, in Sutherland (1990, p. 159).
20. Officer, in Sutherland (1990, p. 161).
21. Monica Wichfeld, in Sutherland (1990, p. 161).

22. Sutherland (1990).
23. Ibid.
24. Muus and Muus (1955).
25. Gerner Nielsen, in Sutherland (1990, p. 183).
26. Unnamed judge, in Muus and Muus (1955, p. 141).
27. Monica Wichfeld, in Muus and Muus (1955, p. 142).
28. Ibid.
29. Unnamed judge, in Muus and Muus (1955, p. 142).
30. Monica Wichfeld, in Muus and Muus (1955, p. 142).
31. Muus and Muus (1955).
32. Sutherland (1990).
33. Unnamed companion, in Sutherland (1990, p. 220).
34. Muus and Muus (1955, p. 154).

Chapter 4

1. Khan, in Fuller (1971, p. 156).
2. *London Gazette* (April 5, 1949).
3. Keay (2001, p. 399).
4. Basu (2007, p. 4).
5. Fuller (1971).
6. Basu (2007, p. 10).
7. Ibid.
8. Ibid., p. 20.
9. Ibid.
10. Fuller (1971, p. 49).
11. Basu (2007, p. 22).
12. Copland and Perlis (1984, p. 62).
13. Fuller (1971).
14. Basu (2007).
15. Ibid., p. 24.
16. Fuller (1971, p. 53).
17. Basu (2007, p. 33).
18. Ibid.
19. Fuller (1971).
20. Ibid., p. 96.
21. In Basu (2007, p. 43).
22. In Binney (2002, p. 162).
23. Ibid, pp. 163–164.
24. Ibid., p. 164.
25. Escott (1991, p. 64).
26. Escott (p. 75).
27. Binney (2002, p. 170).
28. Ibid.
29. Ibid.
30. Escott (1991).
31. Basu (2007, p. 147).
32. Ibid., p. 149.

33. Fuller (1971).
34. In Escott (1991, p. 76).
35. Escott.
36. Fuller (1971).
37. Ibid., p. 209.
38. Binney (2002, p. 170).
39. Escott (1991, p. 79).
40. Basu (2007).
41. In Fuller (1971, p. 246).
42. Binney (2002).
43. Unnamed staff member, in Fuller, (1971, p. 243).
44. Ibid.
45. In Basu (2007, p. 179).
46. Ibid.

Chapter 5

1. Sugihara (1995).
2. Gold (2000, p. 141).
3. Ibid., p. 143.
4. Dürer, in Sugihara (1995, p. 86).
5. Gold (2000, p. 143).
6. Ibid., p. 11.
7. Levine (1996, p. 118).
8. Sugihara, in Levine (1996, p. 125).
9. Chiune Sugihara, in Sugihara (1995, p. 2).
10. Ibid., p. xiii.
11. Kasai, in Levine (1996, p. 102).
12. Sugihara (1995, pp. 5–6).
13. Gold (2000, p. 63).
14. Foreign Ministry communiqué, in Gold (2000, p. 65).
15. Levine (1996, p. 225).
16. Ibid., pp. 225–226.
17. Sugihara (1995, p. 17).
18. Chiune Sugihara, in Sugihara (1995, p. 17).
19. Levine (1996).
20. Chiune Sugihara, in Sugihara (1995, p. 24).
21. Sugihara (1995, p. 24).
22. Gold (2000, p. 82).
23. Ibid., p. 96.
24. In Gold (2000, p. 97).
25. Sugihara (1995, p. 56).
26. Ibid.
27. Levine (1996).
28. Gold (2000, p. 128).
29. Okazaki, in Sugihara (1995, p. 109).
30. Levine (1996, p. 278).
31. Sugihara (1995, p. 142).
32. Leon (October 23/31, 2008; 2011).

Chapter 6

1. Pearson (2005, p. 34).
2. Ibid.
3. Howarth (1980, p. 190).
4. Nowicki (1992, p. 152).
5. Ibid., p. 152.
6. Pearson (2005).
7. McIntosh (1998, p. 150).
8. O'Donnell (2004, p. 173).
9. Hemingway (1964, p. 211).
10. Pearson (2005, p. 51).
11. Ibid., p. 59.
12. Ibid.
13. Atkins, in Binney (2002, p. 113).
14. Pearson (2005).
15. Ibid., p. 66.
16. Stafford (1986, p. 8).
17. Foot (1984, p. 66).
18. Ibid.
19. Stafford (1986, p. 9).
20. Foot (1984, p. 67).
21. Ibid., pp. 67–68.
22. Binney (2002).
23. Gilbert (2003, p. 260).
24. Mazower (2008, p. 419–420).
25. Binney (2002).
26. Cowburn (1960, 2009; p. 54).
27. Ibid., p. 106.
28. Foot, in Cowburn (1960, 2009; p. xi).
29. Ibid., p. 93.
30. Pearson (2005, p. 122).
31. Ibid.
32. Cowburn (1960, 2009; p. 112).
33. Ibid., p. 112.
34. Elliott (2009).
35. Ibid., p. 234.
36. Ibid., p. 148.
37. Pearson (2005, p. 137).
38. Weitz (1995, p. 105).
39. Pearson (2005).
40. Ibid., p. 137.
41. White (1964, p. 350).
42. Glass (2009, p. 276).
43. Pearson (2005).
44. Elliott (2009, p. 156).
45. Pearson (2005).
46. Ibid.
47. Ibid.
48. O'Donnell (2004, p. xvii).
49. Ibid., p. xvii.
50. *What Was OSS* (June 28, 2008; p. 1).
51. Pearson (2005).
52. Cannel, in Glass (2009, p. 351).
53. Pearson (2005).
54. Lacouture (1965, p. 113).
55. Binney (2002).
56. Schoenbrun (1980, p. 246).
57. Ibid., p. 246.
58. Weitz (1995, p. 287).
59. Evans (2009, p. 623).
60. Shaw (2010, p. 145).
61. Pearson (2005).
62. Dwork and van Pelt (2002, p. 335).
63. Pearson (2005, p. 205).
64. Ibid.
65. Ibid.
66. Elliott (2009, p. 112).
67. Weiner (2007, 2008; p. 13).
68. Ibid., p. 14.
69. Ibid., p. 27.
70. Ibid., p. 27.
71. Ibid., p. xviii.
72. Pearson (2005).
73. Weiner (2007, 2008).

Chapter 7

1. Dafne, in Atkinson (1985, p. 127).
2. Partisan, in Hay (1986, 1989; p.162).
3. Hannah Senesh, in Hay (1986, 1989; p. 164).
4. Ibid., p. 23.
5. Catherine Senesh, in Senesh et al. (2004/2007; p. xvii).
6. Ibid.
7. Ibid., p. 18.
8. Catherine Senesh, in Senesh et al. (2004/2007; p. xxiii).
9. Masters (1972).
10. Ibid., p. 37.
11. Senesh et al. (2004/2007; p. 26).
12. Atkinson (1985).
13. Ozsváth (1997, p. 107).
14. Senesh et al. (2004/2007; p. 67).
15. Ozsváth (1997, p. 108).
16. Catherine Senesh, in Senesh et al. (2004/2007; p. xxv).
17. Hay (1986, 1989; p. 38).
18. Senesh et al. (2004/2007; p. 86).
19. Ibid., p. 156.
20. Ibid., p. 155.
21. Ibid.
22. Masters (1972, p. 118).
23. Senesh et al. (2004/2007; p. 157).
24. Ibid.
25. Masters (1972, p.119).
26. Ibid.

27. Hay (1986, 1989; p. 138).
28. Ibid., p. 140.
29. Masters (1972, p. 148).
30. Dafne, in Masters (1972, p. 151).
31. Schur (1986, p. 73).
32. Masters (1972).
33. Gilbert (1998, p. 554).
34. Hannah Senesh, in Palgi (2003, p. 14).
35. Atkinson (1985, p. 138).
36. Hay (1986, 1989; p. 173).
37. Ibid., p. 174.
38. Masters (1972).
39. Catherine Senesh, in Senesh et al. (2004/2007; p. 258).
40. Ibid.
41. Hay (1986, 1989).
42. Senesh et al. (2004/2007).
43. Masters (1972, p. 236).
44. Palgi (2003).
45. Hannah, in Palgi (2003, p. 172).
46. Senesh et al. (2004/2007).
47. Ibid.
48. Gilbert (1985).
49. Ibid., p. 751.
50. Palgi (2003).
51. Hannah Senesh, in Palgi (2003, p. 202).
52. Ibid., p. 202.
53. Palgi (2003, p. 205).
54. Ibid.
55. Ibid.
56. Captain Simon, in Senesh et al. (2004/2007; p. 292).
57. Catherine Senesh, in Senesh et al. (2004/2007; p. 291).
58. McCain (2008).
59. Ibid., p. 134.
60. Ibid., p. 135.
61. Ibid., p. 137.
62. Ibid.
63. Senesh et al. (2004/2007; p. 306).

Chapter 8

1. Masson (1975/2005, p. 53).
2. Ibid., p. 54.
3. Christine Granville (2012).
4. Masson (1975/2005, p. 8).
5. Ibid.
6. Evans (2009, p. 5).
7. Miles and Cross (2008, pp. 362–363).
8. Churchill, in Foot (1984, p. 48).
9. Miles and Cross (2008, p. 365).
10. Masson (1975/2005, p. 64).
11. Masson (1975/2005).
12. Ibid.
13. Oliphant (September 16, 2009).
14. Masson (1975/2005, p. 129).
15. Miles and Cross (2008, p. 365).
16. Masson (1975/2005, p. 133).
17. Ibid.
18. Ibid., p. 197.
19. Ibid.
20. Oliver (2005, p. 149).
21. Ibid.
22. Miles and Cross (2008, p. 365).
23. Masson (1975/2005, p. 224).
24. Binney (2002).
25. Masson (1975/2005).
26. Ibid.
27. Ibid., p. 237.
28. Ibid., p. 253.
29. Miles and Cross (2008, p. 366).
30. Masson (1975/2005, p. 250).
31. Fleming (1953, p. 32).
32. Ibid.
32. Fleming (1953, p. 33).
34. Pearson (1996, p. 213).
35. Fleming (1957).
36. McCormick (1994).

Bibliography

Atkinson, Linda (1985). *In Kindling Flame: The Story of Hannah Senesh, 1921–1944*. New York: Lothrop, Lee & Shepard Books.
Axelrod, Toby (2001). *Hans and Sophie Scholl: German Resisters of the White Rose*. New York: Rosen Publishing Group.
Baker, Jean-Claude, and Chris Chase (1993). *Josephine: The Hungry Heart*. New York: Random House.
Basu, Shrabani (2006/2007). *Spy Princess: The Life of Noor Inayat Khan*. New Lebanon, New York: Omega Publications.
Binney, Marcus (2002). *The Women Who Lived for Danger: The Agents of the Special Operations Executive*. New York: William Morrow.
Brown, Anthony Cave (1987). *"C": The Secret Life of Sir Stewart Graham Menzies, Spymaster to Winston Churchill*. New York: Macmillan.
Casey, William (1988). *The Secret War Against Hitler*. Washington, DC: Regnery Gateway.
Christine Granville (2012). Encyclopedia of World Biography. Retrieved 1/15/12, http://www.notablebiographies.com/supp/Supplement-Fl-Ka/Granville-Christine.html.
Copland, Aaron, and Vivian Perlis (1984). *Copland: 1900 Through 1942*. New York: Saint Martin's/Griffin.
Cowburn, Benjamin (1960, 2009). *No Cloak, No Dagger: Allied Spycraft in Occupied France*. London: Frontline Books.
Dumbach, Annette, and Jud Newborn (1986/2006). *Sophie Scholl and the White Rose*. Oxford: Oneworld Publications.
Dwork, Debórah, and Robert Jan van Pelt (2002). *Holocaust: A History*. New York: W. W. Norton.
Elliott, Geoffrey (2009). *The Shooting Star: Denis Rake, MC, A Clandestine Hero of the Second World War*. London: Methuen.
Escott, Beryl E. (1991). *Mission Improbable: A Salute to the RAF Women of SOE in Wartime France*. Somerset, England: Patrick Stephens.
Evans, Richard J. (2009). *The Third Reich at War*. New York: Penguin.
Fleming, Ian (1953). *Casino Royale*. New York: Penguin.
____ (1957). *The Diamond Smugglers*. London: Jonathan Cape.
Foot, M. R. D. (1984). *SOE: An Outline History of the Special Operations Executive, 1940–1946*. London: British Broadcasting Corporation.
Fuller, Jean Overton (1971). *Noor-un-nisa Inayat Khan (Madeleine)*. London and The Hague: East-West Publications.
____ (1989). *Déricourt: The Chequered Spy*. Salisbury, England: Michael Russell.
Fussell, Paul (1975/2000). *The Great War and Modern Memory*. Oxford: Oxford University Press.

Gilbert, Martin (1985). *The Holocaust: A History of the Jews of Europe during the Second World War*. New York: Henry Holt.
_____ (1998). *A History of the Twentieth Century, Volume Two: 1933–1951*. New York: William Morrow.
_____ (2003). *The Righteous: The Unsung Heroes of the Holocaust*. New York: Henry Holt.
Glass, Charles (2009). *Americans in Paris: Life and Death Under Nazi Occupation*. New York: Penguin.
Gold, Alison Leslie (2000). *A Special Fate: Chiune Sugihara — Hero of the Holocaust*. New York: Scholastic Press.
Halpern, Sue (August 17, 1986). Students Against the Reich. *New York Times*. Retrieved 3/11/12, http://www.nytimes.com/1986/08/17/books/students-against-the-reich.html?pagewanted =print.
Hanser, Richard (1979). *A Noble Treason: The Revolt of the Munich Students Against Hitler*. New York: Putnam.
Hastings, Max (1981). *Das Reich: The March of the 2nd SS Panzer Division Through France*. New York: Holt, Rinehart and Winston.
Hay, Peter (1986, 1989). *Ordinary Heroes: The Life and Death of Chana Szenes, Israel's National Hero*. New York: Paragon House.
Helm, Sarah (2005). *A Life in Secrets: Vera Atkins and the Missing Agents of WWII*. London: Nan A. Talese.
Hemingway, Ernest (1964). *A Moveable Feast*. New York: Scribner.
Higonnet, M., J. Jenson, S. Michel, and M. Weitz (1987). *Behind the Lines: Gender and the Two World Wars*. New Haven, CT: Yale University Press.
Hitchcock, William I. (2008). *The Bitter Road to Freedom: A New History of the Liberation of Europe*. New York: Free Press.
Howarth, Patrick (1980). *Undercover: The Men and Women of the OSS*. London: Phoenix Press.
Jacobsen, Helge Seidelin (1986). *An Outline History of Denmark*. Copenhagen: Høst & Søns Forlag.
Jens, Inge, ed. (1984). *At the Heart of the White Rose: Letters and Diaries of Hans and Sophie Scholl*. New York: Harper and Row.
Kater, Michael H. (2004). *Hitler Youth*. Cambridge, MA: Harvard University Press.
Keay, John (1990). *India: A History*. New York: Atlantic Monthly Press.
Kramer, Rita (1995). *Flames in the Field: The Story of Four SOE Agents in Occupied France*. London: Penguin.
Lacouture, Jean (1965). *De Gaulle*. New York: New American Library.
Leon, Masha (October 23/31, 2008; 2011). Remembering Yukiko Sugihara: On the Go. Forward Association. Retrieved 3/3/11, http://www.forward.com/articles/14441/.
Levine, Ellen (2000). *Darkness Over Denmark: The Danish Resistance and the Rescue of the Jews*. New York: Holiday House.
Levine, Hillel (1996). *In Search of Sugihara: The Elusive Japanese Diplomat Who Risked His Life to Rescue 10,000 Jews from the Holocaust*. New York: The Free Press.
Lifton, Robert Jay (1986). *The Nazi Doctors: Medical Killing and the Psychology of Genocide*. New York: Basic Books.
London Gazette (April 5, 1949). Supplement number 38578, p. 1703. Retrieved 4/9/11, http://www.london-gazette.co.uk/issues/38578/supplements/1703.
Martin, Douglas (June 27, 2000). Vera Atkins, 92, Spymaster for British, Dies. *New York Times*.
Masson, Madeleine (1975/2005). *Christine: SOE Agent and Churchill's Favorite Spy*. London: Virago.
Masters, Anthony (1972). *The Summer That Bled: The Biography of Hannah Senesh*. New York: St. Martin's.
Mazower, Mark (2008). *Hitler's Empire: How the Nazis Ruled Europe*. New York: Penguin.
McCain, John, and Mark Salter (2004). *Why Courage Matters: The Way to a Braver Life*. New York: Ballantine.
McCormick, Donald (1994). *17F: The Life of Ian Fleming*. London: Peter Owen.

McDonough, Frank (2009/2010). *Sophie Scholl: The Real Story of the Woman Who Defied Hitler.* Stroud, Gloucestershire, UK: The History Press.
McIntosh, Elizabeth (1998). *Sisterhood of Spies: The Women of the OSS.* New York: Dell.
Miles, Rosalind, and Robin Cross (2008). *Hell Hath no Fury: True Profiles of Women at War from Antiquity to Iraq.* New York: Three Rivers Press.
Millar, George (1979). *Road to Resistance.* London: Arrow.
Mommsen, Hans (1986/2000). *The German Resistance Movement 1933–1945* (English Edition, Information and Documentation Exhibition arranged by the Federal Republic of Germany). Stuttgart: Institut f(r Auslandsbeziehungen.
Muus, Flemming (1956). *The Spark and the Flame.* London: Museum Press.
____, and Varinka Wichfeld Muus (1955). *Monica Wichfeld: A Very Gallant Woman.* London: Arco.
Newborn, Jud (2006). *Solving Mysteries: The Secret of "The White Rose"*—Historical Addendum to Sophie Scholl and the White Rose. (Unpublished Afterword). Retrieved 3/3/12, http://www.judnewborn.com/docs/Solving%20Mysteries%20-WhiteRoseArticle-Newborn.pdf.
Nowicki, Ron (1992). *Warsaw: The Cabaret Years.* San Francisco: Mercury House.
O'Donnell, Patrick K. (2004) *Operatives, Spies, and Saboteurs: The Unknown Story of WWII's OSS.* New York: Citadel.
Oliphant, Roland (Sept. 16, 2009). Russia and Poland continue to argue over the Second World War. *The Telegraph,* p. 1.
Oliver, David (2005). *Airborne Espionage: International Special Duties Operations in the World Wars.* Stroud, Gloucestershire, UK: Sutton Publishing.
Ozsváth, Zsuzsanna (1997). Can Words Kill? Anti-Semitic Texts and Their Impact on the Hungarian Jewish Catastrophe. In *The Holocaust in Hungary—Fifty Years Later.* Randolph L. Braham and Atilla Pók, eds. New York: Columbia University Press.
Palgi, Yoel (2003). *Into the Inferno: The Memoir of a Jewish Paratrooper behind Nazi Lines.* New Brunswick, NJ: Rutgers University Press.
Pattinson, Juliette (2007). *Behind Enemy Lines: Gender, Passing and the Special Operations Executive in the Second World War.* Manchester and New York: Manchester University Press.
Pearson, John (1966). *The Life of Ian Fleming.* London: Companionship Book Club/Jonathan Cape.
Pearson, Judith (2005). *Wolves at the Door: The True Story of America's Greatest Female Spy.* Guilford, CT: Lyons Press.
Plant, Richard (1986). *The Pink Triangle: The Nazi War Against Homosexuals.* New York: Henry Holt.
Rothfels, Hans (1961). *The German Opposition to Hitler.* London: Oswald Wolff.
Schoenbrun, David (1980). *Soldiers of the Night: The Story of the French Resistance.* New York: Dutton.
Scholl, Inge (1970). *Students Against Tyranny: The Resistance of the White Rose, Munich, 1942–1943.* Middletown, CT: Wesleyan University Press.
Schur, Maxine (1986). *Hannah Szenes—A Song of Light.* Philadelphia: Jewish Publication Society.
Senesh, Hannah, Eitan Senesh, David Senesh, Ginosra Senesh, Foreword by Middlemarsh, Inc. (2004). Afterword by Roberta Grossman (2007). *Hannah Senesh: Her Life and Diary—The First Complete Edition.* Woodstock, VT: Jewish Lights Publishing.
Shaw, Antony (2010). *World War II: Day by Day.* New York: Chartwell Books.
Shirer, William (1960). *The Rise and Fall of the Third Reich.* New York: Simon & Schuster.
Spoto, Donald (2006). *Enchantment: The Life of Audrey Hepburn.* New York: Harmony Books.
Stafford, David (1986). *Camp X: OSS, "Intrepid," and the Allies' North American Training Camp for Secret Agents, 1941–1945.* New York: Dodd, Mead.
Stevenson, William (2007). *Spymistress: The Life of Vera Atkins, The Greatest Female Secret Agent of World War II.* New York: Arcade.
Sugihara, Yukiko (1993/1995). *Visas for Life.* San Francisco: Edu-Comm Plus.
Sutherland, Christine (1990). *Monica.* New York: Farrar, Straus & Giroux.

Vinke, Hermann (1980). *The Short Life of Sophie Scholl.* New York: Harper & Row.
Weiner, Tim (2007, 2008). *Legacy of Ashes: The History of the Central Intelligence Agency.* New York: Anchor Books.
Weitz, Margaret Collins (1995). *Sisters in the Resistance: How Women Fought to Free France, 1940—1945.* New York: John Wiley and Sons.
What Was OSS? (June 28, 2008). Central Intelligence Agency. Retrieved 10/15/11, https://www.cia.gov/library/center-for-the-study-of-intelligence/csi-publications/books-and-monographs/oss/art03.htm.
White, Dorothy Shipley (1964). *Seeds of Discord: DeGaulle, Free France and the Allies.* New York: Syracuse University Press.

Index

Abortion *see* Federal Security Department for Combating Abortion and Homosexuality
"Ackuin, Abbé" (code name) *see* Alesh, Robert
Alesh, Robert 141, 145
Andersen, Hans Christian 55
André (Gestapo agent) 98–99
anti–Semitism 9, 10, 30, 86, 127, 133, 160, 161, 166
"Aramis" (code name) *see* Harratt, Peter
Arrow Cross 177, 180, 181
Astor-Drayton, Margaret 57
Atkins, Vera (Rosenberg): awards 23; background 8–12; Déricourt debacle 17, 22; inspiration for *Miss Moneypenny* 26; interrogates Rudolf Hoess 22; later years 23–26; searches concentration camps 19–22; sexual orientation 10, 23; SOE activities 12–19; war crimes investigations 20–21, 24
Auschwitz extermination camp 22, 169–170, 176, 182
Avenue Foch 96, 99, 102
Awakening of Epimenides 28

Baastrup-Thomsen, Else 76–77
Baker, Josephine 3–4
Baker, Nora *see* Khan, Noor Inayat
Baker, Ora Ray 82
Balachowsky, Alfred 92
"Bang Away Lulu" 88
Bankhead, Talullah 56
Barbie, Klaus 140–141, 145–146
Barnard College 124
Basu, Shrabani 15, 17, 83, 84
Battle of Britain 87
Battle of Stalingrad 46
BBC *see* British Broadcasting Corporation
Beaulieu (SOE training site) 131–133
Beaverbrook, Baron Maxwell 57
Beekman, Yolande 103
Bégué, Georges 138

Bel Age 86
Beleyme Prison 136–138
Bellows, George 128
Ben-Gurion, Prime Minister David 182
Benzedrine *see* stimulants
Berdichev, Abba 168
Bernanos, Georges 35
Bernhardt, Sarah 83
"Bill for the More Effective Protection of Social and Economic Life" *see* "First Jewish Bill"
Binney, Marcus 17, 95
Blessed Is the Match 170, 183
Blitzkrieg 189
Blitzstein, Marc 84
Blixen-Finecke, Baron Bror 54
Blixen-Finecke, Baroness Karen 54
Bloch, Marie 136, 137
Bloch, Pierre 99, 136, 138
Bloy, Leon 35
BMW (Bavarian Motor Works) 97
Bohr, Niels 68
Bond, James 26, 211
Borman, Martin 46
Boulanger, Nadia 84
Box Horn Farm 126, 149, 154
"Brideshead Revisited" 37
British Broadcasting Corporation (BBC) 58, 203
Brown, Anthony Cave 12
Buchardt-Hansen, Claire 72, 75
Buchenwald concentration camp 145
Buckmaster, Maurice 13, 14, 16–19, 90–91, 95, 129
Bund Deutscher Mädel see League of German Girls
Bushido Code 121
"Butcher of Lyon" *see* Barbie, Klaus

Cammaerts, Lt. Col. Francis 198–203
Campo dei Fiori 56–57, 59

Index

Carpathian Mountains 184
Cartaud, Pierre 99
Casals, Pablo 83
Casey, William 12
Casime-bi, Princess 82
Catholicism 35, 37, 160
Central Intelligence Agency (CIA) 12, 155
Central Intelligence Group 154
Chanel, Coco 52, 56
Chicago Times 146
"Chicago Typewriter" *see* Thompson submachine gun
Chopin, Frédéric 186
Chorleywood (SOE training site) 91
Christian X 59–60, 66, 79
Christianity 28, 37, 40, 162
Churchill, Clementine 56
Churchill, Winston 12–13, 56, 63
CIA *see* Central Intelligence Agency
Cinema (SOE circuit) 92
Copland, Aaron 84
Corsica (SOE mission) 135–138
"Country and Folk" (periodical) 61
Coward, Noël 56
Cowburn, Benjamin 136, 198
Curaçao 114
"Cuthbert" *see* Hall, Virginia
cyanide capsules 167, 172, 198

D-Day *see* Normandy Invasion
Dachau concentration camp 21, 104–105, 181
Dafne, Reuven 157, 168–169, 177, 183; "Geri" (code name) 177
Dalton, Hugh 12
Damerment, Madeleine 103
Danish Communist Party 61
Danish National Socialist Party 60
Danish Resistance 52–53, 61, 63–64, 68, 77, 79
Dayan, Moshe 163
Dayka, Margit 176
death march (Hungary) 180
Debussy, Claude 83
Decapitation 49
de Gaulle, Charles 95
De Géulis, Jacques 129
de La Tour, Clare 128
DeMille, Cecil B. 155
Déricourt, Henri 17, 22, 91, 93
Deutsche Jungenschaft see German Boys Federation
"Diane" (code name) *see* Hall, Virginia
Dinesen, Isak *see* Blixen, Countess Karen-Finecke
Diplomatic Academy of Vienna 125
Dr. Dynamo *see* Dalton, Hugh
Il Duce see Mussolini, Benito
Dulles, Allen 155
Dunford, Michael 207
Dürer (officer) 107–109

L'École des Services Politiques 125
L'École Nationale d'Agriculture 92
L'École Normale de Musique de Paris 84
Eddy, Mary Baker 82
Eickemeyer, Manfred 43
Einstein, Albert 29
Eisenhower, Dwight D. 155
El Al Airlines 182
Engestofte estate 54, 57, 60–67, 69–71, 79, 80
Eretz Yisrael 178

F Section (French Section) *see* Special Operations Executive
FANY *see* First Aid Nursing Yeomanry
Faye, Colonel Léon 101
Federal Security Department for Combating Abortion and Homosexuality 33
Fiat Company 188, 193
Le Figaro 85–86
First Aid Nursing Yeomany (FANY) 15, 90, 198
"First Jewish Bill" (Hungary) 161
Fleischmann 170
Fleming, Ian 26, 210
Foot, M. R. D. 12, 15, 131–132, 136
Ford Motor Company 13
Franco, Generalísimo Francisco 144, 146
"Free Denmark" (periodical) 61
Free Zone (*Zone Libre*) 133, 135–140, 142–144, 154; "Vichy France" 133
Freedom Council of Denmark 66
Freisler, Roland 47
French Resistance 2, 14, 18, 86, 92–93, 95–97, 99, 105, 184
Frit Denmark see "Free Denmark"
Fröbel Institute 34
Fuller, Jean Overton 22, 85, 100, 104
Fussell, Paul 9

Galen, Bishop Clemens Graf von 35
Gandhi, Mohandas K. 83
Garry, Henri 92, 96, 98, 100
Garry, Marguerite 100
Garry, Renée 98–99
"Geri" (code name) *see* Dafne, Reuven
"Germaine" (code name) *see* Hall, Virginia
Germans Boys Federation (*Deutsche Jungenschaft*) 33
Getlich, Charles 188
Geyer, Wilhelm 43, 49
Girls' Agricultural School (Palestine) 162
Gizycki, Jerzy 189
Glass, Philip 84
Goethe, Johann Wolfgang von 28
Goillet, Lt. Paul 153, 154, 155
Goldberg 84–85
Goldfeder, Stephanie *see* Skarbek, Countess Stephanie (Goldfeder)
Goldstein, Peretz 168, 174
Graf, Wilhelm (Willi) 36

Graham, Miss 53
Grand Duke Dimitri 55
Granville, Christine (Skarbek, Krystyna): "Armand, Pauline" (code name) 198; awards 212; background 186–189; inspiration for *Vesper Lynd* ("Bond Girl") 210–211; journey to Egypt 194–196; marriage 189; murder 209; relationship with Dennis Muldowney 208–210; SOE mission in France 199–203; SOE missions in Poland and Hungary 190–193
Grauer Orden see Gray Order
Gray Order (*Grauer Orden*) 37
Great Depression 10, 52, 56
"Great Slump" 126
Green Heart (SOE circuit) 142, 145
Guérin, Madame 134, 135, 145, 153
Guillet, Anton 102

Haecker, Theodor 35
Haganah 165
Hall, Barbara 125
Hall, Edwin 125
Hall, Virginia: awards 153; background 125–127; Central Intelligence Agency (CIA) 155; Central Intelligence Group 154; Corsica incident 135–138; "Diane" (code name) 148; escape from France 144–145; "Germaine" (code name) 132; "LeContre, Brigitte" (cover name) 132, 137, 139; "Limping Lady," 141; loses leg in accident 126; "Monin, Marie" (cover name) 141; OSS mission in France 148–153; "Philomène" (code name) 141; prosthetic limb ("Cuthbert") 129, 132, 144; SOE mission in France 133–144; SOE mission in Spain 146; SOE training 130–132
Hardeburg Castle 55
Harnack, Falk 37, 49
Harratt, Peter 148
Harrods 206
Harrogate (SOE training site) 87
Heckler (SOE circuit) 135, 142, 145, 150–152
Heemstra, Baroness Ella van 4
Helm, Sarah 8, 19, 24
Hemingway, Ernest 127
Hepburn, Audrey 4
Herzl, Theodor 182
Himmler, Heinrich 33, 46, 68
Hitchcock, Alfred 88
Hitler, Adolf 10, 27, 31, 38, 46, 47, 73, 112, 128
Hitler Youth (*Hitlerjugend*) 31–34, 45
Hitlerjugend see Hitler Youth
Hoess, Rudolf 22
Holocaust 37, 115, 123, 158, 176, 182
Homosexuality *see* Federal Security Department for Combating Abortion and Homosexuality
Horserød Camp 73

Horthy, Adm. Miklós 167, 177, 193
Horthy, Miklós, Jr. 193
Hotel Metropolis (Berlin) 118
Hôtel Ritz (Paris) 56
Hotel Victoria (London) 88
House of Commons 20
Hovmand, Hans Christian 65, 71, 74
Huber, Kurt 37, 41, 49
Humphreys, Leslie 11
Hungarian National Defense 172
Hutton, Barbara 56

Ibsen, Henrik 70
Imperial Parliament (Poland) 186
India 82, 88
Industrial Intelligence Center 11
Into the Inferno 176
Irish Regatta 53
Islam 86
Israeli Defense Force 182
Italian Riviera 56–57, 59
Iwate Prefecture 109

"Jacob" (code name) 63–64, 70–71, 74
Jacobsen, Thune 68,
Jahn, Marie-Luise 37
Jepson, Selwyn 88
Jewish Brigade 182
Jewish Burial Society 180
"Jewish Problem" 68
Jones, Quincy 84
Joulian, Ms. and Mdm. 134–135, 145, 153
Jungsmädel see Young Girls League

Kallós 170–172
Kauffman family 69, 71
Kaunas, Lithuania 111–114, 116, 118–120, 123
Kennedy, Andrew *see* Kowerski, Andrew (Andrzej)
Khan, Hidayat 86, 87
Khan, Khair 86
Khan, Moula Bakhsh 82
Khan, Noor Inayat: arrest 100; award 105; background 82–86; betrayed to Gestapo 98–99; escape attempts 100, 101, 102; imprisonment 101–104; interrogation 100–101; "Madeleine" (code name) 92; "Nora Baker" (code name) 100; "Nurse" (code name) 92; "Regnier, Jeanne-Marie" (code name) 92; sexual assault 104, 105; SOE training 88–91; Women's Auxiliary Air Force (WAAF) 87–88; writings 85–86
Khan, Vilayat 83, 86–87
Kibbutz Sdot Yam 164–166
Kieffer, Hans 100–101
Kierkegaard, Søren 35
Kiersgaard, Erik 62
Kikuchi, Setsuko 112, 118, 119,120
King George VI 79
"Kirsten" (code name) *see* Wichfeld, Varinka

Kistarsca internment camp 176
Konsularacademie *see* Diplomatic Academy of Vienna
Kowerski, Andrew (Andrzej) 187, 190, 194
Kramer, Rita 13
Krauss, Wilhelm 102

LaFrenz, Traute 37, 39
Land og Folk see "Country and Folk"
László, Count Geró 178
League of German Girls (*Bund Deutscher Mädel*) 31–32
Leahy, Ambassador William 137
Le Chambon-sur-Lignon, France 152
"LeContre, Brigitte" (cover name) *see* Hall, Virginia
Ledochowski, Count Wladyslaw 191
Legacy of Ashes: The History of the CIA 154
Le Provost, Robert 134
"Limping Lady" *see* Virginia Hall
Lithuanian Soviet Socialist Republic 113
Loire Valley 24, 91, 136
Lolland, Denmark 54, 60, 64, 76
London Gazette 82
Los Alamos, New Mexico 68
Lund, Kai 70
Lutheranism 28–29, 35, 65, 78
Lycée Saint Cloud 84
Lysander aircraft 91, 93, 97

Maccabee Society 161
Macskás, Dr. 178
Madrid, Spain 146
Mancussen, Pastor 65, 71
maquis 2, 7, 18, 150, 152, 198–204
Marusarz, Jan 184, 190
Masson, Madeleine 185, 187, 191, 196–197, 203, 207, 209–210
Massy-Beresford, Jack 54, 194
Massy-Beresford, Monica *see* Wichfeld, Monica (Massy-Beresford)
Massy-Beresford, Tim 57
"Master Race" 3
Mata Hari 83
Mauthausen concentration camp 181
McCain, Sen. John 182
Meir, Golda 166
MI5 (Military Intelligence — Internal Counter-intelligence) 24, 131
MI6 (Military Intelligence — Foreign Intelligence) 11, 14, 22
Millar, George 7
"ministry of ungentlemanly warfare" 13, 190
Mir Yeshiva 118
Miss Moneypenny 26, 211
Mission Improbable 98
Mitchell, Basil 87
Mohr, Robert 40, 45
Møller, Jørgen 63
Moltke, Count Carl-Adam "Bobby" 62
Monica Fifty-Five 52
"Monin, Marie" (cover name) *see* Hall, Virginia
Montgomery, Gen. Bernard 202
Mount Herzl 182
Muldowney, Dennis 208–210; execution 210
Müller, Franz 38
Munich University 28
Mureska Sobatica, Hungary 170
Musketeers 195, 196, 197
Mussolini, Benito 57
Muth, Carl 35
Muus, Flemming 61, 63–64, 66–67, 70, 73, 79
Mysore (India) 82

Nacht und Nebel (Night and Fog) 21, 102–103
Nagel, Heinrich 72
Nakskov Shipyard 66, 71
National Committee for a Free Europe (NCFE) 155
National Democratic Party (Poland) 186
National Labor Service (Germany) 32, 34
National Socialism 3, 10, 28, 31–33, 36, 38–39, 50, 57, 60, 120, 142, 175
Natzweiler-Struthof concentration camp 20–21, 24
New York Post 132, 139
New York Times 21, 26, 50, 148
Newborn, Jud 30, 36
"Newspaper of the Little Seneshes" 159
Nielsen, Gerner 65, 69, 71, 74
Normandy, France 97, 100, 151, 198
Normandy Invasion 14, 18, 19, 76, 151–152
Northumberland Hotel (London) 129, 133
Nuremburg Seventh Party Congress (1935) 32
"Nurse" (code name) *see* Khan, Noor Inayat

Occupied Zone (*Zone Occupée*) 133
Office of Strategic Services (OSS) 125, 147
Okazaki, Vice Foreign Minister 121
Olympic Ski Team (Poland) 184
O'Malley, Sir Owen Saint Claire 194
Operation Barbarossa 197
Operation Torch 143, 147
Orient Express 9
Orly Airport 97
OSS *see* Office of Strategic Services
Out of Africa 54
Oxfordshire (SOE training site) 146

Palestine 5, 157, 162–167, 172–173, 181–182, 196–197
Palgi, Yoel 168–169, 174, 176, 179, 181–182; suicide attempt 175
Palmach 165–166
Paris Soir 95
passive resistance 27–28, 36, 38, 41
Pattinson, Juliette 3

Pearl Harbor 137
People's Court (Germany) 46–48
Perpignan, France 143, 144
Pétain, Marshal Philippe 133
Pforzheim Prison 101–104
"Philomène" (code name) *see* Hall, Virginia
Piazolla, Ástor 84
Plewman, Eliane 103
Poiana Brasov, Romania 106, 120
Polish government-in-exile 196
Polish Supreme National Tribunal 22
Polizeigefängnis 173
POWs *see* prisoners-of-war
Prince Aage of Denmark 55
prisoners-of-war (POWs) 2, 4, 121, 130, 135, 165, 184, 188, 190–191, 193
Probst, Christl 36, 43, 45–49
Prosper (SOE network) 81, 92–94
Protestantism 49, 152, 160–161
Pyrénées Mountains 136, 139, 144–145, 167

Radcliffe College 124
Radio Free Europe 155
Radio Paris 85
RAF *see* Royal Air Force
Rake, Denis 139–140, 142–144
Rasmussen, Halfdan 61
Rauhine 208, 210
Ravensbruck concentration camp 20
Red Army 41, 106–107, 180
Red Cross: Denmark 75, 78; France 86; Great Britain 87
Red Scare 24
"Regnier, Jeanne-Marie" (code name) *see* Khan, Noor Inayat
Renault factories 97
Renner, Officer 72–73
Renoir, Auguste 201
Renoir, Claude 201
Resistance Movement of Germany 40
Reventlow, Kurt 52, 56–57, 80
Rise and Fall of the Third Reich 48
Rodin, Auguste 83
Rosen, Yonah 165, 168
Rosenberg, Hilda 8–11, 16
Rosenberg, Max 8–10, 14
Rosenberg, Vera *see* Atkins, Vera (Rosenberg)
Rousset, Dr. Jean 134–135, 142–143, 145, 153
Royal Air Force (RAF) 65, 87, 101
Royal Musicians of Hindustan 82, 83
Ruppert (guard) 104
Russian Orthodox Church 36

Sacré-Coeur Convent 187
Saint Hubert's (manor) 53
Saint Margaret's Church, Westminster 54
Samurai 121
Schalburg Corps (SS Force) 67
Schlesinger *see* Senesh, Béla

Schmid, Jakob 44
Schmorell, Alexander (Alex) 36
Scholl, Elisabeth 29
Scholl, Hans 28–41, 43–51, 55, 65, 71, 74, 100; same-sex affair 33–34, 45; spiritual development 35
Scholl, Inge 29
Scholl, Magdalene (Müller) 29
Scholl, Robert 29–31, 34, 45, 48; arrest and imprisonment 39
Scholl, Sophie: arrest 45; background 29–34; execution 49; League of German Girls 31; religious beliefs 37–38, 50; trial 46–49; White Rose Movement 28, 36–45, 50–51; Young Girls League 30
Scholl, Werner 10, 29, 33, 48
Schüddekopf, Katharina 37, 49
Schulenburg, Count Friedrich Werner von der 10, 13
Science and Technology Agency (USSR) 122
Scotland Yard 131
Sea of Galilee 165, 182
"Second Jewish Bill" (Hungary) 162
Second SS Panzer Division 18
Secret Intelligence Service (SIS) 11
Seifert, Detective 173
Senesh, Béla 5, 158–160; Schlesinger, original surname 158
Senesh, Catherine 158–162, 173–177, 180–182, 193; suicide attempt 174
Senesh, Gyuri 158–159, 162, 167, 173, 181–182
Senesh, Hannah: arrest 171; background 158–163; *Blessed Is the Match* (poem) 170, 183; British/Israeli training program 166–167; enters occupied Hungary 170–171; escape attempt 172; execution 179; honors 182; imprisonment 172, 173–177; life in Palestine 163–166; suicide attempt 172; trial 178; Yugoslavian partisans 157–158, 168–170; Zionism 161–162
Sereni, Enzo 168
Services Sanitaires de l'Armée 124
sexual abuse 3, 104, 105
Seymour, Reverend Dean John 79
Shelbourne Hotel (London) 209
Shirer, William 46
Sibelius, Jean 107, 111
Siege of Budapest 181
Simon, Capt. Elemér 178, 181
Simpson, Flight Lt. 124
SIS *see* Secret Intelligence Service
Skarbek, Alexander 186
Skarbek, Andrew 186
Skarbek, Frederic 186
Skarbek, Count Jerzy 186
Skarbek, Krystyna *see* Granville, Christine
Skarbek, Countess Stephanie (Goldfeder) 186–189, 191
SOE *see* Special Operations Executive
Söhngen, Josef 36, 43, 49

South Africa 8, 11, 209
Special Operations Executive (SOE) 7, 12–13, 63, 79; Atkins, Vera 7, 17, 19, 22–24, 26; F Section (French Section) 13–21; Granville, Christine 194, 198, 203–205; Hall, Virginia 125, 129–130, 135–136, 146–147, 153; Khan, Noor Inayat 89, 97, 105
Spooner, Colonel Frank 90
Spy Princess 83
Stadelheim Prison 47
Stalin, Joseph 112, 155
Star of David 175; "yellow star" 173, 180, 181
Starr, John 101
Stevenson, William 10
stimulants 42, 43; Benzedrine 144
Student Medical Corps (Germany) 35
Sufi Order of England 83
Sufi Publications Society 83
Sufism 5
Sugihara, Chiune 106, 107, 109–123
Sugihara, Yukiko: background 109–110; children 110, 111, 112; diplomatic life, Finland 110–111; diplomatic life, Lithuania 112–119; postwar Japan 121–123; rescue of Polish Jews 113–119; siege in Romanian forest 106–109; trek across Siberia 120–121
"Sugihara Survivors" 123
Sutherland, Christine 55
Szabo, Violette 20
Szálasi, Ferenc 177
Szelecsényi, Dr. Andre 178
Szenes, Chana *see* Senesh, Hannah

Tangmere Airfield 91
Tatra Mountains 188
Third Reich 1, 10, 12, 25, 27, 35, 47–48, 50, 86, 128, 131, 139, 170, 178
Thompson submachine gun 166
Threlfall, Lt. Col. Henry 205
Tipu, Sultan 82
Tissandier 170–172, 178
Tito, Marshal Josip Broz 174
Tolstoy, Leo 83
Tolstoy, Count Serge 83
"Tommy gun" *see* Thompson submachine gun
Trans-Siberian Railway 115, 210–121
Transylvania 182
Traven, B. 136
Treasure of the Sierra Madre 36
Treaty of Non-Aggression between Germany and the Soviet Union 112, 185, 195
Treaty of Versailles 54, 57
tuberculosis 65, 188, 193
Twenty Jakata Tales 85

The Ugly Duckling 55
United Nations 206
U.S. State Department 124, 126, 132, 144, 154; Foreign Service 124–128

University of Lyons 162
Vercors Plateau 199, 200
Vesper Lynd 211
Vesserau, Colonel 150–151
Vester Faengsel (West Prison) 71, 72, 75–76
Vichy, France 133
"Vichy France" *see* Free Zone (*Zone Libré*)
Viennot, Monsieur 95
Viereck, Pastor Emil 78
Visas for Life 106

WAAF *see* Women's Auxiliary Air Force
Waem, Max 202, 203
Waldheim Prison 77–79
Wanborough (SOE training site) 90, 130
War Cabinet (Great Britain) 15
War Crimes Investigation Unit 20
Warhaftig, Zorach 114, 123
Washington, DC 56, 125, 130, 143, 153, 154, 155
waterboarding 141
Die Weisse Rose 36
White Rose Movement 27–28, 34, 36–46, 48–50
Why Courage Matters 182
Wichfeld, Ivan 55, 71, 73, 80
Wichfeld, Jørgen 52, 54
Wichfeld, Monica (Massy-Beresford): affair with Kurt Reventlow 55–57, 80; arrest 71; background 53–54; Danish Resistance 61–70; escape plot 72–73; imprisonment 71–76, 77–79; life on Italian Riviera 56–59; Paris business ventures 52, 56; rescue of Jewish family 69–70; trial 73–76
Wichfeld, Varinka 53, 55, 62, 64–65, 67, 71, 73, 79; "Kirsten" (code name) 64
Wickey, Lt. Col. 104
Witherington, Pearl 18
Wittelsbach Palace 45
Wittenstein, Jürgen 37
Wolves at the Door 138
Women's Auxiliary Air Force (WAAF) 87, 90, 204
World War I 9, 13, 28, 54–55, 57, 83, 139, 160, 189
Wulff, Hilmar 61, 63–64, 67

"yellow star" *see* Star of David
Yom Kippur 176
Young Girls League (*Jungmädel*) 30–31

Zakopane, Poland 188, 189
Zichy, Countess 174
Zionism 114, 158, 165
Zone Libré see Free Zone
Zone Occupée see Occupied Zone
Zupnik, Rabbi Moshe 118
Zwartendijk, Jan 114
Zyklon-B 22

www.ingramcontent.com/pod-product-compliance
Ingram Content Group UK Ltd.
Pitfield, Milton Keynes, MK11 3LW, UK
UKHW041947140426
5217IPUK00014B/692